Studies in Consciousness / Russell Targ Editions

S ome of the twentieth century's best texts on the scientific study of consciousness are out of print, hard to find, and unknown to most readers; yet they are still of great importance. Their insights into human consciousness and its dynamics are still valuable and vital. Hampton Roads Publishing Company—in partnership with physicist and consciousness research pioneer Russell Targ—is proud to bring some of these texts back into print, introducing classics in the fields of science and consciousness studies to a new generation of readers. Upcoming titles in the *Studies in Consciousness* series will cover such perennially exciting topics as telepathy, astral projection, the after-death survival of consciousness, psychic abilities, long-distance hypnosis, and more.

BOOKS IN THE STUDIES IN CONSCIOUSNESS SERIES

An Experiment with Time by J. W. Dunne

Mental Radio by Upton Sinclair

Human Personality and Its Survival of Bodily Death by F. W. H. Myers

Mind to Mind by René Warcollier

Experiments in Mental Suggestion by L. L. Vasiliev

Mind at Large edited by Charles T. Tart, Harold E. Puthoff, and Russell Targ

Dream Telepathy by Montague Ullman, M.D., and Stanley Krippner, Ph.D., with Alan Vaughan

Distant Mental Influence by William Braud, Ph.D.

Thoughts Through Space by Sir Hubert Wilkins and Harold M. Sherman

The Future and Beyond by H. F. Saltmarsh

Mind-Reach by Russell Targ and Harold Puthoff

RUSSELL TARG EDITIONS

UFOs and the National Security State by Richard M. Dolan

The Heart of the Internet by Jacques Vallee, Ph.D.

STUDIES IN CONSCIOUSNESS

Russell   Targ   Editions

The Future and Beyond

Evidence for Precognition and the Survival of Death

A one-volume edition of *Foreknowledge* and *Evidence of Personal Survival from Cross Correspondences*

H. F. Saltmarsh

HAMPTON ROADS
PUBLISHING COMPANY, INC.

Hampton Roads Publishing Company, Inc.
1125 Stoney Ridge Road
Charlottesville, VA 22902

434-296-2772
fax: 434-296-5096
e-mail: hrpc@hrpub.com
www.hrpub.com

If you are unable to order this book from your local
bookseller, you may order directly from the publisher.
Call 1-800-766-8009, toll-free.

Library of Congress Control Number: 2004104870
ISBN 1-57174-392-8
10 9 8 7 6 5 4 3 2 1
Printed on acid-free paper in Canada

Publisher's Preface

The Future and Beyond by Harold Francis Saltmarsh, the tenth volume in the Studies in Consciousness series, publishes as one volume two classic titles originally published separately in Great Britain in 1938 by G. Bell & Sons, Ltd.

In *Foreknowledge,* which summarizes and analyzes well-documented cases of precognition, Saltmarsh proposes the existence of an extended subliminal present from which we obtain information about the apparent future. In *Evidence of Personal Survival from Cross Correspondences,* he unravels and explains the famous post-mortem communications of F. W. H. Myers to show that these messages could not have been telepathic or clairvoyant perceptions.

Both volumes were reprinted once in the United States, more than a generation ago, and since then, to our knowledge, have remained out of print and all but unavailable. They belong together, and belong in the library of anyone endeavoring to understand psychic phenomena. Publishing them together as *The Future and Beyond* allows us to make them available at an affordable price. The volume you hold in your hands contains every word published in the original two volumes, in the original format.

Foreword
Charles T. Tart

Precognition (an incomprehensible idea about the future) and survival of bodily death (an enormous hope, operating in the service of coping with our greatest fear): Can we say anything useful or sensible or hopeful about either of them? Or will we just go down dead-end paths that have been well trodden by many thoughtful people before, without arriving at a satisfactory place?

Sometimes in our lives, the world seems to give us signs that we are on the right track—like a little precognition as one is getting ready to write about precognition?

This morning I had decided on awakening that immediately after breakfast I should begin working on writing the forward to these two wonderful books by H. F. Saltmarsh. I had put the task aside for more than a year because of the pressure of other projects. As I sat down to breakfast I noticed I was quietly singing an old song to myself, a song whose words (as I was remembering them) were:

> *I sailed on the sloop John B.,*
> *My grandfather and me.*
> *Around this old town*
> *We did go . . .*

A couple of minutes later I looked at the daily newspaper crossword puzzle I planned to do with my breakfast. One across, the first word called for, was "sailing ship." The word "sloop" was of course what was needed.

I wryly remarked to my wife that my "psychic powers" seemed to be hard at work on what was really important in life, thinking I was making a little joke about the relative triviality of crossword puzzles. I hadn't yet made the connection that perhaps this was a little precognitive sign.

Precognition has always been a covertly difficult subject for me. I say covertly, or maybe unconsciously, because for much of my life I had no idea just how difficult it was. I had been studying the literature of psychical research and experimental parapsychology since my teenage years and, as a scientist, had almost immediately accepted the reality of precognition. Besides well-documented spontaneous cases of it in people's lives, such intriguing cases you will read in the first Saltmarsh book, the experimental evidence for its reality was excellent.

Basically, an experimenter would ask a percipient to predict some future target, typically the order of a deck of cards. The predictions would be written down, and at a designated time in the future, a deck of cards would be thoroughly randomized by repeated, blind shuffling and the final order then compared with the predictions. Not always, but far too often for chance to account for it, there was more than just guessing in the percipients' predictions. They were getting extra "hits," and the reality of occasional precognition was demonstrated.

The logic of this was very simple and clear, and, in the more than 45 years of a career partly devoted to parapsychological investigations, I have always included precognition as one of the five psi phenomena that is established beyond any reasonable doubt.[1]

"Reasonable doubt"—good old reason. A very handy tool, but perhaps not always up to the full spectrum of reality.

Here's what opened my eyes to my covert problem with precognition:

In the mid-1970s, my students and I began some studies trying to train other student percipients to use their ESP (extrasensory perception) more effectively. This was based on a theory of mine (Tart 1966) that the traditional method of testing people for their ESP ability contained a major flaw. That method involved percipients guessing decks of hidden cards over and over and over. While results in general were significantly above chance expectation, showing that various forms of ESP existed, there was a common trend for percipients to get worse as they continued the tests. This was called the decline effect.

I looked at this situation as a psychologist with some knowledge of learning theory, and realized that the testing situation involved repeated trials with no immediate feedback of results. That is, you guessed all the way through a deck, typically of 25 special cards, and only at the end were the cards turned over and compared with your guesses.[2] Psychologists had long ago discovered that withholding or delaying feedback constituted what was called an extinction paradigm, a way to confuse a subject and destroy any skill that subject, animal or human, had at a particular task. Thus, it was not at all surprising that a decline effect in ESP performance was common. For all its logic, this was not a welcome idea to parapsychologists because of its implication that we had been killing off the very phenomena we wanted to study.

In our studies at the university, the percipients worked at an electronic machine, the Ten-Choice Trainer, which provided immediate feedback on each guess.[3] A sender/experimenter in another room tried to send the percipient each target number, so we thought of this as a telepathy study. This was a "real-time" telepathy study: Each percipient's goal was to correctly guess the target number currently being sent by his or her experimenter on each trial. Our initial studies were quite successful in getting high ESP scores in a telepathy mode, in not having any signs of declines, and in some people apparently showing the beginnings of learning. The results are described in detail elsewhere (Tart 1976).[4]

Some time after my initial data analyses for telepathy, it occurred to me that, as had often been done in others' parapsychological research, I should further analyze the data to see if there were other effects than simply hitting on the intended, real-time telepathy targets. Among these analyses, I looked for precognition. I found massive precognition effects on the target one ahead of what the percipient was aiming for on each trial. That is, they were guessing a target that had not yet been selected by the random number generator. These were highly unusual precognition effects also, for they involved extremely significant (odds of millions to one) *avoidance*[5] of the correct target!

One of my major research projects all through my life, and still underway, is myself. I've always been interested in observing and understanding the way my own mind works. I noticed strong and unusual feelings as I discovered these precognition effects, so, looking inward, I discovered that while I had *consciously* and *rationally* long accepted the reality of precognition, at a deeper level the concept of predicting the future through some form of precognition was totally nonsensical to me! So nonsensical that I wasn't really specifically resistant to it nor did I defend against it: You don't need to defend yourself against what isn't there.

Now I had some deeper understanding of one of the reasons some people argue so strongly (and often irrationally) against the possible reality of precognition. All because precognition had snuck into my own laboratory when I wasn't looking!

Have I come to terms with precognition? Not really. Intellectually, I still accept it on the basis of the same kind of experimental evidence that initially convinced me, but now I remind myself that I still have some non-intellectual, perhaps non-conscious resistance and rejection of precognition, and I had better be careful not to let my rational processes be covertly influenced by that resistance.

So back to the sloop. Did it really sail into my mind through precognition, as a little reminder from the universe that I was on the right track to start writing the forward to these books and, hopefully, stimulate brighter minds than my own to think about precognition and survival, and so help us understand these vitally important topics better?

Well maybe. But then maybe not. Perhaps in my earlier unfolding of the newspaper section to where I could later retrieve the puzzle I unconsciously read the clue. I would take an oath in a court of law that I didn't look closely at the puzzle section while unfolding the paper, and certainly didn't consciously read any of it, but I can't *completely* rule out the possibility that my eyesight is better than I think it is when used by my unconscious mind, and so perhaps it got a peek that then stimulated the song coming into my head.

How about just coincidence? Perhaps I think about sloops all the time? Not likely. I don't know exactly what a sloop is, just some kind of old-time sailing ship. I doubt that I've ever used the word aloud in conversation, and I can see no reason for the word to pass through my mind more than once every few years, if that often. I'm not a boat person.

And perhaps my memory is making the story a little better than it actually is? Are the words "I sailed on the **sloop** *John B.*" a memory distortion after seeing that "sloop" was the needed word in the crossword puzzle, the actual words being "the *ship John B.*"? But I think I've sung it as sloop over the years, or perhaps as either sloop or ship.

Or is my resistance to precognition still coming out by thinking of these alternatives?

And isn't this still a good sign that we are on the right track? Being able to illustrate the difficulties of evaluating possible precognition in ordinary life? I once had some marvelous synchronicities happen when I was writing an article on synchronicity that I took as a good sign that the article was on the right track (Tart 1981), so perhaps this was something similar?

All of this discussion illustrates some of the problems in deciding whether precognition is real, much less what it means about the nature of reality. Saltmarsh's precognition book deals with all these issues in a reliable, sophisticated, and quite readable way that is very intriguing. And, regardless of my (or your) personal psychological resistances, the laboratory evidence for the reality of occasional precognition is still very, very good.

Too, while many of us prefer the intellectual clarity of laboratory studies, where we have a limited set of known conditions, it is the richness of spontaneous precognitive events in life, even if complex, that gives us the most important hints as to their nature and function. Saltmarsh's cases, though old, are rich indeed.

Needless to say, precognition makes no sense in terms of common sense or physics' classical views of the material universe, or in terms of the doctrine prevailing in almost all of contemporary science of materialism which makes the mind nothing but the operations of the physical brain. Whether the strange physical world of quantum mechanics, where time is much stranger, has anything to do with the human brain, is still a hotly debated, and generally doubted, topic among physicists and neurophysiologists. And this is what makes precognition so interesting and challenging, of course. The day we understand it will call for a major deepening of our understanding of reality.

Speaking of materialism, insofar as the mind is nothing but the operation of the brain, the topic of Saltmarsh's second book, possible survival of bodily death, is clearly *a priori* nonsense. Why bother to think about it? Mind equals brain, brain stops at death, end of story. . . .

But if a human mind can sometimes reach into the future, pre-cognize, that's a very "mind-like" thing to do, rather than a "brain-like" thing. Indeed all of the five robustly established forms of psi (telepathy, clairvoyance, precognition, psychokinesis, and psychic healing) establish a general case that a dualistic view of humankind, that mind may be something of a quite different order than simply matter, needs to be taken seriously. If mind is different from matter, the ending of the material substrate of ordinary consciousness is not necessarily the end of mind. So perhaps our personal life-stories are not automatically ended by death?

One of the main thrusts of early psychical research was the question of postmortem survival. Although contemporary parapsychology largely ignores that issue, preferring the clarity of simplified laboratory work, the evidence collected by careful investigators over the years has been very impressive. Whether you can say survival has been *proven* is a tough question: Some say yes, some say no, some say maybe, and the vast majority of humanity outside the very small circle of psychical researchers is almost totally ignorant that there is any evidence on the issue.

My best understanding at this time is that the *possibility* of survival has been firmly established, and so we should be devoting enormous resources to investigating an issue like this which has vital implications as to how we will live our lives. Of course we are not doing so in our crazy, modern world,[6] so the old evidence, including that discussed by Saltmarsh in this book, is still of great importance.

I will very briefly summarize this evidence. People go to spiritu-alist mediums, who claim to "channel" or relay information from deceased people. The vast majority of communications obtained in this way are not really evidential in proving the identity of the osten-sible surviving communicator: They are too general or more involved with emotional interaction that, while very valuable to those going to mediums, is not evidential. This is to be expected: The vast majority of ordinary telephone calls are not particularly evi-dential of anything either. But some mediumistic communications involve detailed, factually correct information from the deceased (I won't keep saying "ostensible" every time I used "deceased" or "com-municator" as it's awkward, but technically that's what I mean) that seems to prove the identity of the deceased. Once you've ruled out deliberate fraud—and there are some fraudulent mediums, of course, just as there are charlatans in all walks of life—doesn't this prove that at least some people survive death sometimes?

This is where a major complication comes in, a complication that helped divert modern parapsychology to simpler laboratory studies and generally discouraged survival studies to the point where the amount of effort going into the question is quite trivial com-pared to its importance.

The complication: When a medium relays information from a communicator that is correct, might that information simply be telepathically picked up from the sitter's mind and unconsciously worked into an impression of the deceased? We have robust evidence that living people sometimes have telepathic contact with each other. We have robust evidence that telepathy (or the other forms of ESP) can be used in an unconscious way. So a medium may honestly believe she or he is simply relaying information from surviving spir-its, when it's actually their unconscious mind putting on a good impersonation, fortified by psychically acquired information about the deceased.

If we could put firm limits on the operation of ESP, we might rule this out, but at this stage of our knowledge we can't. We don't have any evidence to show ESP can pick up specific *kinds* of infor-mation. Once the possibility of unconscious impersonation in con-cert with ESP was recognized as an alternative to the reality of surviving spirits, survival research reached a major stumbling block, an obstacle still very much with us today.

Here we come to the major contribution of Saltmarsh's second book—the evidence for survival from the cross-correspondences. As is detailed in the book, several psychical researchers struggled with this problem while alive, then died. They then apparently got together on the other side and figured out a way to cooperatively send messages through various mediums that taken separately would make no sense, but put together by living researchers would provide much stronger proof of survival. It would seem preposterous for the unconscious minds of a number of mediums to be able to telepathically cooperate in such a sophisticated fashion, so the possibility that we actually survived death would gain much stronger support.

Were the cross-correspondences, the demonstration organized from the other side, successful? Personally, I can't tell in any final way: The cases involve quotations and allusions to classical literature that I don't know enough about for me to reach a firm conclusion. The experimenters and educated people of those times were far more familiar with the classics than most of us today; it was a natural language for them. But is the material fascinating? Yes! Is it one of the most interesting ideas to come along? Yes! And perhaps most importantly, I hope this example of ingenuity will inspire new researchers to devise other ingenious ways to study the survival question. We need to know!

Charles T. Tart
Institute of Transpersonal Psychology,
Palo Alto, and University of California, Davis

Notes

1. The others, when ordinary sensory communication is ruled out, are telepathy or mind-to-mind communication; clairvoyance, the direct perception of the state of the physical world; psychokinesis (PK), the direct effect of mental intention on the state of matter;

and psychic healing, the direct effect of mental intention on biological processes. The last may be a form of PK.

2. This procedure was necessary for statistical reasons. If you had immediate feedback, that is, saw what each card was right after guessing it, you could, consciously or unconsciously, count cards and then make better guesses knowing, for example, that all of one type of card had already been played so you shouldn't call that one anymore. This would wreak havoc with statistical analysis, so immediate feedback was not given.

3. Unlike card guessing studies, this setup used an electronic random number generator where the odds of a particular number coming up were not affected by what had come up previously, so the statistics were not affected.

4. Interestingly, Russell Targ, the editor of this series of classic books in parapsychology, had been thinking along similar lines and later incorporated fast, unconfusing feedback into the remote viewing procedure he helped develop: Declines in performance have not been reported in remote viewing.

5. Think about guessing red or black with ordinary playing cards. Obviously, guessing all of them correctly, instead of the approximately 50 percent expected by chance, is amazing, odds of millions to one. Now think about getting *none* of them correct. This is just as amazing and statistically unlikely. Thus scoring significantly below chance must involve as much psi as scoring above it: Some part of your mind has to use ESP to know the correct answer in order to be sure you *don't* accidentally guess it.

6. As a psychologist I have many ideas why we act so insanely as to not look at the actual evidence for survival, but it would take us too far afield to discuss that here.

References

Tart, C. T. (1966). Card guessing tests: Learning paradigm or extinction paradigm. *Journal of the American Society for Psychical Research, 60*, 46–55. Available online at www.paradigm-sys.com/cttart/.

————. (1976). *Learning to Use Extrasensory Perception.* Chicago: University of Chicago Press, 1976. Print-on-demand edition from Authors Guild back-in-print editions, 2001, www.iUniverse.com.

————. (1981). Causality and synchronicity: Steps toward clarification. *Journal of the American Society for Psychical Research,* 75, 121–141. Available online at www.paradigm-sys.com/cttart/.

FOREKNOWLEDGE

by

H. F. SALTMARSH

LONDON
G. BELL & SONS, LTD
1938

This volume is based on material in the possession of the Society for Psychical Research and is published with the consent of the Council, who, whilst they do not necessarily endorse any opinion expressed in the book, welcome this opportunity of bringing the evidence before the public.

PRINTED IN GREAT BRITAIN
BY WESTERN PRINTING SERVICES LTD., BRISTOL

GENERAL INTRODUCTION

THIS book is one of a series on the subject of Psychical
Experiences. The Society for Psychical Research, it
should be stated at once, is in no way responsible for
any of the deductions made, or theories advanced. All
it has done as a Society is to allow members of the
various groups who have been preparing the books to
have access to unpublished records in its possession,
and to grant permission to reprint records published in
its *Proceedings*, and, in special cases, records privately
printed in its *Journal*.

The stories of Psychic Experiences that appear in this
series are on a completely different level from the
majority of such stories published in most papers and
magazines. Few people realize the meticulous care
which the Society's investigators have always taken to
test the good faith and the accuracy of those whose
experiences have appeared in the *Proceedings* and
Journal, as also the good faith and the accuracy of those
who contribute corroborative evidence.

The object of this series is to put before the ordinary
reading public examples of the evidence for various
super-normal occurrences and faculties which the
Society has been collecting for over half a century, and
is still collecting.

The lack of interest shown by ordinary readers in this
body of carefully tested evidence may be due to its
bulk and complexity, and partly, perhaps, to their

awareness of the fact that the majority of men of science fight shy of it. One reason for the aloofness of most men of science is probably the absence of any theory which successfully attempts to bring the various phenomena into even a semblance of unity.

In the present series no attempt can, of course, be made to supply such a theory. Nevertheless, it is much to be desired that someone with a thorough knowledge of the evidence should try, as Frederic Myers did nearly forty years ago in his Scheme of Vital Faculty (*Human Personality*, Vol. II, pp. 505–54,) to construct 'a connected schedule or rational index of phenomena so disparate that the very possibility of their interdependence is even now constantly denied.' And that such an attempt should be made afresh is all the more to be desired because since Myers's death phenomena of a new type have been observed.

While, then, the authors of these small books recognize the need for some unifying theory, they have confined themselves to the less ambitious and less arduous task of marshalling a quantity of well-attested evidence for phenomena of many different kinds. For such views and comments as may be found in any of the books the individual writer, as has been stated above, is alone responsible.

THE author desires to make acknowledgement of his debt to the Council of the Society for Psychical Research for permission to print summaries of cases from *Proceedings* and *Journal*, also to the Hon. Mrs. Alfred Lyttelton, G.B.E., for similar facilities in regard to her book, *Some Cases of Prediction. A Study.*

CONTENTS

CHAPTER   PAGE

   I INTRODUCTION   I

  II SOURCES OF EVIDENCE AND CLASSIFICA-
      TION   6

 III ALTERNATIVE EXPLANATIONS   .   .   29

  IV CASES OF PRECOGNITION   .   .   .   46

   V NORMAL EXPLANATIONS   .   .   .   67

  VI METAPHYSICAL THEORIES   .   .   .   83

 VII IMPLICATIONS   103

      GLOSSARY   118

CHAPTER I

INTRODUCTION

It is a common saying that 'Coming events cast their shadows before.'[1] I am inclined to treat such sayings with some respect; the words of a poet may embody, in a concentrated form, the accumulated experience of generations of mankind and, even though they be not strictly true, they can hardly be completely at variance with the truth or they would not survive. Of course, one does not accept them without question, but they can claim to set up a prima facie case for inquiry.

What I propose to discuss in this book is the question whether there is any evidence that coming events ever do 'cast their shadows before' in the sense that people sometimes have knowledge, fugitive and fragmentary glimpses it may be, of the future. Do we ever hear the vague rumour of approaching disaster as we hear the rumble of the oncoming train while it is still out of sight in the distance? Are all the stories of prophecies and warnings mere fables, the outcome of the child-like imagination of mankind?

History and legend are full of such stories, but they are also full of marvels of many different sorts—marvels which we have no hesitation in rejecting as entirely mythical.

It is true, of course, that much prediction of the

[1] Thomas Campbell. 'Lochiel's Warning.'

future is not only possible but commonplace. We make all our plans for the morrow on the strength of such knowledge of the future. I can arrange an appointment at a distant place for a certain time knowing that it will take me so long to get there. More specific and definite examples of prediction may be taken from the tide tables which give the hour of high-water for any day of the coming year, or from the calculated dates of eclipses and other astronomical phenomena. In these predictions, as well as in many others made by scientific men, a high degree of accuracy and certainty is attained. In our dealings with other people we rely, to a great extent, on prediction, or rather on estimates, very often unconsciously formed, of the future behaviour of those with whom we are concerned. Knowing something of the character of a man, and having had many experiences of how character reacts to environment, we are able to forecast how he will behave in certain circumstances. In politics, business and general social intercourse we rely on such estimates of future behaviour and, although we may make mistakes now and then, due to imperfect knowledge, faulty calculation or unforeseen factors in the coming situation, we are, for the most part, substantially correct in our forecasts; in fact, were this not so, an ordered society would hardly be possible.

There is, however, one common feature in all these diverse examples of forecasting, viz., they are all based upon inference from knowledge of the present and past, together with the assumption that causes which have produced a certain effect in the past will do so again in the future.

They are so commonplace that we accept them without questioning and see nothing mysterious about them at all, though, when examined by philosophers and metaphysicians, difficulties and obscurities crop up by the dozen. These difficulties need not worry us, however, for it is not with predictions based upon inference from present and past knowledge that we are now concerned; the subject with which we have to deal is the evidence for non-inferential prediction, or, to use the usual and more accurate term, precognition.

What we want to discover is whether there are any cases where knowledge of the future, which is not based upon inference from knowledge of the past and present, is ever given to man. Do coming events cast their shadows before so that we have glimpses of what the future will bring to us?

The philosophical implications of non-inferential precognition are very far-reaching and even revolutionary in character. Ideas which would ordinarily be scouted as fantastic and ridiculous claim serious attention, and, unless one rests content with the extreme agnostic position, any attempt at explanation seems to involve the entertainment of hypotheses which appear, on the surface, to be wildly improbable.

Apart, however, from the embarrassment caused to professional philosophers, the reality of precognition[1] raises points of difficulty for that everyday working philosophy of life which is possessed, in some degree, by nearly everybody. For example, if events can be

---

[1] I shall in future usually use the single word 'precognition' for all cases of apparently supernormal, or non-inferential foreknowledge; it will not be used to mean normal prediction based on inference.

known before they happen, does not this imply that the future is completely fixed and determined? If so, what about our freewill and moral responsibility? Can we save freewill and morality by adopting the fatalist theory, that is to say, the theory that 'every man's fate is written on his forehead' and do what he will, he cannot avoid it? Whether such a theory be logically tenable I will not here discuss, but seeing that it is held by a large section of the human race, it would mean discounting human intelligence too profoundly to sweep it contemptuously to one side as being unworthy of serious attention.

If we fail in salvaging morality by adopting the fatalist theory, must we accept whole-heartedly the extreme determinist position and hold that the future is completely and inexorably fixed? On this view, whatever happens, all human action, thoughts, emotions and volitions included, is the inevitable out-come of what has already happened. The laws govern-ing phenomena admit of no exception, our apparent freewill is nothing but a subjective illusion, we are all parts of an immense mechanism which goes on its way regardless of our desires and sufferings.

A dismal theory, perhaps, but one which has been firmly held by some of the greatest thinkers of ancient and modern times. To embrace it whole-heartedly seems to entail the relinquishment of much which we hold to be of the highest value, viz., our inalienable right to decide for ourselves in the final issue, and to behave as morally responsible agents. For if the future be completely predetermined and unchangeable, we are not free to make moral decisions. The choices which we make, though apparently autonomous, are really the inevitable outcome of the past, and we could not, in fact, have chosen otherwise than we did. Yet, if this be so, can we be morally responsible?

I do not say that fatalism or determinism are the only possible theories which can be held consistently with the reality of precognition, in fact, as I shall hope to show later on, there is a third alternative which permits, though it does not necessarily entail, the existence of freewill and, thereby, our status of morally responsible agents.

It is clear that this matter of precognition is one which touches us very nearly and has a bearing on the most important aspect of human life. It is, therefore, of interest, not only from the standpoint of psychical research, but also from that of ethics and the ordinary everyday conduct of life, to determine, first of all, whether precognition be a reality, and secondly, if it be so, what implications flow from it.

CHAPTER II

THE records of antiquity are full of accounts of pre-cognition; soothsayers and prophets were more or less respectable practitioners in olden days. The Old Testament provides several examples, Grecian Mythology others. Belief in witches and magicians, who were sometimes able to foresee the future, was commonly held until quite recent times. I imagine that Shakespeare did not consider that he was writing mere nonsense when he introduced the three Weird Sisters into Macbeth. Had we any adequate supporting evidence, that incident would be a good and, in some respects, a rather typical case of precognition. But supporting evidence is necessarily lacking in all ancient cases; they show, however, that the idea that precognition is possible is not of recent growth but has been present in the minds of humanity for as long as we have any record. Since the beginning of serious scientific interest in supernormal phenomena, roughly, that is to say, from the date of the foundation of the Society for Psychical Research some fifty odd years ago, investigators have taken the trouble to collect supporting evidence and thus establish a sounder foundation on which to build a reasonable belief – or the reverse – in the reality of odd and unusual happenings.

The records of the Society contain an immense mass

of valuable material, of cases which have been carefully investigated and examined from the evidential standpoint.

A few years ago I searched the printed records of the Society, i.e., the *Proceedings* and *Journal*, for the first fifty years of their existence and extracted therefrom all the cases of apparent precognition which I could find; a report on the results of this search was published in *Proceedings* of the Society, Volume XLII, February 1934, and it is from this report that I shall draw much of the matter to be contained in this book. I may find it desirable to quote from other sources in order to illustrate some particular point, but I shall confine myself to the S.P.R. cases as far as possible. I think that it is a convenience to the reader who wishes to verify references if the field from which they are drawn is made as narrow as possible.

During the first fifty years of its life the Society published, according to my count, 349 cases of apparent precognition. One must not take these figures too exactly, as some of the cases are multiple, that is to say, more than one instance of precognition is given in the same account. I studied the records of all these cases and came to the conclusion that some twenty of them were not really precognitive at all, they were either clearly chance coincidences, or else cognitions, whether supernormal or not, of contemporary, rather than future, events. I therefore rejected them from my collection.

In addition to these rejected cases, I found others, numbering forty-eight in all, which were so vague that it was doubtful whether a precognition had occurred. As an example of the kind of vagueness which I mean, suppose a person were to hear the ticking of the death watch beetle and then, within the next week or so, learn of the death of a relative or friend, I should consider such a case to be far too vague to be of the slightest value. I admit that few of the cases which I have put into this class are so crude and naive, in fact, I do not think that the Society would have accepted for publication a narrative so obviously worthless. Another example, more characteristic of the type of case which I have in mind, would be where someone has a vague feeling of depression or of approaching calamity, and subsequently experiences some misfortune to which there had been no obvious reference in the impression. An unidentified hallucination, followed by the death of a friend or relative, would be classified as too vague to be worth considering.

Some of these cases may, of course, have been genuine instances of precognition, but it is safer to reject them all.

In a few instances the evidential value of a case was not sufficiently good for it to be included among those retained, but, owing to the strict rules laid down by the Society in this matter, I had to reject very few on these grounds.

Deducting these 68 rejected cases, we still have the respectable total of 281. Since the publication of my report in 1934 there have been further cases published. I, personally, have come across quite a considerable number of others which, although I have been satisfied as to their genuineness, have not been such as to be capable of formal verification and thus, under the rules of evidence of the S.P.R., have not been published.

I first made a rough classification of the remaining cases into 'Good' and 'Ordinary'. A 'Good' case is one in which the precognition is particularly definite and full of detail, and where the evidence is satisfactory. There were 134 of these. An 'Ordinary' case is one which, although it may not attain to the standard of the Good cases, is sufficiently evidential of precognition to be significant when it is taken along with a mass of other evidence. Standing by themselves these Ordinary cases would not afford a sufficient basis for belief in precognition, but when they are considered as a part of the whole evidence, they certainly lend collateral support, besides sometimes being useful as illustrating some particular point. It was, of course, a matter of personal opinion as to the class to which any particular case should be assigned, although in many instances there was little room for doubt. However, it may be said with considerable certainty that roughly one half, or slightly more, belong to the 'Good' class.

In making the classification I adopted a system of marking, allotting marks for evidential value, also for the amount and kind of detail foreseen and the completeness or otherwise of the fulfilment.

I also drew up a specification of the ideal case; needless to say, I have not yet found one.

The ideal case of non-inferential precognition must comply with the following conditions:

(1) The precognition must have been told or recorded before fulfilment, or else acted upon in such a manner as to afford objective evidence of foreknowledge.

(2) Details must be given in the precognition, and

B

fulfilled in the event, sufficient to render it unlikely that it was a mere chance coincidence.

(3) If the precognition be of a relatively simple event, it must indicate fairly narrow limits of time for fulfilment, or else contain details which fix the occasion of fulfilment; e.g., visiting a certain place, or meeting a certain person.

(4) It must be of such a nature that inference from knowledge considerably wider than that normally possessed by the subject, and by means of a considerably enhanced power of inference, could not reasonably be held to have afforded the foreknowledge. The bearing of this condition will be made clear when we discuss cases in which hyperaesthesia, that is to say, abnormal acuity of the senses, or where subliminal, or, as some call it, subconscious, knowledge, might have accounted for the precognition.

(5) It must be of such a nature that suggestion, whether auto-suggestion or otherwise, whether conscious or subconscious, could not have brought about the fulfilment. Some cases of precognition of the course of an illness come under this head.

(6) It must be of such a nature that telepathy from another person could not have produced it. An example of what is here meant would be where another person had formed the intention to do so-and-so, and the precognition consists in the subject foreseeing the performance of that action. We assume, in such a case, that knowledge of the intention was conveyed telepathically to the subject.

(7) The time interval between the occurrence of the precognition and the fulfilment must be sufficiently

long to make it certain that they were not really simultaneous, yet sufficiently short to reduce the probability of chance fulfilment to negligible proportions. This latter limit is dependent on the circumstances of the precognition, such as the nature and amount of detail foreseen.

I made the following notes to this specification:

Note A. The interval of time which elapsed between the occurrence of the case and its being reported must be taken into account, both as regards the precognition and the fulfilling event. If documentary evidence is not available – and it very rarely is – the evidence depends entirely on memory, so that it is obvious that the sooner it is reported the better. Confirmation of the subject's statements by other people must be independent. Action inspired by the precognition and taken before fulfilment is, in some respects, as good evidence as confirmatory accounts.

Note B. Details are more readily given in visual precognitions, hence dreams, visual hallucinations and crystal visions are likely to afford the best cases. Auditory hallucinations may approximate to these where actual words are given. The number of details is important as the probability of the fulfilment being due to chance is far less where there are several than where they are few.

Trivial details are evidentially more valuable than broad general features. Incorrect details do not necessarily detract much from evidential value.

This seems a formidable list of conditions to be fulfilled and, naturally, one does not expect to find the perfect case. But we have some which comply very nearly with most of the conditions, failing, partially, in only one or two, while we have other cases which are satisfactory as regards those conditions in which the first set failed, yet failing themselves where those succeeded.

A single case, even if ideally perfect, could not, by itself, establish the reality of precognition. However minute the details foreseen, and however accurate the fulfilment, the possibility of chance coincidence would have to be allowed. We know that the queerest coincidences do occur and a single ideal case might be just one of these. Even if two or three more such cases were to be found, we might, though shaken, still cling to the chance hypothesis. When, however, the numbers mount up and we go from twos and threes to tens, twenties and even hundreds, then the conviction that precognitions occur is almost impossible to resist, even if none of the cases be ideally perfect.

There are, in addition, several published collections, for example, a book by Prof. Charles Richet, entitled *L'Avenir et la Prémonition*, which, while it includes several of the S.P.R. cases, contains a number of others; also a short work recently published by the Hon. Mrs. Alfred Lyttelton, called *Some Cases of Prediction: A Study*; giving full accounts of cases reported to her as a result of her broadcast address on the subject. These have all been carefully investigated and commented upon by her and constitute a valuable addition to the evidence. Dr. Osty of L'Institut Métapsychique of Paris has also made a thorough and searching examination of the subject and has given some excellent examples of precognition in his various books, and in the *Revue Métapsychique*.

There are, moreover, in the literature of Spiritualism and Psychical Research, other than that of the S.P.R., numerous examples of the phenomenon.

I cannot, obviously, give all the evidence in full, it would fill several volumes, but I propose to summarize a number of representative cases, drawn mainly from those of the S.P.R., which can be taken as a sample of the whole.

Before starting to quote actual cases it will be convenient to adopt a system of classification for the purpose of introducing some order into the heterogeneous mass of material, and I shall follow the system which I used in my report, giving the figures for that collection only. I first divided the cases into classes according to the kind of impression by means of which the cognition was received. I drew up the following table:

CLASSIFICATION

	Dream	Border-land	Impres-sion	Hallucin-ation	Medium-istic	Crystal Vision
Good	76	4	14	17	20	3
Ordinary	40	3	25	45	31	3
Totals	116	7	39	62	51	6

I ought, perhaps, to explain that by borderland cases I mean those which occur between sleep and waking. By impression I mean those cases where the precognition comes as a generalized feeling, such as intense depression or elation, a feeling of someone's presence or that some disaster is impending over the head of some person; sometimes it comes in the form of words heard mentally, sentences running through the head. Impression may reach such an intensity that it becomes hallucination, and there might, conceivably, be borderland cases between the two types; I do not, however, know of any. The meanings of the other headings are, I think, clear; crystal vision would, of course, include any form of 'scrying', whether a crystal or some other means were used.

It will be observed that dream is the largest of these classes by a long way, but I do not think that we are entitled to draw from this fact the conclusion that precognition is more likely to occur in dreams than in any other state. I would rather explain it as follows. First compare dream with impression. Dreams which are remembered on waking, or thought sufficiently interesting to be told, are likely to have been particularly vivid. On the other hand we are so constantly getting impressions of one sort or another, such as feelings of mild depression, changes of mood, that we pay no particular attention to them. Moreover we can frequently assign a cause to an impression, whereas we can rarely do so for a dream. Finally dreams are likely to contain more detail than impressions. It is clear, therefore, that whether precognitions occur more frequently or not in dreams than in impressions, those which do occur are more likely to be noticed.

As regards hallucinations, while they are much more striking experiences than dreams, and are also capable of containing much detail, they are so much less frequent in occurrence that we should normally expect the number of cases to be fewer.

Concerning mediumistic predictions, I must confess

that I consider my figures to be quite unreliable. I am inclined to believe that precognitions, mostly of a trivial nature, occur fairly frequently in the utterances of the best trance mediums, but it was obviously too large a task to search through all the available records and pick out the apparent cases of prediction. Even if this had been done it would have been impossible, in the majority of cases, to discover whether or not the prediction had been fulfilled.

There is one point which I might mention here, viz., that, in my opinion, precognitions occur only when the subject is in a state of dissociation, that is to say, they are affairs of the subliminal, or as some people prefer to call it, the subconscious mind.

I then made a further classification based on the kind of event foreseen. It is as follows:

	Dream	Borderland	Impression	Hallucination	Mediumistic	Crystal Vision	Total
Death from natural causes	28	2	3	29	10	–	72
Death from accident	9	–	4	5	6	3	27
Course of illness	6	–	4	3	5	–	18
Accident not involving death	11	1	3	3	2	–	20
Accident to material things, such as fires, etc.	17	1	11	6	2	–	37
Trivial incidents	35	–	6	5	21	3	70
Incidents not trivial	3	1	4	3	1	–	12
Arrival cases	5	1	2	8	2	–	18
Winning numbers, winners of races, etc.	6	1	2	1	6	–	16
	120	7	39	63	55	6	290

The reader will notice that the total number of cases exceeds that in the previous table; this is because some cases exhibit precognitions of more than one type of event.

Two or three significant facts emerge from a study of this table. First: Death is the event which provides the highest number of precognitions, being 72 for natural causes and 27 for accidental. Running this very close, however, are incidents, trivial and not trivial, being 70 and 12 respectively. I should perhaps say here that the distinction between trivial and not trivial incidents is not one which can be very sharply drawn. I do not know that it is of much importance, but I felt that one could not properly put under the same heading so trivial an event as the finding of a brooch, and an incident such as the failure of a bank in which the subject had all her money. The important point to notice is that most of the incidents foreseen were quite trivial and unimportant.

Under the heading of arrival cases, I have included the arrival of persons and messages, letters and telegrams. These might, of course, have been classed as incidents, but there is a theoretical reason for keeping them separate, as will appear later.

Another point to be noticed is that in the case of death, the precognitions by hallucination are nearly equal in number to those by dream, viz., 34 and 37 respectively, while for incidents, dream, at 38 cases, far outnumbers hallucination, which stands at 8.

I think that we can suggest a possible explanation for this. The emotional excitement attendant on death is far greater than that caused by a trivial incident.

There are some grounds for holding that emotional excitement may be connected in some way with the generation of hallucinations. In the census of hallucinations carried out by the S.P.R. in the early days, it was found that phantasms, i.e., hallucinatory appearances, sounds and so on, reached their greatest frequency round about the actual time of death, tailing off rapidly in numbers as the interval between the occurrence of the hallucination and the death increased.

Emotional excitement would naturally tend to be greater when the death was near at hand than when it was some distance away in time.

There are two or three special types of case which require mention. First: Collective, that is to say, where the precognition has been experienced by more than one person. There are only two instances of this in dreams, neither of which is in the 'Good' class.

In the first, to be found in *Proc.*, XIV, 253, Dr. Howard and another student of Columbia University both dreamed on the night before the boat race that Columbia would win. Presumably everybody at the University was more or less excited about the coming race, so there is nothing remarkable in two people there dreaming about it on the night before, nor that they should dream of their own crew being victorious. Had it not been for the fact of being collective I should not have mentioned the case.

The second case, *Journal*, XIII, 118, is of a Mr. E. J. and his wife having apparently simultaneous dreams of his mother. In Mrs. E. J.'s dream she was told that the mother would not live for another three months. This prediction was fulfilled. However, as the mother was eighty-two years of age, and expected to die at any moment, the prediction was not striking. Here again I should have rejected the case as worthless, and probably due to chance, except for the curious fact of collectivity.

Collective hallucinations are more common; I found nine of them in my collection. The following is a summary of one such case. It is taken from *Proc.*, XI, 448–51.

The family of Mme. Isnard were seated at dinner with a friend, while their mother was lying ill in an adjoining room. A sudden and inexplicable gust of wind arose, blowing together with a crash, and then open again, the folding doors between the dining-room and Mme. Isnard's bedroom. Mlle. Isnard then saw an hallucinatory figure of a woman pass into the corridor. The head and shoulders were covered with a veil and the face was hidden. The figure was like that of a nun. She felt an immense sadness and thought, 'My mother will die.' Looking at the others seated at the table she perceived that they, too, had seen the apparition. She spoke of it and the visitor tried to comfort her by saying that it was only a play of shadows. Mme. Isnard, who had been dozing, and had seen and heard nothing, was somewhat worse on waking. The following week the son, Dr. Isnard, was alone with his mother, when the doctor called and she rose to let him in. As she went slowly to the door, Dr. Isnard was struck with the likeness between her and the apparition which he had seen. Mme. Isnard died that month. The story is well attested and is confirmed by the independent account of the visitor.

In this case precognition was not only collective but, for the daughter, the visual hallucination was combined with an impression; in fact, had it not been for the reinforcement given to the hallucination by this means, I should have counted the case as being too vague to be of much value, seeing that there was no certain indication that the appearance of the figure symbolized death, nor that it was in any way concerned with Mme. Isnard. It is not clear from the account whether the rest of the family and the visitor shared the impression with Mlle. Isnard, or whether they took it from her that the apparition was a portent of the death of the mother.

Besides these collective hallucinations I found two cases of collective impressions.

In all these collective cases, while it is possible that the several subjects received the precognition independently from an external source, it seems a more reasonable hypothesis to suppose that one only of the percipients experienced a precognition and that he or she passed on the knowledge to the others by telepathy.

Collective cases are not of any special importance in contributing towards an understanding of the problems of precognition, but they are instructive and interesting in other respects; and the fact of being collective certainly lends an added impressiveness to the evidence.

The next type to which I now refer is that of Recurrent cases. I have 6 instances of recurrent precognitive dreams, 5 of hallucination, 1 of impression and 2 mediumistic.

These cases certainly give the impression that there must have been some persistent cause, either internal

or external. It might be that the knowledge has somehow been acquired by the subliminal mind and that
more than one attempt has been made to transmit it to
the normal consciousness. On the other hand the
external source from which the knowledge has been
derived might have been tapped on several occasions.

The evidential value of these cases is high; not only
is it less likely that mere chance coincidence could
account for the phenomena, but, in the case of dreams,
repetition adds so much to the impressiveness that one
would be more inclined than usual to pay attention
to and remember a recurrent dream, also, possibly, to
tell other people about the experience.

It is true that where the dream is reported as having
occurred twice during the same night, it is always
plausible to suggest that the second occurrence did not
really happen, and that the dreamer was subject to an
illusion of memory. It is particularly difficult, as a
rule, for most people to remember dreams, although
with a little practice the habit can be acquired, when
it often becomes clear that dreams are a great deal
more numerous than is usually thought; that is to say,
the dreams which we should normally remember are
only a small percentage of those which can be remembered after practice, and even these latter are probably
only a few out of a far larger number. Dreams which
contain a supernormal element, whether precognitive
or telepathic, are likely to be more vivid and easier to
remember, but it does not follow that all vivid dreams
consist of anything beyond normal ingredients.

Where the dream has been told, noted either in
writing or by a special act of memory, or somehow or

other acted upon before it recurs, the suggestion of illusion of memory is not so plausible; nor when a comparatively long interval occurs between the original and its repetition.

I now will give a short summary of one of these cases as a sample.

From *Proc.*, V, 319: Mrs. Smith dreamed on three nights running that her mother would soon die. On the last occasion she jumped up and said to her husband, 'Oh, that horrid dream again, and someone has just whispered in my ear, "She will last but five weeks."' In each dream Mrs. Smith tried to get to her mother but could not do so.

At the time her mother, who lived in Ireland, was very well and, in fact, wrote at the time of the dream that 'she had taken a new lease of life.' Four days later she was·stricken by paralysis. She asked for Mrs. Smith to come to her, but, owing to smallpox then raging in Dublin, Major Smith refused to allow his wife to go. Mrs. Smith's mother died exactly five weeks to the very hour after the time of the last dream. The account is confirmed by Major Smith.

Another more impressive example is that of Lady Q, of which I give an account on page 47. Here the dream was three times repeated and the fulfilling event took place six years after the first dream.

Further instances of recurrent precognitions will be found among the other types of case of which I give summaries.

The remaining special class to which I wish to call attention is that in which a warning is conveyed by the precognition. I found 12 of these among dreams,

2 in the borderland cases, 9 impressions, 10 hallucinations, and 1 mediumistic.

These cases are particularly interesting for several reasons. First, evidential. From this point of view, if, in consequence of the warning, the subject makes some change in his course of action, this fact may constitute very good confirmatory evidence. Consider an actual case. *Proc.*, VIII, 400 : Mr. Brighten, sleeping on board a yacht at anchor, dreamed of a voice warning him of being in danger of being run down by another vessel. He woke and went on deck, but finding everything quiet and in order, although fog had come on, turned in again and went to sleep. The dream was repeated and he again woke and went up on deck. He was rendered so anxious by the dream, and by the fog, that this time he went aloft, just in time to see, above the fog, another vessel bearing down on him. He shouted to the captain of this vessel who put his helm over and thus avoided a collision.

There is independent confirmatory evidence, but, even without this, the case is strong. It was in consequence of the warning conveyed by the dream that Mr. Brighten twice went on deck during the night and, on the second occasion, actually went aloft. Actions speak louder than words, and it is hard to doubt that he did actually receive some sort of warning. In this particular case I could, however, find an alternative explanation to that of supernormal precognition. Anyone used to the sea is liable to develop unusually acute sensitivity to sounds or other indications of changes of weather and other matters affecting the safety of his craft. It is quite common for a very slight and, to a landsman, almost imperceptible alteration of the sounds of the ship to cause a seaman to wake up from sleep and turn out to see that all is right. The coming on of fog frequently causes such an alteration in sound : it might have been a steamer blowing, or a lighthouse in the vicinity commencing to sound its fog signal, which was the cause of Mr. Brighten's first waking, and that his dreaming mind dramatized this into the form of a warning voice. Having gone on deck and found fog, he would naturally be somewhat anxious on going to sleep again and his senses would have been subconsciously alert; thus he might have caught some sound from the oncoming vessel, sufficient to cause the warning to recur.

I am aware that this may sound rather far-fetched, and against it may be put the fact that, although Mr. Brighten found that fog had come on, he did not consider that the situation was sufficiently dangerous to make it prudent for him to remain on watch after his first waking.

The next case to this, in *Proc.*, XIII, 401, is one in which Mr. Brighten is again concerned. He was sleeping on board a moored pleasure vessel with a companion. He dreamed that the mooring ropes parted and that the vessel was carried out to sea by the current and swamped on the bar. He woke and went on deck in time to see the bow rope part. His companion also woke and followed him on deck, arriving just as the stern rope parted. They managed to hold on with boathooks until help arrived and the vessel was re-moored.

Here again the warning was successful and the

disaster was averted by action taken in consequence of it. The fact that he went on deck to inspect the moorings during the night is strong confirmation of the story of the dream. He may, of course, have deliberately invented the whole thing, simply desiring to spin a yarn, but there is no reason whatsoever to doubt his veracity; the fact remains that something or other did cause him to go on deck just at the critical moment.

The second point of interest in warning cases is that they appear to exhibit purpose. The majority of the cases of precognition of which I have any knowledge seem to be completely meaningless and devoid of any practical utility. While it may be of great interest to know beforehand when someone is going to die, there is, as a rule, little that can be done about it, nor any practical advantage to be gained, while the precognition of a trivial incident cannot possibly benefit anybody. I merely mention this point here: we may have to return to it later when we come to discuss the theoretical side of the matter.

Some of these warning cases also illustrate very clearly another important distinction which is to be found among precognitions. In them the precognition is recognized as a *prediction* or *premonition*, it has about it the flavour of futurity. When we remember something which has happened to us in the past we get a mental image which bears on it the mark of pastness, there is an inherent reference backwards in time; similarly in warning, and some other types of precognitions, the mental image has a reference forwards in time and bears the mark of futurity. But this is by no means so in all, or even in most, cases of precognition. The image is received by the mind, but it has no special temporal reference, it is recognized as having been a precognition afterwards, that is to say, when the fulfilment is learnt. There is a parallel to this in ordinary memory; for instance, when we get a mental image of a place and afterwards recognize it as having been an image of somewhere we once visited, or when we catch a glimpse of some person who, somehow, seems familiar but cannot be placed, and later on we remember who it was.

This point is of considerable importance, and it must be remembered that most precognitions are not immediately known to be such, they are not predictions in the sense that they are, at the time of their occurrence, consciously recognized as having a reference to the future.

The last feature of warning cases to which I now wish to call attention is very curious and, for theoretical purposes, rather puzzling. In some, but not in all, of these cases the warning is acted upon and, as a consequence of this action, the complete fulfilment of the precognition is averted. In the first of the two cases just cited, there seems little doubt that, had not Mr. Brighten gone aloft and hailed the oncoming vessel, there would have been a collision, but it is not clear that the precognition was of the actual fact, it looks rather more like a precognition of a possibility, viz., the danger of being run down. In the second case, had not the two men gone on deck when they did, the vessel would undoubtedly have been swept away as foreseen in the dream, though whether she would then have been

c

carried out to sea and swamped on a sandbank at the bar it is impossible to say.

To illustrate this point still further, I quote another case, *Proc.*, XI, 497: Lady Z dreamed of driving in a street near Piccadilly and of her coachman falling off the box on to his head in the road, crushing in his hat. Next day, wishing to go to Woolwich, she gave orders to her coachman to start at ten o'clock, though, on account of her dream she half hoped for an excuse to go by train. He demurred at starting at the time proposed but said that by 11 o'clock he and the horses would be fit for the journey. Lady Z was driven to Woolwich without incident; on the return journey, when reaching Piccadilly, she noticed that the drivers of other vehicles were looking at her coachman. She then saw that he was leaning back on the box as though the horses were pulling violently. The carriage turned up Down Street and Lady Z suddenly remembered her dream. She called to the coachman to stop, jumped out and caught hold of her child, who was with her. She then called to a policeman to catch the coachman who was swaying in his seat. Just as she did so, the coachman fell off the box. Had Lady Z been less prompt in calling assistance, he would probably have fallen exactly as she had seen in her dream.

The interesting point about all these cases is that, while the course of future events appears to have been foreseen, those events are not inexorably fixed but are capable of being modified by deliberate action beforehand. It might be put this way: the future foreseen is what might, and most probably would happen if things were left to run their course, but in actual fact does not happen because of the intervention of someone who steps in and performs some action which averts the complete fulfilment of the precognition. A fuller discussion of the matter must be postponed until later.

Before finally leaving these warning cases it may be of interest to refer to a type of case of which we have a fairly large number. These are those where the warning occurs in such close temporal proximity to the event that it is impossible to say whether they should be classed as showing precognitive or contemporaneous knowledge.

Mrs. Lyttelton's daughter, Lady Craik, has kindly given me permission to quote the following account of her experience. She was once on the point of crossing Victoria Street in front of a stationary bus, when she felt a strong hand on her shoulder which pulled her back sharply. At the same moment a motor-bicycle swerved past the bus, going very fast between it and the refuge. She turned to thank whoever had saved her, but, to her surprise, there was no one within reach.

Here the event was practically simultaneous with the warning and it seems probable that the subliminal mind of Lady Craik was aware of the threatened danger and conveyed the warning to the normal consciousness by means of a tactile hallucination.

The bearing of such cases upon precognition is that there appears to be no hard and fast line of demarcation between those where the impression and the event are, so far as can be judged, simultaneous, and those where there is an interval of time between them. In the case quoted on page 42, the event, viz., the explosion of the vulcanizer, happened only a few seconds after the hallucinatory warning voice had been heard, sufficient only for Mr. Smith to run to the window.

Simultaneous and precognitive cases may be arranged in an unbroken series, the first type shading off into the second by imperceptible degrees; moreover it is interesting to note that similar means of conveying the warning are employed in both types.

These facts tend to suggest that the same faculty is at work in both types of case.

CHAPTER III

WE can now consider the bulk of the 281 cases in the collection drawn from the S.P.R. records and see whether any of them can be eliminated as being susceptible to an explanation other than that of supernormal precognition.

In my view there are four possible special alternative explanations which are applicable in certain cases, besides the general alternatives, such as chance, etc.

These four are: (1) Telepathy, (2) Auto-suggestion, (3) Subliminal knowledge and inference therefrom, (4) Hyperaesthesia (i.e., abnormal acuity of the senses). There may, of course, be others, but I have not been able to discover any, nor have I come across any suggested by other investigators. I will deal with them in order and illustrate with examples.

(1) *Telepathy*. Cases where the alternative explanation of telepathy can be put forward are those in which some person, other than the subject, had normal knowledge that the event foreseen would happen, or else had formed the intention to act in a certain manner. The most numerous of the first sort are those called 'Arrival' cases, in which the arrival of a letter or telegram is foreseen. The sender of the letter possesses normal knowledge that it is on its way and will, in due course, arrive; on this hypothesis, it is sup-

posed that this knowledge is conveyed telepathically to the subject. The telepathic message[1] is, of course, sent subliminally.

A variation of this hypothesis which might possibly be applicable in some cases is to suppose that the subject happens to become aware by clairvoyance of the fact that a letter is being written or posted, and that this knowledge is transmitted to the normal consciousness, either in a dream or hallucination, etc., as a precognition. I am not inclined to regard this possibility very seriously, as the element of chance is so large. In the case of telepathy there already exists a conscious link between the writer of the letter and the subject, while for clairvoyance that link is absent, and we have to rely on chance to supply it. However, whichever hypothesis we adopt, such cases may be lifted out of the category of true precognition.

The following cases are illustrations. The first is from *Journal*, X, 27: Mr. J. G. Keulemans dreamed of receiving a postcard in German with two words erased and Latin names substituted. One was the name of a bird 'Zosterops.' The card was delivered two hours later.

The second, from *Proc.*, XI, 461: Mrs. Venn coming down to breakfast, asked A., who was seated at the table, if there were any letters for her. He replied that there was one. Mrs. Venn then asked him to see from whom it came and he replied, 'It has the Deal

---

[1] I speak of a telepathic message being sent. We do not know that anything which could be called sending, or even anything which could be called a message, is involved in the phenomenon of telepathy, but such language is sometimes convenient and does no harm provided that it is not taken to be exact.

postmark, it is from Frances, for you or me.' Mrs. Venn, whose back was towards the table all this time, turned and saw that there was no letter. It was evident that A had had a visual hallucination as he was confident that he had seen the letter, read the postmark and identified the writer by the handwriting. This was at 9 o'clock in the morning. An hour later a letter arrived by the second post. It was for A from Frances and bore the Deal postmark. Frances had been away from Deal and neither Mrs. Venn nor A knew that she had returned there.

From *Proc.*, XI, 503: Professor J. Thoulet was sharing rooms with a friend at Rivanazzaro, in Piedmont. The wife of this friend was then living at Toulon and was shortly expecting a baby. Professor Thoulet woke one night thinking that he had a telegram in his hand. He entered the room of his friend and woke him, crying out, 'You have just got a little girl, the telegram says,' and then began to read the telegram. Before he had completed doing so, it appeared to vanish from his hand and he realized that he had been dreaming. His friend made him write down the words which he had seemed to read and he made a sort of plan of the remainder, although he could not then remember any of the words in spite of the fact that he had read them in his dream. Professor Thoulet left Rivanazzaro after two or three days and went to Turin; eight or ten days later he received a telegram from his friend as follows, 'Come directly, you were right.' He returned to Rivanazzaro and was shown a telegram which his friend had received; the beginning was exactly what he had written down and when he read the remaining words he remembered them as the same as those which he had seemed to read in the dream telegram. The confinement had taken place ten days after the night of the dream. Professor Thoulet was personally known to Professor Charles Richet who vouches for the story.

It will be seen from a consideration of these cases that while the simpler instances can be fairly adequately accounted for by telepathy, in the more complex the telepathic hypothesis requires a good deal of stretching to make it cover the facts. In Professor Thoulet's case, for example, we have to assume that the sex of the child to be born was correctly guessed beforehand, also that the actual wording of the telegram was decided upon ten days before the event took place. Where we have to make additional unsupported assumptions in order to enable any hypothesis to cover the facts, the probability that that hypothesis is applicable rapidly diminishes as the number and intrinsic improbability of the assumptions increase.

We know, or at any rate we are pretty certain, that there is such a thing as telepathy, although we do not know much about it, or how and under what conditions it works; if, therefore we can explain a phenomenon by postulating telepathy we are bound, provisionally, to accept that explanation rather than one which necessitates the operation of a less well established cause, such as supernormal precognition.

But if we have, as here, a graduated series of cases wherein the explanation by telepathy becomes progressively more difficult and the supplementary assumptions more numerous and less likely, the tailing off of applicability tends rather to discredit the hypothesis as a whole. However, supernormal precognition is so extraordinary and intrinsically unbelievable that one feels disposed to grasp at any alternative, even if only barely possible. It seems to me that the safer course to pursue is provisionally to class all these cases as non-precognitive, but to bear in mind that the classification may have to be modified. We can bracket together the two rival hypotheses, but put telepathy first.

The second type of case which may possibly be explained by telepathy is that in which the intention to perform some action has been formed by someone and the subject somehow obtains knowledge of it by means of telepathy or mind-reading. I would remind readers that a large number of what we call pre-cognitions contain no definite reference to the future: it is only after they have subsequently been found to be veridical, i.e., truth-telling, of a future event that they are recognized as precognitive.

Suppose that B forms the intention of visiting A and A dreams of that visit before it actually happens, we should explain the case as being due to telepathy from B, even though A's dream showed the event as being present and not future. B, for example, might be thinking of his proposed visit and picturing himself as being with A, this picture might then be transmitted to A by telepathy.

Of course the action intended may not be a visit, it may be anything whatsoever and not in any way connected with the person who experiences the precognition. In such a case the telepathic message would, as it were, strike at random.

The first case which I cite is one of arrival of visitors; it is taken from *Proc.*, VI, 374. It will be observed that the person who had the precognition was herself a visitor at the house and would, on the face of it, seem to have been the most unlikely one to receive the telepathic message, if such there were. It may have been, however, that she was in some way peculiarly sensitive to such things and thus picked it up while the others missed it.

Here is the story. Miss X, driving in a wagonette with the friends with whom she was staying, when nearing the house remarked, 'You have very early visitors.' None of the others could see anything, but Miss X described a dogcart, with a white horse and two men in it, standing at the door. She saw one of the men get down and commence playing with a fox terrier. She described their appearance and commented on their dress, although the distance was so great that she could hardly have seen them normally. As they reached the house and drove up the drive, Miss X called attention to fresh wheel marks in the gravel; no one else, however, could see them. On entering the house they learned that no visitors had called. Shortly afterwards, a dogcart with a white horse, in which were two men, drove up and the scene was enacted exactly as Miss X had described it. Their appearance, clothes, etc., were as she had described, and one of the men alighted and played with the dog.

Here the hypothesis of telepathy requires a good deal of stretching, although it might be made to cover the facts. We should have to suppose that not only the appearance of the dogcart, horse and the men themselves, was transmitted telepathically, but also that the intention of one of them to alight and play with the dog had already been formed. The hallucinatory wheel marks in the gravel might have been simply the effect of suggestion on Miss X.

In the next case the intention is not of a visit but of a far more sinister action. That the subject received the precognition can be accounted for, if at all, only by the fact that she was on the spot and happened to be peculiarly sensitive. Whether she was always sensitive to such influences is not known. The case is reported in *Proc.*, X, 332. Mrs. McAlpine was sitting by the side of a lake and was absorbed in the beauty of the scene; presently she felt a cold chill creeping over her and a curious numbness, as though she could not move. She felt frightened, yet impelled to stare at the water. Gradually a black cloud seemed to rise and in the midst she saw a tall man in a suit of tweeds jump into the water and sink. Then the blackness passed and the scene became normal again. Mrs. McAlpine told her brother and sister of her experience, but they only laughed at it.

About a week later, Mr. Espie, a bank clerk, who was unknown to Mrs. McAlpine, committed suicide by drowning himself at that place. There was evidence to show that he had been contemplating taking his life for some time.

Mrs. McAlpine's account is confirmed by her sister.

It may be that the man, in contemplating suicide, had decided on the spot where he would do it. The chill and numbness felt by Mrs. McAlpine, also the

black cloud, could be accounted for as being symbolic.

In my collection of cases I have found 9 of dreams,
9 impressions, 9 hallucinations, 2 mediumistic and
1 crystal vision, which might possibly be explained by
telepathy.

The next alternative to be discussed is that of *auto-
suggestion*. The way in which this would work is somewhat as follows. The subject gets an idea that something
is going to happen and this idea acts as an auto-
suggestion and operates so as actually to bring about
the very thing which was anticipated. It is clear that
this is possible only where such things as are capable
of being produced by suggestion are concerned; these
are mainly to do with the state of health of the subject.
If it were a case of performing some specific action,
we should not consider it necessary to invoke any
unusual cause whatsoever. It might conceivably be
that the subject unconsciously influenced another person to act in a certain way and thus fulfil the apparent
precognition, but this assumes the existence of telepathic suggestion. I do not say that telepathic suggestion is impossible, or even unknown, but I do not
know of any cases which could plausibly be referred to
this cause. Dr. Tanagras, of Athens, has elaborated a
theory on these lines by means of which he seeks to
explain many cases of precognition, even those involving accidents to material things, such as railway
disasters, but I am not disposed to regard it very
seriously.

We know, however, that auto-suggestion is potent to
produce effects on the body and mind, and where the

apparent precognition is of such an event, it seems reasonable to adopt the hypothesis that the fulfilment was due to the operation of that cause.

The following case is an illustration. It is taken from *Proc.*, V, 291. The youngest son of Professor Brooks had been ill, but had recovered and was apparently quite well. He told his mother, who had just returned from abroad, that a friend of his, who had died some months previously, had appeared to him and told him that he would die from heart trouble on 5th December at 3 o'clock in the afternoon. Everyone, including the doctor, laughed at him; but the boy remained convinced that he would die as foretold. On 4th December he took leave of his friends, giving them flowers and parting presents. He rose as customary on the 5th, ate an unusually hearty breakfast and was, to all appearances, quite well. At lunch he complained of faintness and died of paralysis of the heart at 3.10 p.m. He was aged 17 years and 5 months at the time of his death.

The number of cases which might plausibly be explained by auto-suggestion I found to be 3 dreams, 2 impressions, 7 hallucinations and 1 mediumistic. It may possibly be significant that there are more of them to be found among hallucinations than in all the other classes put together. It seems reasonable to explain this on the grounds that hallucinations, being much rarer and more exciting events than dreams, impressions, etc., would thereby tend to be more likely to produce an effective auto-suggestion.

The next class to be discussed is that in which the knowledge shown in the precognition might possibly have been derived from inference from *subliminal knowledge*. It is known that our subliminal knowledge may sometimes be wider and fuller than that of our normal consciousness. We frequently notice things which never come into the focus of our ordinary attention; for example, we may be reading in a room in which a clock is ticking and be quite unconscious of the sound until something brings it to our notice, when we recognize that we have been hearing it all the time.

It is clear that this type of alternative explanation is one which is capable of almost indefinite expansion. We cannot set any precise limit to our subliminal knowledge, especially if we are prepared to admit the possibility of acquiring it by telepathy or clairvoyance. Moreover, it is abstractly possible that our powers of subliminal inference may greatly exceed our normal capacity in that respect. We must not, however, push the explanation too far. In many cases the requisite amount of knowledge would be so great, and the powers of inference therefrom so fantastically acute, that the hypothesis is quite untenable.

The cases which may plausibly be held to come under this heading are mainly those which are concerned with the state of health or the course of illness. It is not unreasonable to suppose that the subliminal mind may possess a wider and deeper knowledge of the state of the organism, and become aware of developments in the course of a disease some time before the effects of these are apparent to the supraliminal.

It is further possible that this cause of apparent precognition may be supplemented by auto-suggestion; thus the subject may become subliminally aware of the development of his illness, and infer therefrom the probability of a change in his bodily state; auto-suggestion may then step in and operate to bring about the exact fulfilment of the inference.

The following is an example of this, though, as a case, it is rather defective, as the prediction was only partially fulfilled. It is taken from *Journal*, IV, 292–3. Mrs. Edwards had an auditory hallucination predicting her death at a certain hour. At the exact time she had a severe haemorrhage and very nearly died. The clock was actually striking when the haemorrhage started.

Other instances of cases which might possibly be attributed to inference from subliminally acquired knowledge are:

Proc., XI, 432, Dr. Suddick, with his wife and two friends, was sitting for table-tilting. One of the sitters, Mr. Cottnam, inquired concerning his friend, Mr. Chris Varis, then lying ill in another town and expected to die at any moment. Mr. Varis's doctor had told Mr. Cottnam that he would probably live only a few days at most. In answer to the inquiry, the table rapped forty times. Taking this to mean that forty days would elapse before the date of the death, which would bring it to 8th October, Mr. Cottnam asked, 'Will he pass out on 8th October?' The table replied, 'Yes.' Asked if he would pass in the forenoon, it again answered 'Yes.' Mr. Cottnam then asked whether a telegram would be sent to him on the morning of the 8th, giving the information. The table replied 'Yes.' A night or so later, Mr. Cottnam, sitting at another house with different sitters, had a message purporting to come from a friend, recently deceased but of whose death he was unaware. This message confirmed that Mr. Varis would die on 8th October.

The prediction was fulfilled: Mr. Varis died at 6 a.m. on 8th October, and a telegram was sent to Mr. Cottnam that morning.

Fourteen people signed a statement to the effect that they knew of the prediction before the event.

Mrs. Varis, the widow, stated that neither she nor her husband knew anything about the prediction having been made.

Proc., XI, 446. A lady staying with a relative in Paris, saw, while she was in bed, a hallucinatory figure resembling him, but shrunken, partially paralysed and apparently imbecile, crossing the room. He was asleep at the time. Some time later he was attacked by softening of the brain, and became nearly as she had seen him in the hallucinatory vision.

Counting all those cases which, without undue stretching of the hypothesis, might be accounted for as being due to inference from subliminal knowledge, I found 10 among dreams, 2 borderland, 5 impressions, 19 hallucinations, and 1 crystal vision.

It must be remembered, however, that there was no independent evidence in any of these cases that the subject actually did possess the requisite subliminal knowledge: all we can say is that it might possibly have been so, and thus an alternative to supernormal precognition must be allowed.

The last of the possible alternatives is explanation by *hyperaesthesia*, that is to say, unusual or supernormal acuity of the senses. There is excellent independent evidence that hyperaesthesia occurs, sometimes to an extent which appears almost miraculous. It is, as a rule, a sporadic occurrence, not the kind of thing which can be called up at will; although there are grounds for believing that in certain cases it can sometimes be induced by hypnosis.

It is quite possible that the hyperaesthetic sensation may not be consciously received as such, but may reach only the subliminal mind, in which case the knowledge acquired might rise in symbolic form to the supraliminal, or might be transmitted as a vague feeling of uneasiness, an hallucinatory warning, and so on.

Here are some cases. The first is from *Proc.*, XI, 418. A lady, living in a wooden house in the Rockies, while sitting one evening in the porch, had an hallucinatory vision of a fire in the distance. After watching for about ten minutes, she heard a faint crackling sound and, being disturbed by the hallucination which, at the time, she took to be real, she went to investigate and found her own house on fire. She was just in time to save her child. There was no other fire in the vicinity.

As lending support to the hypothesis of hyper-aesthesia, it is interesting that the same subject experienced a second somewhat similar occurrence. While in England, she was wakened one night from sleep by the impression of hearing her name called. On waking she found the nightlight blazing.

The second is from *Proc.*, XI, 421. M. H. Gray had an hallucinatory vision of flames. On investigation she found that the clothes in the laundry were on fire. This might have been hyperaesthesia of smell or of hearing, although two closed doors intervened.

The following, though possibly due to hyperaesthesia,

D

requires a considerable stretching of that hypothesis to make it fit. It is from *Proc.*, XI, 424. Mr. F. O. Smith, a dentist, was working at his bench on a set of false teeth using a copper vulcanizer, when he heard a quick, imperative voice call twice, 'Run to the window, quick.' Without stopping to think where the voice came from, he obeyed, and at that instant the vulcanizer exploded, partially wrecking the room. He thus escaped death or serious injury. It was found later that the safety valve of the vulcanizer had become inoperative. Mr. Smith may have had a hyperaesthetic indication of this, or of the undue pressure in the vessel; for example, there may have been some slight alteration in the sound emitted by the boiling.

I did not find many cases where this explanation could fairly be applied: there were 1 borderland, 6 impressions and 4 hallucinations.

In making all these selections I have stretched the various hypotheses as far as they could reasonably stand it, on the principle that explanation by an independently known cause was to be preferred to postulating anything so antecedently unbelievable as non-inferential knowledge of the future. However, if subsequent investigation should provide grounds for accepting supernormal precognition as actually happening at all frequently, it may be that the stretching in which I have indulged will have to be considered as having been too liberal, and that some of the cases assigned to the alternative categories could more plausibly be reckoned as instances of true precognition.

It is better, nevertheless, to be on the safe side and

disallow all cases where an alternative is even remotely probable. We are then left with the following cases of precognition : 94 dreams, 4 borderland, 17 impressions, 23 hallucinations, 41 mediumistic and 4 crystal vision, making 183 in all. This is a sufficiently formidable array of evidence to challenge us to find an explanation —we cannot lightly set it aside.

Besides these cases collected from the first fifty years of the records of the S.P.R., there are a few which have been published since I made my report. There is also the collection made by the Hon. Mrs. Alfred Lyttelton, contained in the book already referred to; these number thirty-two. The general standard of evidential value of these cases is high, in none has an unsupported narrative been accepted, confirmation of some sort has always been obtained. They are classified under four headings, viz., (1) those which may be attributed to coincidence, (2) those which could be accounted for by telepathy, but which cannot be dismissed as examples of coincidence, (3) those in which the fore-knowledge shown could conceivably have been derived from telepathy, but telepathy of a very complex kind, (4) true precognition. There are 7 cases in the first class, 5 in the second, 4 in the third and 16 in the last. The types of incident precognized range from winning horses to accidental death, trivial incidents to serious disasters, including the loss of the Airship R101. There are dreams, hallucinations, impressions, etc.

I need not enter into any discussion of the individual cases: this has already been so well done by the author that anything further would be redundant. For those who desire fuller acquaintance with the evidence for precognition I would recommend reading the book itself.

In the other work to which I have referred, viz., Professor Richet's *L'Avenir et la Prémonition* there is a collection of some 140 or 150 cases; some, however, have been drawn from the records of the S.P.R. and have thus already been counted in my collection. Roughly one may say that there are some 100 cases in this book additional to those which are reported in *Proceedings* and *Journal* of the Society for Psychical Research. Here the average evidential value is, perhaps, not quite so high as in the other collections, but there is quite a number of cases which appear to be satisfactory in this respect.

Besides these authorities, numerous examples of precognition are to be found scattered about in the literature of psychical research and spiritualism. It is, of course, out of the question to make a comprehensive collection from all sources, nor would the result repay the labour. The total mass of evidence is so great that it would be impracticable to attempt to classify and analyse it all: the only method is to take a large, and fairly representative, sample and confine investigation to that, assuming that what is found to be true therein will apply roughly and generally to the whole mass.

I would, however, just mention one other authority, Dr. Osty of the Institut Métapsychique of Paris. In the publications of that institute, viz., the *Revue Métapsychique*, as well as in his various books, may be found many examples of precognition, investigated and analysed with care. Dr. Osty arrives at the conclusion that it is sometimes possible for a suitably sensitive subject to obtain supernormal knowledge of the future (*le déroulement*) of his own life, or of that of another human being.

Were all the reported cases of apparent precognition collected from all these various sources and subjected to analysis, I am sure that, after the rejection of doubtful cases and those which could reasonably be ascribed to chance coincidence or other normal causes, as well as those which can be accounted for on the basis of the four alternative hypotheses which I have discussed, there would remain a very considerable mass of evidence to be reckoned with, that is to say, cases of true precognition or non-inferential foreknowledge.

If, in discussing cases of this kind I confine myself to those drawn from the *Proceedings* and *Journal* of the S.P.R., it is not because I think that they are in any way superior in value, it is because I am more familiar with them, and also for the reason that it is more convenient for those readers who may wish to verify my summaries by turning to the original reports, if the field from which they are drawn is made as narrow as possible. *Proceedings* of the Society for Psychical Research are available to the public and can always be obtained from the Society itself; the *Journal* is printed for private circulation among members of the Society.

CHAPTER IV

CASES OF PRECOGNITION

In this chapter I propose to give summarized accounts of a selection of cases illustrating the various types of incident which form the subject of precognitions. I shall draw them mainly from those remaining over from my original collection, after deduction of all those which can be assigned to alternative causes.

I will start with a few cases where the event foreseen was natural death.

From *Journal*, IV, 222: A girl, sixteen years old, dreamed that she was walking with her cousin, having been to a musical entertainment. Suddenly the cousin, B, appeared to faint and leaned for support against some railings. She tried to support her, but gradually B sank to the ground and died.

About a week later B, who had been to an operatic performance, fainted in the street on her way home and died. Subsequent inquiries showed that she had leaned for support against some railings and gradually subsided dead. The account is confirmed by the mother and sister of the dreamer, who had been told of the dream before the event.

In this case the dream was not an exact representation of the actual event, as the dreamer herself played a part therein, whereas she was not present when B

died. This discrepancy may be taken as mere drama-
tization by the dreaming mind.

Proc., XI, 577: Lady Q, living with her uncle, who
was like a father to her, dreamed that she was sitting
in the drawing-room of his house with her sister. It
was a brilliant spring day and there were many flowers
showing in the garden, over which, however, there was
a thin coating of snow. In her dream she knew that her
uncle had been found dead by the side of a certain
bridle path about three miles from the house and that
he was wearing a dark homespun suit; his horse was
standing by him. She also knew that the body was
being brought home in a two-horse farm waggon with
hay in the bottom. They were waiting for the waggon
with the body to arrive at the house. Then, in the
dream, she saw the waggon come to the door and two
men, well known to the dreamer, carry the body
upstairs with considerable difficulty as the uncle was
a very tall and heavy man. During this proceeding the
body's left hand hung down and struck against the
banisters as the men ascended the stairs. This detail
gave her unreasonable horror and she woke.

In the morning, feeling much upset, she told her
uncle and begged him to promise that he would never
ride that particular road alone. He promised that he
would always make an excuse to have a groom with
him when he rode that way in the future.

Gradually the memory of the dream grew fainter
until, two years later, it was repeated in every detail.
Lady Q taxed her uncle with having broken his promise, and he admitted that he had occasionally done
so. Four years after this, Lady Q, having married and

left her uncle's house, was living in London and was expecting her first baby. On the night before she was taken ill she dreamed the dream again with the variation that she seemed to be in her bedroom in London and not in her uncle's drawing-room as previously. She was, however, able to perceive the whole scene as in the former dreams. Then came another fresh point; a gentleman, dressed all in black, whose face she could not see, stood beside her bed and told her that her uncle was dead. She awoke in great distress but, being then so ill, ceased to dwell on the dream.

After a few days she was allowed to write a few lines in pencil to her uncle. This note reached him two days before his death.

During her convalescence, she wondered at not hearing from him, until, one morning, she was told that her step-father wished to see her. He entered the room dressed in black and stood beside her bed. Lady Q cried out, 'The Colonel is dead. I know all about it. I have dreamed it often.'

Subsequent inquiries showed that the dream was fulfilled in every detail, including that of the left hand striking against the banisters. The men who carried the body upstairs were those seen in the dream. The only detail which was not correct was that of the flowers and snow, but Lady Q discovered that dreams of flowers and snow were considered as symbolic of death by members of her family.

I have summarized this case rather fully as it seems to me that it is a particularly interesting one. Not only are the details of the precognition very full and numerous, but the fact of recurrence makes it specially impressive. Also it is an example of long-distance pre-cognition, the first dream having occurred six years before the event.

There is another point to which I should like to call attention as I shall discuss it later. It will be noticed that the precognition falls into two distinct parts; in one the dreamer knows certain facts without there having been any imagery of the events, in the other the events are actually seen in the dream.

Lady Q's account is confirmed by her husband and her step-father.

The next is from *Journal*, XVII, 145: Madame Bouscarlet, of Geneva, dreamed of seeing a friend of hers in Russia driving in a carriage. The details of the scene were symbolic to her of death. The friend said, 'Madame Nitchinof leaves the Institute on the 17th.' Mme. Bouscarlet wrote an account of her dream to another friend in Russia, and the letter with post-mark was examined by the investigator, who was convinced that it had been written and posted before the event. Mme. Nitchinof, who was head of the Institute, died, quite unexpectedly, on the 17th, having been first taken ill some five or six days *after* the date of the dream. Thus she did leave the Institute as foretold.

This is a simple case though the prediction of the actual date of the death gives it value. It is interesting, however, as being one of the few in which documentary evidence was available.

I will now pass to cases of accidental death.

The first is from *Proc.*, V, 322: Mrs. Schweitzer dreamed that she saw her younger son, F, with a stranger, on some cliffs. Her son suddenly slipped down the side of the cliff. She turned to the stranger and said, 'May I ask who you are and what is your name?' He replied, 'My name is Henry Irvin.' Mrs. Schweitzer then said, 'Do you mean Irving the actor?' and the stranger replied, 'No, not exactly, but something after that style.' On waking she was very worried by the dream and told her elder son, begging him to recall his brother, who was away travelling for the firm on business. He ridiculed the matter, saying that F was quite safe as he was in Manchester.

About eight days later F was killed on the cliffs at Scarborough, where he had gone for a week's holiday after completing his business in Manchester. Mrs. Schweitzer, on visiting the place, met the man who had accompanied him on the fatal occasion and recognized him as the stranger of her dream. She inquired if his name were Henry and being told that it was, recounted her dream. He then said that he used to recite at concerts, etc., and was always introduced on such occasions as Henry Irvin, Jr. His real name was Deverell.

This case is very interesting, not only as being quite a good precognition covering a considerable amount of detail, viz., the site of the accident, the presence and appearance of the dead man's companion, but also the very curious matter of the companion's name. This seems an odd and irrelevant fact to be included in the dream; granted the possibility of precognition, one can understand, more or less, that knowledge of the approaching death of her son might be transmitted to, or acquired by, his mother, but one can conceive no reason whatsoever why a fancy name of a chance acquaintance should have been included. It was knowledge which was, presumably, in the possession of Mr. Deverell alone, out of all the actors in the affair, and we can only assume that it was somehow derived from his mind. Yet at the time of the dream the dead man and Mr. Deverell were not acquainted. The strange allusive manner, also, in which the fact is conveyed in the dream is noteworthy.

This detail appears to me to be utterly inexplicable unless we adopt the rather unlikely hypothesis that the precognition occurred in the first place to Mr. Deverell and never reached his normal consciousness, but was transmitted telepathically to Mrs. Schweitzer, and that the detail of the name, 'Henry Irvin,' was added as a sort of extra identification.

Next from *Proc.*, XI, 517. At the end of February, or the beginning of March, 1883, Thomas Carbert, porter at Escrick Station, Yorks, dreamed that he saw Mr. Thompson, the stationmaster, lying with his legs cut off, close to a heap of coal and against a small cabin at the back of the station. The accident had been caused by what was called a 'pick-up' goods train, and, in his dream, Carbert knew that it occurred in the month of May. He told his dream to Mr. Thompson the next day, who laughed at it, though it made him uneasy. The same morning Mr. Thompson told of the dream to a Mr. Hartas Foxton, who confirms the account.

On 18th May of the same year, Mr. Thompson was run over by a 'pick-up' goods train and both his legs were cut off. The accident happened at the back of the station exactly in the place seen by Carbert in his dream.

Mrs. Sidgwick, commenting on this case, appeared to think that accidents of this kind to railway officials were not rare enough to raise the incident above chance. While I hesitate to differ from so great an authority, I cannot help thinking that the number of stationmasters killed every year on the railways of this country is a relatively small percentage of the whole, and when the details of the precognition are taken into account, viz., the cutting off of both legs, the exact place of the accident, the month when it was to occur, and the fact that it was caused by a certain type of train, it appears to me that chance is a very improbable explanation.

I now turn to accidents not involving death.

The first case which I shall cite is interesting as it exemplifies the recurrent dream and a warning which was acted upon. It is that of Mrs. Reay, *Proc.*, V, 313. Mrs. Reay dreamed that the carriage which was sent to meet her at Mortlake Station to take her to her sister's house at Roehampton was upset in the road close to the house. The dream caused her to wake, but she went off to sleep again, when it was repeated. She again woke feeling very nervous, but eventually went to sleep for the third time. On waking in the morning she had forgotten the dream.

As had been arranged, she went to Mortlake and was driven from the station in a pony carriage. On nearing her sister's house, the horse became restive and the groom got down but could find nothing wrong, this happened three times; while he was examining the horse on the third occasion, the memory of the dream came back to Mrs. Reay and she decided to get out and walk the remaining distance to the house. The groom then drove off by himself; in a short distance the horse became unmanageable and the carriage was upset and smashed. The groom managed to extricate himself, but said that he was thankful that Mrs. Reay had alighted as he could not otherwise have saved her from a serious accident.

Mr. Reay, who heard of the dream on the evening after the accident, confirms. Although this dream was not told beforehand, Gurney, a widely experienced psychical researcher, who investigated the case, stated that, after a personal interview, he felt quite convinced that the account was correct.

The following is a relatively simple case. It is taken from *Proc.*, V, 340. Mrs. Donaldson, on Sunday morning, 29th September, 1878, roused her husband by moaning and speaking in her sleep. She said, 'Oh, B! What is the matter with your face?' and then began to sob. She told her husband that she had dreamed of seeing B, her nurse, standing in the nursery with her back turned to her; on being spoken to, B had half turned round, when she saw that her face wa' terribly cut and bruised.

The following evening B did not appear as usual family prayers and Mrs. Donaldson was informed t! she had met with an accident. She went upstair' the nursery and saw B precisely as she had appe in the dream with her face cut and bruised.

Mrs. Donaldson's account is confirmed b' husband.

I will now give one case of accident to material things. Here the dream, which was itself quite vague, was reinforced by an impression on waking, which focussed and made definite the reference of the precognition. It is another instance of a recurrent dream. I take the account from *Proc.*, V, 335. Frau K dreamed of an outbreak of fire and, on waking, thought that her securities, which were kept in the fireproof safe at a brewery, were in danger. She could not remember dreaming anything about the securities but felt that they were somehow connected with the fire. She told her dream to several people. Three days later it was repeated with even greater distinctness, and her anxiety for her securities increased. She begged her husband to have them removed and he, after much objection, finally consented. As soon as they were deposited in a bank her anxiety ceased. About six weeks later she again dreamed of a fire, but this time with no feelings of anxiety, rather with relief. Simultaneously with the dream the brewery was burnt down and the safe so exposed to the fire that all papers therein were destroyed.

The account is confirmed by five witnesses.

Turning now to trivial incidents, in the first case which I give the lady to whom it occurred might have been inclined to dispute my judgment in treating holes burnt in her new carpet as trivial. However, here it is. It comes from *Proc.*, V, 343. Mrs. Mackensie dreamed that she was in her drawing-room with several people, including a Mr. J. She left the room to see whether supper was ready; on returning to the drawing-room she found the carpet, a new one, covered with black spots. She was very angry and, when Mr. J said that they were inkstains, replied, 'I know it has been burnt and I counted five patches.' She told the dream at breakfast. It being Sunday, the party went to church; afterwards Mr. J joined them for lunch, a thing which he had never done before. Mrs. Mackensie went into the dining-room to see if lunch were ready. On returning to the drawing-room, she noticed a spot on the carpet. Mr. J said that it was surely ink and then pointed to some more spots. Mrs. Mackensie cried out, 'Oh, my dream! My new carpet burnt!' This proved to be correct; it was afterwards discovered that the housemaid, having allowed the fire to go out, had carried live coals from another room to relight it and had spilled some on the carpet. Five holes were burnt. This account was confirmed by Miss Mackensie. It was investigated by Gurney, who knew the family and vouched for the accuracy of their story after having personally interrogated them.

There is one discrepancy: the meal was lunch and not supper as in the dream.

The following case is taken from *Proc.*, XI, 491: Mr. Haggard, British Consul at Trieste, had a vivid dream in which he was invited to dine with the German Consul-General. He was ushered into a large room on the walls of which were hung trophies of arms from East Africa. (He, himself, had been much in East Africa.) After dinner he went to inspect the arms and noticed a beautiful gold-mounted sword which he pointed out to the French Vice-Consul, who at that moment joined him. As they were talking the Russian Consul came up and joined in the conversation, remarking on the small size of the hilt of the sword. He became very excited while talking and waved his arm above his head as though wielding a sword.

Mr. Haggard was much impressed with the vividness of this dream and recounted it to his wife on waking.

Some six weeks later he was invited to dine with the German Consul-General when the events of the dream were repeated in every detail. While the Russian Consul was talking and waving his arm about, Mr. Haggard withdrew quietly from the group, walked to where his wife was standing and called her attention to the scene. She remembered the dream perfectly and was able to witness its fulfilment.

Mr. Haggard's account is confirmed by his wife and two other witnesses.

The next case is that of Mrs. Atlay, *Proc.*, XI, 487. She dreamed that her husband, the Bishop of Hereford, was away from home and that she read morning prayers in the hall of the palace. After doing so, on entering the dining-room, she saw an enormous pig standing between the dining table and the sideboard. This dream amused her and she told it to the governess, who confirms the account, and to her children, before reading prayers. After prayers, she opened the dining-room door and saw the pig standing between the dining table and the sideboard in the exact spot in which she had seen it in the dream.

The pig had escaped from its sty while prayers were being read.

On page 488, *Proc.*, XI, there is reported another case of a very unusual, though trivial, incident having been foreseen in a dream. It is shortly as follows:

Mrs. C dreamed that she was being persistently followed by a monkey, which terrified her extremely as she had an intense horror of monkeys. She mentioned the dream to her husband and family at breakfast, and Mr. C suggested that she should go for a short walk to throw off the unpleasant impression caused by the dream. Quite contrary to her custom, she went out for a walk with her children. After a short while she saw, to her horror, 'the very monkey of her dream.' The monkey commenced to follow her, causing her great distress.

Her account is confirmed by Mr. C and by Mrs. C's nurse.

This case is queer in that it was due to the dream that Mr. C suggested that Mrs. C should go for a walk, a thing which she would not otherwise have done. Thus the dream itself brought about circumstances which rendered the fulfilment possible. It need hardly be stated that it is a most unusual event to be followed by a monkey in the streets of London, where the incident happened.

The last of these cases is perhaps the most important of them all. I said earlier that I had not found a perfect case. The one which I am now about to cite, however, runs perfection very close. I can find very little fault with it. It is from *Proc.*, XX, 331. Mrs. Verrall, writing automatically on 11th December, 1901, had the following in her script: 'Frost and a candle in the dim light. Marmontel. He was reading on a sofa or in bed – there was only a candle's light. She will surely remember this. The book was lent, not his own – he talked about it.' On 17th December she again wrote: 'Marmontel is right. It was a French book, a memoir,

E

I think. Passy may help, Souvenirs de Passy or Fleury. Marmontel was not on the cover – the book was bound and was lent – two volumes in old-fashioned binding and print. It is not in any papers – it is an attempt to make someone remember – an incident.'

On 1st March, 1902, a Mr. Marsh mentioned to Mrs. Verrall at dinner that he had been reading *Marmontel's Memoirs*. Being interested on account of the references in the script, she asked him for particulars about his reading. He said that he had borrowed the books from the London Library and had taken the first volume with him to Paris, where he had read it on the evening of 20th February and again on 21st. On each occasion he read by the light of a candle, on the 20th he was in bed, on the 21st he was lying on two chairs. The weather was very cold but there was no frost. The books were bound, as are most of the books in the London Library, not in modern binding, but the name Marmontel was on the back. The edition is in three volumes but at the time of his visit to Mrs. Verrall he had read only two.

Asked whether 'Passy' or 'Fleury' would help, he replied that Fleury's name certainly occurred in the book, but was not sure about Passy. On returning to town Mr. Marsh wrote to Mrs. Verrall saying that on 21st February, while lying on the two chairs, he had read in the first volume of *Marmontel's Memoirs* a chapter describing the finding at Passy of a panel, etc., connected with a story in which Fleury plays an important part. It will be seen that the description given in the script was in the main accurate. The only errors were that there was no frost, though the weather was cold, that the book was in three volumes, though Mr. Marsh had read only two, and that the name Marmontel was on the back.

In spite of these discrepancies it seems to me that the coincidences between the statement in the script and the account given by Mr. Marsh are far too many and too detailed to be ascribable to chance. It is only on account of these errors that I have hesitated to claim perfection for this case. I do not think that any attention need be paid to the fact that the concluding words of the scripts seemed to imply that an incident in the past was being described.

From the evidential point of view the case is unassailable. The actual scripts were sent by Mrs. Verrall before the 1st March, when she met Mr. Marsh, to one of the investigators of the Cross Correspondences,[1] which were occurring about this time. There is, therefore, completely satisfactory documentary evidence for the precognition, while, as for the truth of Mr. Marsh's account of the event, no one in their senses would venture to question it. The only alternative is the obviously absurd one of collusion between Mrs. Verrall and Mr. Marsh.

I will now leave these trivial incidents and give a case which cannot be classed with them, although it is an incident. As I have already mentioned, the distinction between the two classes is quite arbitrary. I made it, in the first instance, because I wanted to emphasize the fact that so many of the events foreseen are com-

---

[1] The first volume of this series, *Evidence of Personal Survival from Cross Correspondences*, gives a brief and simple account of this branch of psychical research.

pletely unimportant and meaningless. I consider that
this fact is of primary importance in trying to understand the problem.

The first of these cases is to be found on page 505,
Proc., XI: it is a borderland case.

Mr. Alfred Cooper, a medical man, who was attending professionally the late Earl of L, called on the Duke
of Hamilton, whom he was also attending. After the
consultation they both went into the drawing-room
where the Duchess was. The Duke said, 'Oh, Cooper,
how is the Earl?' 'What Earl?' asked the Duchess.
Mr. Cooper replied, 'Lord L.' The Duchess then said,
'That is very odd,' and then recounted a vision which
she had had between sleeping and waking in which she
saw Lord L in a chair as if in a fit; there was a man with
a red beard standing by his side. Lord L appeared to
be by the side of a bath over which there was a red
lamp. Mr. Cooper said that there was very little the
matter with Lord L and that he would soon be all right.

Lord L did get better and was very nearly well,
when, after six or seven days, he contracted inflam-
mation of both lungs and became very ill. He had two
male nurses. When Mr. Cooper called to see him, he
found him as in the vision of the Duchess, in a chair by
the side of a bath over which was a red lamp; the male
nurse with him had a red beard.

The account is signed by both the Duchess of
Hamilton and Mr. Cooper.

There seems to be no reason whatsoever why this
scene should have been foreseen by the Duchess. It looks
like a perfectly meaningless and sporadic happening.

In the next case there is a warning which is acted

upon. On the face of them such cases are easier to understand than the meaningless trivialities reported above; that is to say, if we assume that the motives to which we are accustomed somehow hold good in the environment from which precognitions come. They do not, however, lead us any nearer to a satisfactory explanation of the origin of the foreknowledge.

It is another borderland case and is reported in *Proc.*, XI, 481.

Miss Graham, between sleep and waking, heard a voice saying, 'Miss Graham, take your money out of the bank.' She had all her money in a bank in Boston. She paid no attention to the warning and went that morning to her dressmaker. On arrival she was obliged to wait, and another lady, also waiting, seemed determined to talk to her. Miss Graham was not socially inclined and did not respond freely, until the stranger asked, "Do you know anything of Howe's Bank?' Miss Graham replied that she had her account there. The lady then proceeded to tell her that the bank was unsafe, and said that she had felt impelled, against her will, to tell her this. Miss Graham succeeded in withdrawing her money; the bank stopped payment the next day.

This is confirmed by Dr. Caroline E. Hastings, who was with Miss Graham when she went to the bank.

This case is interesting as, if we can accept the statement of the strange lady who spoke to Miss Graham, that she had felt impelled against her will to tell her about the bank, it looks as though some external agency were involved – as if two persons, mutually unacquainted, had come under the influence of whatever it was that was trying to convey the warning. The whole set of circumstances is worthy of note. Had Miss Graham and the other lady not decided to go to the dressmaker on that particular morning, and had they not been compelled to wait, it seems probable that the original warning would have failed of its purpose. How so complicated a set of coincidences could have been brought about I cannot imagine.

It is possible that this was only an instance of illusion of memory and that Miss Graham falsely imagined that she had had the dream; alternatively, the dream warning may have been a telepathic communication from some one who actually knew that the bank was unsafe, and that she had her account there.

The next case might have been classed as an accident. It is given in *Proc.*, XI, 489. I give only a very condensed account. Colonel Coghill received a letter from a friend, telling of a dream in which she saw him lying under his horse with several people trying to assist him. The dream was fulfilled exactly two days later. The letter written by the lady telling her dream was unfortunately lost, but had been seen by Sir Joseph Coghill, who confirms it. However, a letter from Colonel Coghill referring to the dream, written before the event, is preserved; there is, therefore, some documentary evidence.

I have already given instances of 'Arrival' cases and need add no more here. I will now give two examples of cases of precognition of 'Winners.' The first is from *Proc.*, XIV, 251. Professor Haslam, between sleeping and waking, was thinking of a forthcoming horse-race, and saw a jockey in scarlet pass before him; he appeared to be pulling his horse in hard, and finally won the race. He thought, 'Scarlet is a common colour,' then the vision of the jockey passed before his eyes again. Next day he told various friends. He attended the meeting, and went to the saddling paddock to find a jockey who was in scarlet. He found his man and put a little money on the horse. The jockey pulled in his horse hard during the race and finally won. The case has good independent confirmation.

I think that the most impressive of these 'Winners' cases is that of Mr. John H. Williams, reported in *Journal*, XXVIII, 216.

Mr. Williams, a quaker, aged eighty or more, was an ardent opponent of betting. He awoke from sleep at 8.35 am. on 31st May, 1933, from a dream in which he had listened to a detailed account by radio of the Derby, which was to be run that day at 2 p.m. He heard the names of the first four horses, Hyperion, King Salmon, and two others which he failed to remember. He listened to the whole running commentary from start to finish. At 11 o'clock that morning he had to go out on business, and related to a neighbour, whom he met in a bus, his morning's experience. He also told it to another person whom he met on business matters.

Though so opposed to betting and entirely uninterested in horse-racing he decided to listen to the running commentary on the radio, when he heard the identical expressions and names as in the dream.

I corresponded personally with Mr. Williams and the two gentlemen to whom he had told his dream that morning; they very kindly answered my questions and gave ample confirmation of the account.

It seems most inappropriate that precognition of a horse-race should have come to one who was so strongly opposed to racing and betting, and we can assign no reasonable explanation of the occurrence.

It is curious that another case of foretelling the winner should have to do with the same horse and the same race. The case will be found on page 46 of Mrs. Lyttelton's book, *Some Cases of Prediction,* to which I have already referred. The prediction, which was made some time before the race, gave, however, only the first three letters of the horse's name, as P Y H (not necessarily in that order). Mrs. Barrett, who made the prediction, knew nothing about racing.[1]

I will conclude with another case from Mrs. Lyttelton's book. It is given there in full on page 106 *et seq.* I will give only a very brief summary.

Mr. Calder, the Headmaster of the Grammar School at Goole, wrote to Mrs. Lyttelton, after her broadcast talk on precognition, giving a full account of two precognitive dreams experienced by his wife.

In 1928 he was appointed headmaster of Holmforth Secondary School in Yorkshire. Before leaving Middlesex, where they then resided, Mrs. Calder, who had never been to Yorkshire, dreamed of an old greystone house, set in a lovely valley through which ran a stream of clear but black-looking water. In their house-hunting near Holmforth they came across the very house which Mrs. Calder had seen in her dream; they took it, or rather one half of it, and moved in in August

[1] It is worth mentioning that the Research Officer of the S.P.R. studied the racing calendar for the year and was unable to find any other horse whose name began with the three letters P Y H in any order.

1928. They found that the water of the stream was frequently discoloured by indigo from a near-by dye-works. In her dream Mrs. Calder had seen that only one half of the house was occupied and that outside the door of that half was a barrel which was used as a dog kennel. When they went to live there, though the other half was occupied, there was no barrel. A year or so later, there was a change of tenants of the other half of the house. When the new people arrived they brought with them a dog and placed a barrel outside the door for its kennel. So much for the first dream.

In December 1930 Mr. Calder was appointed head-master of Goole Grammar School, which, of course, meant another move. On 28th December Mrs. Calder dreamed of a dark red house standing on a corner of two streets. She described it to Mr. Calder next day and said that she felt convinced that they would have to live in it, though she was depressed at the prospect. Her precognition was fulfilled in every respect.[1]

The confirmatory evidence of this case is excellent.

Although there are several instances of persons having dreams of places they have never seen, but subsequently visit, this case is specially interesting in

[1] Since the publication of Mrs. Lyttelton's book, Mrs. Calder has experienced another dream of a similar nature, in which she saw details of a house and grounds unknown to her. A few days later, she visited the house of the parents of one of the scholars and recognized it as identical with the one seen in her dream. Circumstances arose which led to her and Mr. Calder occupying half of the house. Though there is no doubt that the dream itself had an influence in determining their decision to take part of the house, it is also true that some of the circumstances were quite independent and that the dream was precognitive. The case is fully reported in the *Journal*, Vol. XXX, 198, April 1938.

One can only comment on this remarkable case by saying that Mrs. Calder seems to be endowed with the power to precognize the houses in which she will live in the near future.

several respects. It is particularly detailed, and the two experiences are exactly similar in character in so far as they both refer to a house in which the dreamer is going to live. In the second dream, it might have been contemporary clairvoyance, but if so, why should Mrs. Calder have had an image of that particular house? That in itself constitutes a precognition. The detail of the colour of the stream in the first case is good.

But perhaps the most interesting point about the case is that of the dog kennel. It really looks as though the prevision were dated. It was not an image of the appearance of the house as it was at the time of the dream, or when Mr. and Mrs. Calder first went to live there, as one would have imagined it would be, but it was of its appearance at a later date. Why these queer details should be given is most puzzling; I cannot help feeling that if we could understand them, and be able to account for the trivialities which we so often find, we should be a long way towards solving the problem of precognition itself.

This, then, is the representative sample of the kind of evidence which we have for precognition. I submit that it is of such quality and of such amount that it cannot lightly be set aside as mere coincidence or imaginative nonsense.

CHAPTER V

In this chapter I propose to discuss those theories which seek to explain away true precognition and to account for the phenomena by normal causes. I fear that it may prove to be somewhat dull, tiresome and perhaps difficult to read, but, if we are to form an opinion as to the reality or otherwise of true precognition, the matter must be faced.

Many people overcome the difficulties involved in the problem by the simple expedient of ignoring the whole thing: they refuse to listen to the evidence and behave as though it did not exist. But, I submit, it is not reasonable, it is grossly unscientific, to adopt this attitude. Even if the evidence were confined to one single case, it should not be ignored; a single fact may upset a generalization just as thoroughly as a whole host. Where the volume of evidence is so large, and so impressive in regard to quality, as is here the case, though its right to be considered may, in strict theory, be no greater than that of a single case, the task of finding an explanation is obviously more urgent.

For a single case could reasonably be ascribed to chance coincidence, illusion of memory or some other normal cause, and need, therefore, create no disturbance in any philosophic system. A multitude of cases, however, cannot thus lightly be waved aside; the pros and cons of all available alternatives must be carefully weighed and their consequences for our general outlook on life worked out. I have already briefly indicated what some of these consequences may be if the hypothesis of supernormal, that is to say, non-inferential precognition be forced upon us. They are far-reaching and revolutionary in a high degree; there is scarcely a system of philosophy which would not be profoundly affected, and, in saying this, I include among systems of philosophy the inchoate and usually almost unconscious systems which are held by the ordinary man as distinguished from the professional philosopher.

If we admit the possibility of foreknowledge of the kind now under discussion, and face up to the implications of that admission, I think that we shall find that our outlook on life and our attitude towards the universe is profoundly modified.

It behoves us, therefore, to give the matter our most careful consideration; for any system, whether it be the closely reasoned, logical structure of the professional philosopher or the vaguer general outlook of the ordinary man, must take into account all relevant facts. I do not, of course, suggest that complete and adequate explanations must be found for all such facts – that is impossible – there are bound to be loose ends in any system; but the implications of unexplained, or even of apparently inexplicable, facts cannot be evaded, particularly if these facts appear to be in contradiction with general principles.

The implications of precognition are so strange that we shall be justified in straining to the utmost any normal hypothesis which can be put forward in explanation. But this straining must not be overdone, or we may find ourselves in the position of postulating greater miracles to explain away lesser.

Quite obviously, the most plausible hypothesis based on normal causes is that of chance coincidence. There can be no question that it is quite within the bounds of *possibility* that all cases of apparent precognition are nothing more than chance coincidence; but mere possibility is not sufficient unless it can be shown that all alternatives are impossible. Where there are other possible explanations, what we are concerned with is the relative probabilities of the various alternatives.

I will state the argument for chance coincidence as strongly as I can, and will take the type, viz., dreams, most favourable for that hypothesis. Now it cannot be denied that many millions of people dream every night. It is not necessary for our present purpose to go into the theory of dreams, it is sufficient to note that they consist of mental images, made up for the most part of material drawn from ordinary experience of daily life. This material is woven into more or less coherent patterns, sometimes fantastic and absurd, but very often reproducing, fairly closely, scenes and events such as might normally happen.

Now it is argued that if, out of the enormous number of dreams which are dreamed, a good proportion are images of the kind of event which may be expected to happen in ordinary life, it is not surprising that some of them should apparently be precognitive.

There is a further point, viz., that we tend to count the hits and ignore the misses. If we have a dream which turns out to be apparently precognitive, we are likely to be struck by the coincidence and remember the experience, while the thousands of dreams which might just as well have been fulfilled, but have not been so, are completely forgotten.

I think that it is probable that a dream which contains some supernormal element, whether telepathic, clairvoyant or precognitive, is, as a rule, more than usually vivid, or else is characterized by some quality which distinguishes it from the normal. I do not say, of course, that all vivid or disturbing dreams contain a supernormal element: many may be due simply to indigestion.

In all the cases of apparently precognitive dreams with which we have been concerned, the dreamer has either told someone of the dream or acted upon it in such a manner as to show that it had made an unusual impression. We do not, as a general rule, allow our conduct to be influenced by any dream which we happen to remember, and as to telling others about them, while there are those who habitually bore the breakfast table with accounts of their dreams, to the credit of humanity it must be admitted that the number of such public enemies is comparatively small.

It has been argued that before we can arrive at any conclusion as to the probability that all apparently precognitive dreams are due solely to chance coincidence, we must know how many of such vivid and striking dreams have been fulfilled, and how many have failed of fulfilment.

Were a widespread census of dreams to be taken, I have no doubt that we should find quite a number of apparent precognitions. Something of this sort was done on a small scale by members of the S.P.R. A number of people, among whom I was included, were asked to write down on waking as much as they could remember of their dreams. I, personally, found that, with a little practice, I was able to remember two or three separate dreams for each night. During the period in which I recorded my dreams they were all of a commonplace nature; many of them were of the kind of event which might very well happen, such as driving a car. None of them, however, was apparently precognitive, that is to say, no event such as had been dreamed of happened in the immediate future. I do not, of course, mean that if I dreamed of driving a car, I did not actually do so during the next few days. No one would suggest that so simple a coincidence was anything out of the ordinary.

The same negative result was obtained from all the other experimenters. But there seems little doubt that had the experiment been continued long enough, we should have found a dream, here and there, which might possibly have been considered precognitive.

However, in the ordinary course of events people do not make special efforts to remember their dreams and, as I have pointed out, it is only the more vivid or disturbing ones which are likely to be recorded, told to others, or acted upon.

There is one further point which must be borne in mind, viz., that only a very small proportion of apparently precognitive dreams would be reported to the S.P.R. or other organization interested in psychical research, and that, of those reported, many would not reach an evidential standard sufficiently high to merit publication. In the case of the S.P.R., at any rate, this standard is set very high and no case is published which does not conform thereto. Thus it happens that many of the reported cases have to be rejected for the sole reason that confirmatory evidence is lacking. This does not imply that such cases are worthless;[1] I have myself come across many instances which I have had no reasonable doubt were genuine precognitions, but the circumstances have been such that I could not obtain any confirmation; I could not, therefore, put them forward for publication, although, knowing the narrators, and being completely satisfied as to their honesty and general powers of observation, I have accepted their accounts as substantially correct.

It follows from what I have said that the number of cases actually published is only a very small fraction of those which occur. The result of all this is that we have whittled down very considerably the number of dreams available for the chance theory, though that number undoubtedly still remains very large.

Let us now consider the other factor in the matter, viz., the possible number of the incidents which can be dreamed about. The advocate of the chance theory, while he requires the number of dreams to be as large as possible, must reduce the number of incidents capable of being dreamed about to the lowest extent in order to make his argument plausible. I will try to make this statement clearer by an example. Suppose that I am looking at a collection of photographs, say a

---

[1] Many cases collected by the S.P.R. which are not deemed sufficiently evidential for publication are nevertheless preserved in the files of the Society, where they are available for study.

family album. Now, if I know that these are all por-
traits of one particular family and that there are
two hundred relatives in that family, I can put my
finger on any photograph without looking at it, and
say, 'That is your Uncle John,' and the chance that I
shall be right is one in two hundred. If the family
consisted of only twenty relatives, the chance would be
one in twenty. But, if, instead of being photographs of
relatives, the album contained photographs of a much
larger group, say, the inhabitants of the British Isles,
then the chance that I should be right in naming any
particular portrait without looking at it would be one
in forty-five millions, or thereabouts.

Now, although it is true that most dreams are made
up of material drawn from ordinary experience, this
material is immensely varied; moreover, the separate
elements therein are capable of being combined in so
many different ways that the possible number of
different patterns is almost infinite. We should not
count as a precognitive dream one of a simple ordinary
event; for example, suppose that I dream of meeting
some friend whom I am accustomed to see every now
and then, and that during the next week I actually do
meet him. Such a dream might, of course, be truly
precognitive, but the fulfilment was so likely to be due
to chance that it could not be considered significant.
But if the simple event be combined with others, such
as meeting my friend in some particular place, or in
some special circumstances, or if, in my dream, he says
certain words which he actually does say when I meet
him, then the probability of chance fulfilment is very
much less. The greater the number of details in the

F

dream and the fulfilling event the less is the plausibility of the chance hypothesis.

Consider one or two actual examples. In Mrs. Atlay's case, she dreamed of seeing a pig in a certain position in the dining-room after she had read prayers. Now such a dream as this cannot be very common, still less usual is it to find a pig in the dining-room; and when this event is combined with the other circumstances, such as the time, i.e., after reading prayers, and the particular place, between the table and the sideboard, the chance of such a combined event occurring to any particular person within any reasonably short period after it has been dreamed about is almost infinitely small. I venture to think that very few people have ever experienced such a combination of events, or have known anyone who has.

Or consider the case of Lady Q summarized on page 47. She dreamed of her uncle lying dead by the side of the road. This, taken by itself, might be considered as being only a rather curious coincidence, though the fact that the dream occurred three times goes against that view. But when the details are added, details such as the body being brought home in a farm waggon, the identity of the two men who carried it upstairs and the very unusual feature of the left hand striking against the banisters, I think that no one could reasonably suggest that the fulfilment was due to chance. Such a combination of circumstances must be unique, in fact, if one takes into account that three particular individuals were involved, viz., the dead man and the two who carried the body, it is clear that it can have happened only once in the whole history of the world.

Finally, consider the case of Mrs. C, page 57, who dreamed of being followed by a monkey while walking in the London streets. How often does one see a monkey roaming free in London, and how many people have had the experience of being followed by one while walking there?

I think that I need labour this point no further. Impartial consideration of the details of the evidence is sufficient to destroy any superficial plausibility which the chance hypothesis may have, and I submit that it may be confidently rejected as an explanation of the many well-evidenced cases of precognition which we possess.

Were it a matter of only one or two such cases, we might, perhaps, say that curious coincidences do sometimes occur, but where there are hundreds to be accounted for, it would be to strain the chance hypothesis beyond all reasonable limits to ascribe them all to that cause.

I have purposely considered only dreams in connection with this argument as it applies to them with much greater force than to the relatively far less frequent experiences, such as hallucinations. In the matter of impressions, though it is true that these are of common occurrence, they comparatively rarely reach an intensity sufficient to call for a special notice.

If the chance hypothesis fails for dreams, *a fortiori* it fails for the other types.

Another possible alternative explanation which must be considered is that of illusion of memory. We all know from personal experience how easily false memories may arise and how convincing they may be.

If I may intrude another personal experience, I give the following illustration. I promised to post a book to a friend and after a month or so, not having had any acknowledgment, I wrote to inquire whether it had been received, and was told that it had not arrived. I had a perfectly clear and definite memory of wrapping it up and addressing it, yet it was entirely false for I found the book on my shelves.

Now it may be said that if false memories such as this may arise, it is possible that the reported cases of precognition are of a similar nature. It may be that the dream, impression or whatever it was never happened at all, or else that it occurred after, and not before, the event, or it may be that the degree of fulfilment was much exaggerated. Where independent corroboration is forthcoming, however, we should have to suppose that two or more persons happened to have been similarly affected, and this seems highly improbable. In cases where documentary evidence exists the explanation is clearly inapplicable.

Where the precognition is taken as a warning and acted upon in some way, illusion of memory can hardly be suggested, unless we make the very far-fetched assumption that the action was taken for some other reason, and that, later, by a false memory, it was ascribed to a fictitious precognition.

To anyone who has actually experienced a precognitive dream or hallucination, this hypothesis of illusion of memory must seem quite untenable. I have myself had one such experience; it is fully reported in the book by Mrs. Lyttelton (pp. 94 *et seq.*) to which I have already referred, but I will summarize it here.

Some two or three years ago I dreamed that I was passing by a field in which were some ewes and lambs, also two dogs. There was a great noise going on and the dogs kept running up to the lambs, some of which were bleeding at the throat. In my dream I took it to be a case of sheep-worrying. It was a very vivid dream and the shock of it woke me and prevented me from going to sleep for some time. In the morning I told my wife what I had dreamed, and all that day I could not get rid of the unpleasant memory of the scene. Some ten days later I was driving in my car along a country road some few miles from my home, when my wife called my attention to two dogs in a field alongside the road in which were a lot of ewes and lambs. As in my dream, there was a great deal of noise and the dogs kept running up to the lambs; it looked as though they were biting them. Many of the lambs were bleeding, but, unlike the scene in my dream, it was their tails and not their throats which were bloody, though I did not recognize the difference at once. I immediately remembered my dream but, taking it to be a case of sheep-worrying, I thought of practical matters first. I could find no one about, so drove on to a village about a mile away and found a policeman, whom I brought back in the car. On returning to the spot, we found that the farmer had arrived. He explained that the lambs had been having their tails docked in the field and that the dogs belonged to him.

Now, although the fulfilling event contained one discrepancy from the dream, I have no doubt that it was a genuine precognition. The suggestion that I suffered from an illusion of memory, and either never had the dream at all, or else dreamed it after having seen the dogs and lambs, seems to me to be simply nonsensical. Had it been so, how did it come about that on seeing the dogs and lambs, I immediately thought of my dream? Did the illusion of memory suddenly spring fully fledged into being at that moment? I am perfectly sure that I had the dream before the event, but, it might be said, 'You were perfectly sure that you had wrapped up and posted the book. It is just that false sense of complete confidence which constitutes an illusion of memory.'

I submit, however, in answer to this, that there is all the difference in the world between a false memory of so simple and commonplace an incident as posting a book and one of so highly complex, unusual and striking an occurrence as my dream. The difference between the two is analogous to that between a mere visual illusion and an hallucination; in fact, if my memory of the dream were false, it would amount to a kind of non-externalized hallucination.

Of course, the fact that independent corroboration was forthcoming renders the hypothesis of illusion of memory practically untenable; but I have thought it desirable to discuss the matter apart from that consideration as it is frequently brought forward as an explanation of those cases where independent confirmatory evidence is not obtainable, but which are otherwise acceptable on the strength of our confidence in the good faith and accuracy of the narrator. Though I have not included any such cases in the evidence cited in this book, I have, as I have already said, personally come across a considerable number.

The only other normal explanation of which I can think—normal, that is to say, in the sense that it is based upon ordinary, well-known causes such as are accepted by everyone—is that of fraud. It is, of course, theoretically possible that all the reported cases of apparent precognition are mere fabrications, but I submit that such a suggestion is too fantastic to merit serious consideration. Though we know that some people occasionally lie, as a general rule, they have some motive for doing so, and it seems impossible to discover any adequate motive which could have operated in all these cases.

This brings us to the end of our discussion of normal explanations, and the failure to find an adequate hypothesis based upon well-known, generally accepted causes, leaves us up against the problem of accounting for the phenomena by some other means. I confess that I face the task with considerable trepidation, and I admit that I have no completely satisfactory hypothesis to offer. Other writers on the subject, notably Mrs. Lyttelton, Professor Richet and Dr. Osty, have frankly accepted the position of complete agnosticism; it may be that they have been wise in so doing.

When subjected to searching analysis, it is found that most, if not all, of our mental activities have their foundations shrouded in mystery. Philosophers are not agreed on any theory of perception, of memory, or the body-mind relation. Many of those put forward are so complex, and involve subtleties so difficult to grasp, that they cannot be appreciated by the ordinary man. In fact, owing to his familiarity with the phenomena, he does not, as a rule, understand what all the fuss is about—he cannot see the difficulties. Familiarity, it is said, breeds contempt, it also obscures the understanding. We accept the commonplace without question just because it is commonplace, and we rarely stop to analyse it; thus we are blind to the mysteries which enshroud our being. Now, it may justly be said that if we cannot understand fully our normal mental processes, such as perception and memory, it is no great matter that we are unable to render a plausible account of so odd and sporadic a phenomenon as precognition. Let us first of all tackle the major questions, and get a plan of the general foundations mapped out, then it will be time enough to fill in the details.

This attitude sounds reasonable enough, but there is another side to the question. It frequently happens in scientific research that the examination of apparent anomalies has thrown a light upon general theory which could not have been obtained from any amount of study of the normal phenomena. For example, our knowledge of normal psychology has been greatly advanced by the study of mental abnormalities, or, to cite the usual instance, our understanding of health has been brought about, to a large extent, by the study of disease.

It may be that a study of the queer abnormality called precognition may throw a light upon some of the dark places of general philosophy and lead to a better understanding of our nature and destiny.

I think that it is clear that the crux of the whole problem is Time. Now, time is, par excellence, one of those mysteries which are generally accepted without question by reason of their familiarity. It is true that the nature of time has been discussed by professional philosophers for many hundreds of years, but we are very little nearer to a clear understanding. Kant reduced it to a mere *a priori* form, McTaggart denied its existence altogether, and accounted for its fictitious appearance of reality by holding that it was due to a misperception of an entirely non-temporal series.

With these and similar metaphysical theories we have no need to concern ourselves here, unless we may say that, if time be not a reality, that, whatever it is, which we normally take for time, is so good an imitation that it does just as well for all practical purposes as real time, if there be such a thing as real time.

Any explanatory theory of precognition must, I consider, be somehow or other based upon time. What we have to explain is how an event which, being still in the future, does not, apparently, exist, can enter into a relation of cognition, that is to say, a relation of known to knower. There have been a few hypotheses put forward and, in the next chapter, I shall try to give a simple non-technical account of some of them, though, owing to their rather abstruse metaphysical nature, it may well prove beyond my powers to render them intelligible.

I will first dispose of one explanation which is sometimes suggested. Those who accept the reality of spiritual beings, whether the surviving spirits of deceased human beings, or whether belonging to a different order altogether, sometimes attempt to account for precognition by saying that such beings have a wider knowledge of the future than is possible for embodied man, and that precognitions are due to their influence.

Now I, personally, am not prepared to accept as *proved* that any such disembodied spirits exist—they may do so, or they may not—I prefer to suspend judgment. But even if they do exist, and do possess a wider knowledge of the future than is possible for us, the problem of precognition is simply shifted from the earthly to the spiritual sphere. We are still faced with the difficulty of seeing how a mind can know something which has not yet happened, and it does not make it any easier if we postulate a discarnate mode of existence for that mind. We have to give a plausible account of the temporal conditions which would permit of precognition, whether those conditions govern the mind of a ghost or a living man.

CHAPTER VI

METAPHYSICAL THEORIES

THE theories which I shall briefly discuss in this chapter all involve some rather subtle metaphysical arguments, and many people, in fact, I imagine that I might reasonably say, most people, have no taste for metaphysics.

It is difficult, probably impossible, to render the concepts of metaphysics into language which will be easily understood by those who have had no previous acquaintance with, or training in, that subject. I am fully aware that the accounts which I shall give of the various theories are woefully deficient in clearness and intelligibility. Moreover, in my attempt at simplification I have had, perforce, to omit much of the argument, so that my summaries are not only inadequate, but also partially distorted.

I would recommend, therefore, that readers who are not particularly interested in metaphysics should omit this chapter, the more so as, in my opinion, none of the suggested hypotheses can be regarded as being even provisionally acceptable.

The first theory with which I must deal is that put forward by Mr. J. W. Dunne in his well-known book, *An Experiment with Time.* I cannot possibly go into all the details of his theory of Serialism, but must content myself with a very brief and inadequate indication of how he proposes to use it to account for precognition.

He starts with the proposition that time has length. For example, it is roughly 872 years since William the Conqueror landed, it is four hours since I had breakfast, in another twelve hours it will be midnight, and so on. All these statements involve lengths of time.

On this view the events of history are spaced out in a single dimension, along a line as it were.

But, he says, this is not all: time flows; we experience events in succession. It is as though the observer travels over the length of time and thus comes to one event after another.

Now, if time flows, it must flow at some particular rate: when we specify a rate of flow or other motion, we find that we require two factors, viz., length travelled over and time occupied in doing so. For example, my rate of walking is four miles per hour, or fifteen minutes per mile.

Thus if time flows over the 'length of time' there must be a second kind of time by which to rate the flow. This is what Mr. Dunne calls Time 2. But we cannot stop here: Time 2 also flows at a certain rate, which, of course, involves a Time 3, and so on to infinity.

Mr. Dunne further argues that this infinite series of times would involve an infinite series of observers. He also draws many other conclusions and endeavours to show, with great ingenuity, and some plausibility, how this theory of serialism may be made to account for some odd and little understood phenomena; he even applies it to advanced physics and claims that it throws light in obscure places.

However, that is not our present concern, all that we are interested in is to see how serialism can account for precognition. The world of Observer 1 has three dimensions of space, i.e., length, breadth and depth, and one of time, i.e., Time 1. In the world of Observer 2 Time 1 becomes transformed into a spatial dimension, so he has four dimensions of space and one of time, viz., Time 2, similarly for Observer 3. The number of spatial dimensions increases with each Observer, while the temporal dimension remains single.

Now, what is contained in space is there all the time as space is not successive; the milestones along the road do not spring into being as I walk. I can go from one to the other as often as I please, and in any direction.

As I have said, Time 1 of Observer 1, which contained the series of events presented to him in succession, is changed for Observer 2 into a space dimension and the events, therefore, are no longer successive. As a general rule the focus of attention of Observer 2 is concentrated on the same point as that of Observer 1, so that, although anything in the Time 1 dimension *could* be presented to him, seeing that it is all co-existent and not successive, in actual fact only that part which is in the focus of attention of Observer 1, that is to say, Observer 1's present moment, is usually so presented. In certain circumstances, however, such as during sleep, Observer 1's attention is withdrawn, so the attention of Observer 2 is free to roam at will over the whole spatial field, viz., the three spatial dimensions proper and the one temporal dimension which has become spatial for him. He cannot, of course, wander about in his own temporal dimension, Time 2; for that is successive, just as Time 1 is successive for Observer 1. But he can fix his attention on any part of Time 1, and thus acquire knowledge of what Observer 1 would call the future. Should he transmit this knowledge to Observer 1, the latter would call it a precognition. Observer 1, Observer 2 and the rest are not different persons but the same: they might be thought of as different levels of one mind. The true man is the observer at infinity.

I might, perhaps, make this a little clearer by an illustration. The time dimension can be looked upon as being like a cinematograph film rolled up on its reel. As it passes through the projector, the individual pictures are presented in succession. There is past, i.e., that part which has already been shown, present, i.e., the part now showing on the screen, and future, i.e., that which has not yet been unrolled.

Now Observer 2 transforms Observer 1's time into a spatial dimension, that is to say, he unrolls the film off its reel and stretches it out in a straight line on a table. If Observer 1 can hold Observer 2's attention focussed on the same spot as his own, viz., the picture which is actually being shown on the screen, i.e., his present moment, all well and good. But let Observer 1 relax his vigilance by going to sleep, Observer 2 can take a peep at any part of the film which he pleases, and thus get a glimpse of what Observer 1 would call the future.

What are we to think about all this? It does, I admit, afford some sort of explanation for precognition, but I cannot feel happy with all these observers, each with his own particular time. I do not like series which extend to infinity, except in certain rather special cases.

One can sometimes deal with an infinite series, for instance when it is what the mathematician calls convergent, that is to say when each succeeding term is less than the one before in a particular manner, but this is because they are finite in at least one respect; but Mr. Dunne's series are not of this kind, the succeeding terms do not grow less. I do not want to argue this point out fully; if the analysis made by Mr. Dunne were inescapable, we should have to accept, provisionally, some sort of infinite series, however much we disliked doing so. But until we are satisfied that there is no alternative to his analysis, we can put that aspect of the matter on one side.

I, personally, do not accept his analysis of the nature of time. I would go even further and submit that it is demonstrably incorrect.

It seems obvious to me that the proper starting place for any theorizing is Change, and not Time at all. Change may be change of place, as in physical motion, change in characterizing attributes, as when an object changes colour or a mind changes in mood, or it may be simply the passage of thought, sensations, etc., through our minds. But change of some sort is the fundamental phenomenon from which arises the idea of time. A world in which there was no change whatsoever would be a timeless world.

Mr. Dunne starts off with such a changeless world; in his time, as length, there is no change; event A is so many units of time before event B, which in its turn, is so many units of time before event C. This is just as static and changeless as the marks on a footrule, it is not real time at all. He introduces real time in his conception of an observer who observes events in succession. Here we get change, i.e., in the presentations to the observer's mind, which follow one another in succession. It is simply due to the fact that he takes something static and non-temporal to be real time that all his difficulties about the speed of time arise. We can intelligibly speak of speed, or rate of change, when one of the factors is non-temporal, e.g., so many feet per second, or the change from optimistic self-satisfaction to pessimistic depression during the course of a day; but to speak of a speed of so many hours per hour seems, on the face of it, to be absurd.

I submit that the proper way to look at it is as follows. Time does not flow; events or changes occur in succession, and it is just this which constitutes time. You can measure the rate at which one particular change occurs by comparing it with another particular change, but to seek to measure change in general is simply nonsense, for there is nothing with which to compare it —nothing to measure it by.

I do not want to go into the metaphysics of Time, even were I competent to do so—it would be quite unsuitable in a book of this sort, but I submit that Mr. Dunne's theory of serialism may be rejected on three general and easily understood grounds. Firstly, an infinite series of observers, even though those observers be only different levels of the consciousness of one person, and an infinite series of times are unacceptable. Secondly, a time dimension cannot be changed into a space dimension, time and space being totally different in essential nature. Thirdly, the fundamental analysis is incorrect. Time does not flow over a static history at a certain rate. History is that which is left behind by the onward surge of change. All rates or speeds are relativities, and time or change is the essential factor in them all.

Another possible explanatory hypothesis was put forward and discussed at the meeting of the Aristotelian Society and Mind Association at Bristol in 1937. The speakers were Professor C. D. Broad and Professor H. H. Price, and the subject was, 'The Philosophical Implications of Precognition.' Now the fact that this subject should be seriously discussed at a meeting such as this is itself noteworthy. The Aristotelian Society and Mind Association hold these meetings for the purpose of hearing discussions of topics of current interest in philosophy, and they are attended by many of the leading authorities in philosophy.

Though neither Professor Broad nor Professor Price committed himself to an opinion as to the reality of the phenomenon of precognition, the fact that they deemed it worth their while to devote their time and thought to the consideration of its philosophical implications shows that the evidence must have made some considerable impression on their minds. Two men of such outstanding position in the world of philosophy would not have thus discussed a mere triviality, an unsupported belief due to the credulity of the superstitious, nor would the other philosophers present at the meeting have listened to them with patience.

I do not desire to make any appeal to authority, I regard such as inadmissible and out of place, and prefer to allow the evidence to speak for itself; but an appeal to authority may have its uses in gaining a hearing for

G

that evidence. People are too fond of simply ignoring an inconvenient problem, and brushing aside as 'all rubbish' that which will not fit in with their preconceived ideas. However, when they discover that men of weight and learning have thought the matter worth their serious attention, they may possibly change their attitude.

I do not propose to attempt to give any summary of this most important symposium, but would recommend those who are interested in the matter from the metaphysical and philosophic standpoint to study thoroughly the three papers contained in the Bulletin issued by the Aristotelian Society and Mind Association. They will find therein the most authoritative exposition of the subject yet available.

I should like, if I can, to give a simple account of the hypothesis discussed by the two Professors. The difficulty to be overcome is how a relation, i.e., the relation of cognition or known to knower, can exist if one of its terms is an event which has not yet happened. Professor Broad pointed out that the true analogue of precognition is not perception, but rather memory. In a precognition there is a present mental image which is perceived,[1] just as is the case with normal memory, but while, in the latter phenomenon, the image refers to, or is somehow derived from, an event in the past, that is to say, an event which has actually existed, in the former the reference is to the future which does not yet exist.

We can conceive means by which the memory

---

[1] I use the word 'perceive' instead of the more correct term 'prehend' because of the unfamiliarity of the latter.

image may be derived from the original event, for we know that any event may set in motion trains of causes and effects, which trains may persist for an indefinite length of time; for example, one commonly held theory of normal memory is based upon the supposition that the experience of perceiving an event leaves a permanent trace in the brain cells and that, if at some subsequent moment these cells are stimulated, a more or less accurate image of the original will be revived.

The difficulty with precognition is that the normal order of cause and effect has to be reversed, that is to say, the effects in the brain – they are called 'traces' – have to be there before the event which causes them has happened. Such a reversal of the normal order appears to be quite inconceivable, yet, unless we dismiss the evidence altogether, precognitive images do occasionally arise in the mind.

One possible method of meeting this difficulty is, according to Professor Broad, to have a two-dimensional time. I shall not attempt to summarize the highly metaphysical arguments which were employed, but I think that I might be able to illustrate, by an analogy, one way in which a two-dimensional time would make precognition logically and causally possible.

When we want to fix the position of an event in a uni-dimensional time, we require a point of reference, say, noon to-day, a distance, say, four hours, and a direction, viz., before or after noon.

If time were two-dimensional, we should still be able to do with one point of reference, but we should want two distances and two directions, just as, when fixing a position on a chart, we need so many degrees of

latitude, north or south, and so many degrees of longi-
tude, east or west.

There would be a further consequence of having
two dimensions of time. With one dimension we must
think of an event as a line, having length but no breadth;
with two dimensions, we may picture it as an area,
having both length and breadth.

I will now try to explain how two-dimensional time
might be made to account for precognition.

Let us, for the sake of simplicity, think of our ordinary
time as a road running from south to north. At the
point, O, where we now are, that is, at the present
moment, all that lies to the south is past, all to the north
is future. We can remember the country to the south,
as we have already passed over it, but the country to
the north is unknown. Let us say that we are standing
facing south, so that we cannot see what is behind our
backs on the road northwards.

Now add a second dimension, that is east and west,
and let us suppose that what lies to the east is future,
and to the west, past, in that dimension. Remember
that an event is now an area and not a line. Any area
which lies in the sector from north to east will then be
absolute future, i.e., future in both dimensions; an area
in the sector from south to west will be absolute past;
but in the sectors from south to east and from north to
west, an area lying therein will be past in one dimension and future in another. In our normal consciousness, however, we know of only one dimension, viz.,
south and nort'ʏ so that knowledge of any area with
south in it will appear to us as due to memory. But
should we gain subliminal knowledge of the westerly

part of an area, lying in the north-west, it would appear to our normal consciousness as a precognition, because the northerly dimension in it is our normal future.

I will try to make this difficult conception clearer by an illustration, although I do not know that Messrs. Broad and Price would approve of it.

Consider a train of causes and effects, for example, a number of billiard balls lying on the table being set in motion by a player striking one of them with his cue. The ball which he has played strikes another and imparts motion to it, the second, in its turn, collides with a third and so on until all the balls are set in motion. Here we have a series of causes and effects arising from the single initial cause. But the striking of the first ball by the player is not the whole of the initial cause; for it to produce its effect there must have been a set of static conditions, gravitation, inertia, the shape, surface and coefficient of elasticity of the balls, the condition of the table, etc. Were any of these static conditions altered, the series of events, viz., the movements of the balls, would also be changed. The static conditions are contemporaneous, not successive; they do not constitute a series of events in time.

Suppose, now, that time has two dimensions; we may regard the series of events as lying along one of them, that is to say, along the dimension which we are facing, while the static conditions, or some of them, lie along the second dimension, i.e., to right and left. If we can imagine ourselves making a right-angled turn in time, it would appear that what had previously seemed to us to be a series of events would now be in the position and take on the appearance of a set of static conditions, while the former static conditions, or some of them, might – I do not say, would – be presented to us as a series of events.

Before making this turn, for me to have knowledge of the movement of one of the balls before it had been struck by one of the others, would have been a precognition (I am purposely leaving out knowledge due to inference). But after making the turn such knowledge would not be precognitive, because what had been a series of causes and effects would have now become a set of static conditions, and be thus contemporaneous throughout.

Whether the conception of a two-dimensional time is anything but sheer nonsense is a matter on which it is very hard to form an opinion. It is not logically impossible; there is nothing inherently necessary about uni-dimensionality of time, even though it may seem absurd to talk of going sideways in time.

But, as both Professor Broad and Professor Price agreed, the phenomenon of precognition is itself so odd and so out of parallel with all our normal experience, that we must not be surprised if any hypothesis to account for it be bizarre and fantastic.

There is a third hypothesis for precognition for which I, myself, am responsible. I first suggested it in a 'Report on cases of apparent Precognition,' published in *Proceedings*, S.P.R., Vol. XLII, February 1934. I should say here that I am not, and never have been, by any means in love with my hypothesis. I put it forward as a means of thinking about the phenomena rather than as an explanation of them. I do not suggest that it is an even approximately correct account of what actually happens.

It is a commonly accepted principle that the present moment, of which we have experience, occupies a certain length of duration; it is not a point which has position and no magnitude. A little reflection will make this quite clear. In the first place, there can be no doubt that we do experience duration – we see things actually moving, and a movement must occupy some duration, however short. In a point-instant, that is to say, an instant of time which had no length, movement would be impossible, for it would stop the very moment it started.

No number of point-instants could, by addition one to another, make up a duration.

The fact is, of course, that points, lines and so on, are simply abstractions from reality having no actual existence: they are primarily made for the convenience of mathematical reasoning.

But what we have to deal with here is reality as it is presented to us in experience; we can therefore say that the only present moment of which we have any knowledge, or for the existence of which we have any grounds for belief, is one which has a definite length. This present moment is usually called the 'specious present'; in what follows I will use that term.

It is an unquestionable fact that a relation of cognition can be set up between a mind and an event which is present to it, or, in ordinary language, I can know what is going on now. A present event is one which is contemporaneous with a part of my specious present.

Now, as my specious present has a definite length,

it may be that more than one event is contemporaneous with it, and that those events are not contemporaneous with each other, but successive.

The average length of the specious present of the normal individual has not been ascertained with any degree of certainty, various estimates have been made, though none can be considered reliable.

To avoid the appearance of accepting any such estimate, let us suppose that the normal specious present endures for three units of duration, the length of the units being left quite undetermined. Thus, my specious present runs from T_1 to T_3. All events which are contemporaneous with any of these T's are present to me. Now it may be that there is a series of successive events, E_1, E_2, E_3, such that E_1 is contemporaneous with T_1, E_2 with T_2, and E_3 with T_3. As they are all within the span of my specious present they will all be present for me, in spite of the fact that E_1 precedes E_2, and E_2 precedes E_3.

But if E_1 precedes E_2, E_2 and E_3 are in the future from the point of view of E_1; from the point of view of E_3, E_1 and E_2 are in the past.

Now let us suppose that there is another observer besides myself, and that his specious present is somewhat longer than mine, let us say that it covers five units of duration, viz., T_0, T_1, T_2, T_3 and T_4. The three events, E_1, E_2 and E_3, will all be present to him, but so also will an event, E_0, which is contemporaneous with T_0, and an event E_4, which is contemporaneous with T_4.

From my point of view, E_0 is in the absolute past because my specious present no longer covers T_0, with which Eo is contemporaneous, while E4 is in the absolute future because my specious present has not yet reached so far. Thus, what may be present to one observer may be either past or future to another, if there should be any difference in the lengths of their respective specious presents.

Suppose now that we substitute for the second observer a stratum of my own subliminal mind. It follows that if the specious present of my subliminal mind be longer than that of my normal consciousness, events which are present to the former may be future to the latter.

There is some ground for supposing that the length of the normal specious present may vary in certain circumstances, such as concentration of attention, fatigue, hypnosis and the influence of drugs, e.g., cannabis indica; there is, therefore, no *a priori* objection to holding that the length of the subliminal specious present may be greater than that of the normal consciousness.

We know that knowledge acquired by the subliminal may occasionally be transmitted to the normal mind, so that, supposing that the specious present of the former were to extend to T4, and that knowledge of E4, an event which is contemporaneous with that moment, were acquired, such knowledge might be transmitted to the normal mind and would then constitute a precognition for it.

I will endeavour to make this rather obscure argument clearer by a fictitious example. Suppose that my normal specious present extends from noon until one second after noon, and that my subliminal specious present stretches as far as one o'clock. All events happening up to one o'clock are present events for my subliminal mind and might, therefore, be known to it.

Suppose that some such event occurs at 12.45 p.m., and that knowledge of it is acquired by my subliminal mind. If that knowledge be transmitted to my normal mind while its specious present extends from noon until one second after noon, it would appear to it as a precognition.

In order to cover all our cases of precognition we should have to suppose that there is a level of the subliminal mind of which the specious present extends over a period of many years; for example, in the case of Lady Q (page 47), the first dream occurred some six years before the fulfilling event. This may seem, on the face of it, to be highly fanciful and far-fetched, although there is, so far as I know, no principle by which any limits can be set to the extension which can be allowed to the specious present, once the possibility of variation in length is admitted.

This theory, therefore, explains precognition by denying it, that is to say, it suggests that what appears as a case of supernormal, non-inferential foreknowledge, is only a fragment of the knowledge of the present of the subliminal mind, or of some stratum thereof, which is thrust up into the surface consciousness.

I will venture on another pictorial illustration or parable in the hope of making the theory more intelligible. Suppose that I am looking at a line of printed words through a narrow slit which passes over it. The width of the slit permits me to see only three letters at a time. As the slit moves along the line, I am able to read what is printed, but cannot see anything which lies ahead of the position of the slit. This represents the normal specious present. Suppose, now, that my subliminal mind is also reading the words, but that its slit is much wider and covers a space of several more letters, both forward and behind. If then, the subliminal mind reads a word which lies ahead of the position of the normal slit and transmits the knowledge thereby acquired to the normal mind, it would appear to it as a precognition.

This theory involves what appears, at first sight, to be a rather queer conception of time, or perhaps I should rather say, of past, present and future. But if it be true that our present moment has a definite length – a view that is generally accepted nowadays – this conception is forced upon us by actual experience. Moreover, it is the only kind of present moment of which we have any knowledge; mathematical time, consisting of point-instants having no length, is an abstraction having no real existence. Are we not, therefore, justified in holding, subject, of course, to correction if further knowledge inconsistent with the view be acquired, that the nature of time is such that the only present moment possible for us is one which covers a span of duration?

The extra assumptions required by the theory, viz., variations in the length of the span of duration covered, and transmission of subliminal knowledge to the normal consciousness, are comparatively small and have, moreover, some backing in experience.

If one tries to think of a timeless consciousness, such as must be ascribed to a personal Creator, one can only do so in terms of an 'everlasting now,' that is to say, of a specious present of infinite length. I must repeat that I am by no means enamoured of this suggestion and that I put it forward more as a mode of looking at the phenomena than as an explanation of them.

The last hypothesis to be mentioned is one which was, I believe, originally suggested by Du Prel; it may be called the 'extra sense' theory. Suppose a man born blind and having no knowledge of the possibility and nature of sight. This man is standing on the platform of a railway station, he can hear the sound of an approaching train. He infers from past experience that such a sound means that a train will shortly pass through the station. This is ordinary inferential knowledge of the future. He has a companion with him who is able to see as well as to hear. Long before the sound of the approaching train is audible, he can see it in the distance coming towards the station. If he then tells the blind man that a train is coming, it will appear to the latter as a non-inferential precognition. The suggestion is, therefore, that there is some stratum of the subliminal mind which possesses an extra sense whereby it is able to obtain sensory knowledge of events that fall outside the range of normal consciousness.

It seems to me that this theory does not carry us very far towards understanding precognition; all that it amounts to is to say that the subliminal mind possesses an unknown faculty of precognition. It explains one mystery by postulating another. If there be, in reality, such an extra sense, we are still faced with the difficulty of explaining the time conditions under which it operates.

I must confess that I do not find any of these four theories at all satisfactory, yet I cannot suggest any alternative. I am, therefore, disposed to adopt the attitude of complete agnosticism as regards explanation of the phenomenon. I do not say, dogmatically, that no adequate theory can be found, but I cannot conceive on what lines it can run.

What we can say, with some confidence, is that our ordinary idea of the nature of time is clearly inaccurate, and that the odd and bizarre phenomenon of precognition must make us prepared to accept radical, and possibly fantastic-seeming, modifications of it.

Recent advances in physical science have clearly demonstrated that the nature of time is more complex than was formerly supposed and that the absolute physical present and absolute physical simultaneity are illusory. Beyond that, however, I cannot see that any of the conclusions of mathematical physics and the theory of relativity help us at all in understanding precognition.

There is one point upon which I must briefly touch. It might be said that if it can be shown that precognition is metaphysically impossible, no evidence, however apparently compelling, should induce us to believe in its reality. Now I cannot accept this view; it implies that metaphysics has reached a position of absolute certainty, an implication which I do not think that even the most enthusiastic metaphysician would claim. No human knowledge can be absolutely certain. In the last resort all logical reasoning rests upon assumption: we can force back all arguments until we arrive at one or more axiomatic principles, principles, that is to say, which derive their validity from self-evidence. To perceive that a proposition is self-evident is a mental experience, and from experience we cannot derive certainty. There are numerous examples of propositions which are held to be self-evident by one philosopher, yet doubted by others. How are we to choose between them? Until, therefore, metaphysics can prove its own infallibility, and a sort of divine right to pronounce on what is possible and what is not possible, the prohibition of belief in precognition may be neglected. I think that the following principle may be laid down. While it is absurd to affirm the existence of the impossible, it is idle to deny the possibility of the actual. It does not, however, help us very much.

I conclude this discussion with a quotation from the novel, *Aylwin*, by Theodore Watts-Dunton. 'Quoth Ja'afar, bowing low his head: "Bold is the donkey-driver, O Ka'dee! and bold the ka'dee who dares say what he will believe, what disbelieve – not knowing in any wise the mind of Allah – not knowing in any wise his own heart, and what it shall some day suffer." '

In this unsatisfactory position, then, we must leave the attempt to find an explanatory hypothesis, and pass to the final task of trying to deduce some of the implications of the evidence.

CHAPTER VII

IMPLICATIONS

IN the previous chapter I have discussed four suggested explanations for the phenomenon of precognition, but have been compelled to confess that none of them seems to me to be even provisionally acceptable. However, inability to explain a fact does not justify us in ignoring it. If we are satisfied, on the evidence before us, that it is really a fact, we must take it into account and accept its plain implications, even if we cannot understand how it comes to be.

Now, the evidence before us is several hundreds of stories of people obtaining what is, apparently, knowledge of future events. We have discussed theories which would explain this fact away, viz., chance and illusion of memory. For my part, I cannot accept either of these as an adequate explanation of the whole mass of evidence.

We cannot simply ignore the evidence, for the stories are there in print for anyone to read. It can hardly be suggested that they are all nothing but a tissue of lies and fabrications; independent confirmation has been obtained in almost every case which I have cited, as well as in the majority of the others of which I have not given details; it is surely absurd to suppose that so many people would have independently entered upon conspiracies to perpetrate silly and

senseless deceptions, with no imaginable motive save
that of spinning yarns. In many instances the manifest
integrity and sincerity of the narrators and witnesses
puts this suggestion quite out of court.

We are left, therefore, in the position of being faced
with a fact which we are unable, for the present at any
rate, to explain. I do not see, however, that this need
worry us unduly, for it is by no means the only inexplicable fact in our world. It might be that, could we find
adequate explanations for the many unsolved problems
of philosophy and psychology, could we fully understand the nature of time and causation, we should find
that the phenomenon of precognition would drop
neatly into its appointed place in the scheme of things.
I only say that it might be so, our ignorance is far too
great for us to *know*.

It is clear, I think, that the crux of the whole problem
is Time and the nature of Time. Were it not for the
abnormality of the time relation in cases of precognition, there would be nothing particularly striking about
them: it is true that some, in fact most, of them exhibit
certain features which appear to be supernormal, such
as telepathy and clairvoyance, but, apart from the fact
that the reference is to the future, and not to the present
or past, they would all fit comfortably into already
existing categories.

Glancing over the whole mass of evidence, and
leaving aside those cases which can be explained on
some alternative hypothesis, there seem to be two
distinct types of precognition. In one type what we get
is foreknowledge of a future event, and this knowledge
may come in a large variety of ways, and be couched

in many different forms of symbolism. Many warning cases show this very well, also precognitions of the approaching death, either of the subject or someone else. Where the precognition occurs in a dream, the scene dreamed of may not represent at all accurately the fulfilling event, but conveys knowledge of that event symbolically, or else the dreamer simply knows that so-and-so is going to happen. I suppose that everyone has had the experience of knowing something in a dream without being able to account for that knowledge.

In cases of precognitive impressions, this absence of sensory imagery is usually well-marked, though there are cases where the impression takes the form of words mentally heard, or 'ringing through the head.' Hallucinations, whether visual or otherwise, are rarely representations of coming events, but convey the knowledge by means of symbols.

The other general type is of those cases where the precognition appears, on the surface, to be an actual glimpse of the future. It is as though a rent suddenly appeared in the veil which covers the future, and then closed again after permitting the subject to take a fleeting glance at what lies ahead.

Precognitions of trivial events, which, as I have noted, form quite a large proportion of the whole, are very often of this type; there is, as a rule, no mark of futurity about them, they are recognized as having been precognitive only after the fulfilling event has been experienced.

Consider such a case as that of Mrs. Atlay (page 56). Her dream was not manifestly prophetic, it was simply a more or less accurate representation of a future event. It was as though she had stepped forward a few hours in time and taken a peep at her dining-room.

Or consider the case of Mrs. Calder (page 64). In this case the first dream was, except for one detail, of a scene probably actually existing at the time; the only reason for classing it as precognitive at all, apart from that detail, is that it was a dream of a house which the dreamer would at some time occupy. It might have been simple clairvoyance, though the fact of future occupation gives a sort of precognitive motive for its occurrence. But the detail to which I refer, viz., the barrel used as a dog kennel by the door, seems to date it as a precognition. This feature did not exist until over a year after the dream. Had it been contemporaneous clairvoyance, motivated, perhaps, by foreknowledge of the fact of future occupation, the barrel would not have been seen in the dream, as it was not, in fact, there at the time.

This case, also, looks very much like a glimpse through a rent in the veil which hides the future.

In some cases we get the two features combined, for example, in that of Mrs. Schweitzer (page 49), where the dream conveys a more or less accurate pictorial representation, sufficiently accurate, at any rate, to enable her to recognize the stranger, Mr. Deverell, when she subsequently met him; yet the knowledge of the appositeness of the name, 'Henry Irvin,' was conveyed in a symbolic and indirect form, viz., in a conversation which did not actually happen, yet which gave a very clear account of real facts.

Now I do not think that we can lay it down, dogmatically, that there is only one type of precognition; there may be, for all we know, two or more different modes in which the faculty is manifested, or there may be two or more different faculties by means of which precognition is gained.

However, if we can see a means of bringing these two types under one head, we shall gain, at least, in simplification.

I think that it is pretty certain that precognition is an affair of the subliminal mind; and we know that in transmission between the different levels of consciousness some form of symbolism is frequently employed. It may be, therefore, that in instances of the first type, i.e., where a sort of non-pictorial knowledge of a coming event is received, the subliminal mind actually gets a glimpse of the future, but is unable to transmit it in all its details to the surface consciousness, and can only get through a symbolic message, or a condensed account of the knowledge gained.

If we accept at their face value those cases where more or less complete and accurate pre-representations of future events are given, and regard them as fugitive glimpses through the veil, it seems impossible to avoid the conclusion that those events already exist in some sense, for we cannot have glimpses of the non-existent. If we reject this view, and class all precognitions together as instances of some unknown faculty of acquiring foreknowledge, we are still faced with the difficulty that a future event is somehow known before it happens; the mind comes into cognitive contact with it, yet how could this be if the event were non-existent – simply nothing?

It seems to me that, unless the entire body of evidence for non-inferential precognition be swept aside or explained away, we are bound to admit that the future does exist in some sense *now* – at the present moment. I have already given my reasons for holding that this evidence cannot be swept aside or explained away. If my readers are in agreement with me in this matter, we must face the implications of it.

Let us first dispose of one misconception which is commonly held. Because certain future events have been foreseen in a supernormal fashion, it has been assumed that *all* future events could, in principle, be the objects of precognition.

Some people have argued from this assumption that the fact of precognition proves that the future is completely determined. This is clearly inadmissible, for the existence of occasional precognitions could, at the very most, prove only that the particular events which were foreknown were determined. To prove by this means that the whole of the future is determined, one would have to show that all future events whatsoever could, in principle, be foreknown, and this, I am quite sure, cannot be done. We know nothing of the conditions which make precognition possible, and it may well be that it occurs only in circumstances of a very rare and special kind. We know that the future is to some extent predetermined by the present and the past, and I suggest that it is only that part of it which is so determined that is a possible object of precognition. There is nothing in the evidence to show that *all* future events could be precognized, in fact, there are some cases which suggest, even if they do not prove, the reverse.

For example, refer to the case mentioned on page 23. The precognition ran as follows: Mooring ropes part – vessel swept away by the tide – swamped on the bar. The fulfilment reached only as far as the first item, when an action by the subject, taken as a consequence of the warning conveyed to him in the dream, intervened and changed the course of events. He went on deck and, assisted by his companion, held on to the bank with boat-hooks, and thus prevented the second item, viz., being swept away by the tide, from occurring. It seems pretty certain that, apart from this action of his, this second item would have been fulfilled; we cannot, of course, say definitely about the third, but it seems quite likely that, had the vessel been swept away, it also might have been fulfilled.

To take another example, that of Lady Z (page 26). Had she not called to the policeman to catch the coachman as he fell from the box, it seems probable that the detail of his hat being smashed in would have occurred.

The view which I am inclined to take on the strength of these and similar cases is that there is *a future* which is now determined by the present and the past, but that it is not inexorably fixed and unalterable – it is, to some extent at least, plastic, and can be modified by actions which we, as beings possessed of some degree of freedom of choice, initiate in the present. Thus, at noon to-day, the events which will occur at noon to-morrow are determined by the total state of affairs now existing. But, into this total state of affairs, I, by my freewill action, thrust an entirely new factor which plays its part in determining the future: so that the events which are determined to happen at noon

to-morrow may be different at five minutes past noon
to-day from what they were at noon, because I, in the
common vernacular, 'have shoved my oar in.' I suggest that if, at noon to-day, I were to have a precognition of what was going to happen in twenty-four hours'
time, it would be of the future as then determined.
If at five minutes past noon I perform a freewill act
which modifies that future, the precognition may be
only partly fulfilled, or may fail altogether.

This notion of a determined yet plastic future is
really one which is quite familiar and commonplace to
us all. Take a very simple example. On going to bed
I wind up an alarum clock and set it for half-past six.
The future in so far as it is determined by that act of
mine is that at 6.30 next morning a certain train of
clockwork will be set in motion, a bell will ring, and a
whole set of other consequences will ensue. Provided
nothing intervenes, that future is completely determined. But suppose that I wake up at six o'clock, get
up and switch off the alarum; by doing so, I alter the
future, the clockwork will not start in motion, the bell
will not sound and all the other consequences may be
quite altered.

If this conception of a determined yet plastic future
be entertained, it is quite obvious that we can accept
the reality of occasional precognitions without in any
way invalidating our claim to be morally responsible
beings; for the plasticity of the future permits us to
exercise a certain amount of control over our destinies.

It is inconsistent with thorough-going determinism,
that is to say, the theory that all events whatsoever are
effects of pre-existing causes, for thorough-going

determinism does not allow the possibility of any free-will, i.e., non-determined, action. I do not think that it is necessarily inconsistent with fatalism, but I find it so hard to state that theory in a way which does not lead to absurdities and contradictions, that I am never quite sure what is, and what is not, consistent with it.

In what I have said up to now I have assumed that the action which causes the complete fulfilment to be averted is a freewill act. I suppose that it is logically possible that it might be any act caused by a non-determined event. I cannot, however, think of any sort of non-determined event other than freewill acts.

I merely mention the point for the sake of logical completeness. I do not consider that it has any other importance.

To sum up on this point. The occurrence of occasional precognitions has no relevance to the question of determinism, unless it can be proved that all events whatsoever could, in principle, be foreknown. This we cannot prove.

If we accept the evidence of certain warning and other cases, we must regard the future as being alterable, or, as I have put it, plastic, by freewill action performed in the present.

This view permits us to hold that we are, to some extent at least, self-determining agents, and thus morally responsible.

I am painfully aware that this discussion is woefully inadequate, and that the language which I have used is deficient in precision; but to treat of the matter exhaustively, and to attempt to meet all possible objections, would entail so lengthy and so metaphysical

a disquisition, that, even were I competent to under-
take the task, it would be quite out of place in a book
such as this. The controversy over freewill and determinism has raged for so long, and has been carried on
by philosophers of such outstanding merit, that it is
unlikely that anything new in the way of argument can
be brought forward. It is possible, nevertheless, that
fresh facts might contribute something valuable towards
arriving at a solution of the problem, and I suggest that
the possibility of non-inferential precognition is such a
fact. Though it has been popularly recognized for many
years, it is only comparatively recently that serious
attention has been given to the evidence, while, so far
as I know, it has been taken into account by very few
indeed of the professional philosophers.

The utmost that the psychical researcher can, or
should, hope to do is to bring the facts to the notice of
the experts, that is to say, the professional philosophers
and moralists, and leave it to them to bring to bear
on those facts the full weight of logical and metaphysical
analysis.

I have ventured, it is true, to attempt to work out
some of the implications, but my attempt is only that of
a layman and amateur. Laymen, that is to say, those
not trained in the study of philosophy, are liable, in
fact almost certain, to overlook relevant considerations,
and to underestimate the logical difficulties in the way
of their arguments. But it sometimes happens that the
professional is stimulated to action by witnessing the
blunders of the layman; I can only hope that this may
be the case in this matter of precognition. I could wish
that some competent philosopher would take my argu-

ments and, after rending them in pieces, show the world what should properly be deduced from the facts.

As regards the facts themselves, I by no means adopt this humble, I might almost say cringing, attitude in the face of the professional philosopher. The evidence was collected and examined by experts in that line of business, my part has been only to select suitable parts thereof. Unless human testimony be rejected altogether as incapable of establishing matters of fact, that evidence cannot, in scientific honesty, be ignored, however inconvenient it may be to those whose philosophic systems it upsets.

After this humble confession, it may seem inappropriate to go further in my attempt to work out the implications of precognition, yet I will make one further venture in that direction, pleading only that it concerns a matter which is more specifically within the boundaries of psychical research.

It seems to me that the occurrence of precognitions indicates that there is something amiss with our ordinary ideas of time.

We commonly think of past events as those which have happened and now no longer exist; of present events as those which are happening now and are, therefore, existent; and of the future as that which has not yet happened and does not yet exist.

Reality extends up to the present and is there cut off sharply. History is continually being made by the events which happen in the present, and may be represented in imagination as a record being written. The pen is always moving onward, but ahead of it is simply a blank page. The difficulties for this view of the nature of time to which the occurrence of precognition gives rise have already been referred to in the chapter wherein I tried to give a brief account of some of the explanatory theories which have been suggested; I will not, therefore, repeat them here. As a matter of personal opinion, and as a result of prolonged and careful study of the evidence, I am forced to the conclusion that non-inferential precognitions do occur, that is to say, that chance, illusion of memory or any other normal cause, cannot account for all the cases of foreknowledge which have been investigated and published. This being so, I hold that the future does, in some sense, exist now, though, as I have tried to show, it is not all immutably fixed but is capable of being altered in some respects.

One implication of this seems to be that at some level of our consciousness we are subject to conditions of what might be called a wider or more elastic time than that which governs our ordinary everyday life.

All that this means for us is, perhaps, impossible to say, but I think that it shows that some of the questions which we ask about life and destiny have been couched in over-simplified terms. Take, for example, the question of the survival of physical death. This, as it is usually formulated, assumes the simple ordinary idea of time, that is of events which follow one another as it were in a straight line. But if time be *not* a simple uni-dimensional affair with an absolutely non-existent future, as seems to be implied by the facts of precognition, the question is ambiguous until the temporal conditions are more precisely specified.

If, as has been suggested, precognition implies a

second dimension of time, so that one could travel in time sideways, so to speak, as well as forwards, it seems possible that a man might die and cease to exist in one temporal direction, yet survive in another.

Or, to take another suggestion, if the present moment of some stratum of the subliminal self covers a considerably longer span of duration than does that of the normal self, when a man reaches the point of death his subliminal self may already be existing in a present which extends beyond that point.

Until we understand more clearly the nature of time, it seems to me that we cannot properly frame our questions about survival so as to be sure of avoiding ambiguities and hidden assumptions. If this be so it looks as though we ought to rest content with opinions much less definite and clear-cut than those which we usually entertain, and which most of us demand.

In conclusion I will enlarge a little on this point.

I think that what most of us mean when we ask about survival may be stated somewhat as follows. After my physical death, will there exist in the continuation of the time stream in which I now seem to myself to live, a personality which is identical or historically continuous with the personality which I now recognize as myself?

This question seems to me to bristle with ambiguities, such as the meaning of identity, the degree of historical continuity, and whether the personality which I now recognize as myself is, in fact, my true and complete self. I will not, however, do more than enumerate these now, but will confine myself to those connected with time.

There are at least five questions which must be settled before the time clause can be made unambiguous.

(1) Is the time stream in which I now appear to live a real time stream?

(2) Is it only a partial, subjective aspect of real time?

(3) Is there another kind or dimension of time?

(4) Can I assume that all parts, or strata, of my personality are subject to the temporal conditions with which I am ordinarily familiar?

(5) Can I assume that a disembodied state of being, if such exist, is subject to time at all?

There are probably other questions which could be raised, and ambiguities which require to be cleared up, but I think that this list is sufficient to show that the formulation of the question is by no means so simple as appears on the surface. If we encounter so many difficulties in asking our questions intelligibly, it cannot be wondered at that the answers are hard to find.

The conclusions, then, to which I have arrived after a prolonged and careful study of the matter are: (a) that I believe that non-inferential precognition does sometimes occur; (b) that I cannot explain it; (c) that it is not inconsistent with regarding man as a morally responsible being; and (d) that we must revise our ordinary ideas about the nature of time. Some of these conclusions may be distasteful to those who demand clear-cut answers to their questions, but until we can attain to a clearer understanding of the problems involved, we must admit a large element of agnosticism in many of our opinions.

Before we can reach such an understanding we must

solve at least two riddles, viz., the nature of normal memory and of precognition.

I fear that this book will have done little towards the solution of the latter problem – I have not touched upon the former – but I believe that the two are some-how bound up together. I hope, however, that, by giving some idea of the evidence for precognition, I may have succeeded in rendering the problem clearer, or, at least, in bringing it into the light of day.

GLOSSARY

Of terms, and special uses of words, commonly
found in the literature of psychical research.

Agent. One who takes the part of transmitter in telepathic
communication.

Automatic writing. Writing executed without the conscious
use of thought or muscular control by the writer. The
term is also applied when the act of writing is consciously
directed but the origin of the words or ideas is unknown
to the writer.

Automatist. One who writes, speaks, or performs other
significant action, without conscious volition. The term
is somewhat widely applied, so as to include cases in
which only the mental action involved is involuntary.

Auto-suggestion. Suggestion applied to oneself. (See
Suggestion.)

Clairaudience. Perception as sound of an impression in some
way true to fact, and not perceptible to the ordinary
senses.

Clairvoyance. Perception of real objects or facts not within
range of the ordinary senses. (Strictly used of perception
in visual form; but the word often denotes paranormal
perception of other kinds.)

Communicator. A personality seeming to be that of a deceased
person or other discarnate being.

Control. (1) A personality regularly represented as using
and taking charge of a medium during trance; (2) The
direction of a medium's speech or action by another
personality.

Discarnate. Disembodied, opposed to incarnate.

118

Dissociation. Independent activity of a part of the mind, which behaves in some way like a separate individual.

Externalized. This word is used of an impression, arising within the mind, which is perceived as though coming from without.

Extra-Sensory Perception. (Abbreviated, E.S.P.) Perception without use of the known senses. A general term, used to include such conceptions as telepathy, clairvoyance and precognition.

Hallucination. A supposed sensory perception which has no objective cause within the range of the sense concerned. (An hallucination may or may not represent a fact underlying the impression received.)

Illusion. The misinterpretation by the mind of something actually perceived.

Influenced Writing. Writing in which the flow of ideas is affected as though by unspoken suggestion from another mind.

Medium. One able to respond to and give expression to paranormal influences, especially those appearing to be personal influences.

Metagnome. An alternative and less question-begging term for 'Medium', introduced by Boirac. Driesch defines it as 'a person from whom supernormal phenomena originate or in express relation to whom these phenomena occur.'

Paragnosis. Equivalent to extra-sensory perception.

Paranormal. Outside accepted experience of cause and effect.

Percipient. One who takes the part of receiver in telepathic communication.

Phantasm. The appearance of a person (in less common usage, also of a thing or event) as conveyed to the mind in hallucination.

Precognition. Perception or awareness of future event, apart from information or inference.

Psychic. This word is applied in general science to all action that has a mental as distinct from a physical basis. In popular speech it has a wide usage denoting anything paranormal. In psychical research the word is largely avoided as ambiguous, but it can occur in either the scientific or in the popular sense.

Purporting. Professing or seeming. It is said that a phenomenon 'purports' to be due to some paranormal cause when the evidence for such a cause is intended to be taken without prejudice for or against.

Retrocognition. Perception or awareness of past event not known to or within the memory of the perceiver.

Script. A piece of automatic writing: the record of an automatist's utterance.

Subliminal. Lying beneath the 'threshold' of consciousness. Practically equivalent to subconscious, or to 'unconscious' as a psychological term.

Suggestion. The impressing of ideas or feelings upon the mind, one's own or another's, so that they become effective without conscious volition on the part of the mind impressed.

Supernormal. See paranormal. The word does not necessarily imply a superior level of action or being.

Supraliminal. Lying above the 'threshold' of consciousness. The contents of the mind which are within the range of, or capable of being reached by normal conscious process.

Telekinesis. The causing of material objects to move without touching them or subjecting them to any known physical force.

Telepathy. Transmission of an image, idea or impulse from one mind to another by paranormal action of the minds concerned.

Veridical. Conveying facts, or ideas that can be shown to have basis in fact.

EVIDENCE OF
PERSONAL SURVIVAL

FROM
CROSS CORRESPONDENCES

by
H. F. SALTMARSH

LONDON
G. BELL & SONS, LTD
1938

PRINTED IN GREAT BRITAIN
BY WESTERN PRINTING SERVICES LTD., BRISTOL

This volume is based on material in the possession of the Society for Psychical Research and is published with the consent of the Council, who, whilst they do not necessarily endorse any opinion expressed in the book, welcome this opportunity of bringing the evidence before the public.

The author desires to make acknowledgment of his debt to the Council of the Society for Psychical Research for permission to print extracts from *Proceedings*, also to Mr. J. G. Piddington for his kind advice and assistance.

GENERAL INTRODUCTION

THIS book is one of a series on the subject of Psychical Experiences. The Society for Psychical Research, it should be stated at once, is in no way responsible for any of the deductions made, or theories advanced. All it has done as a Society is to allow members of the various groups who have been preparing the books to have access to unpublished records in its possession, and to grant permission to reprint records published in its *Proceedings*, and, in special cases, records privately printed in its *Journal*.

The stories of Psychic Experiences that appear in this series are on a completely different level from the majority of such stories published in most papers and magazines. Few people realize the meticulous care which the Society's investigators have always taken to test the good faith and the accuracy of those whose experiences have appeared in the *Proceedings* and *Journal*, as also the good faith and the accuracy of those who contribute corroborative evidence.

The object of this series is to put before the ordinary reading public examples of the evidence for various super-normal occurrences and faculties which the Society has been collecting for over half a century, and is still collecting.

The lack of interest shown by ordinary readers in this body of carefully tested evidence may be due to its bulk and complexity, and partly, perhaps, to their awareness of the fact that the majority of men of science fight shy of it. One reason for the aloofness of most men of science is probably the absence of any theory which successfully attempts to bring the various phenomena into even a semblance of unity.

In the present series no attempt can, of course, be made to supply such a theory. Nevertheless, it is much to be desired that someone with a thorough knowledge of the evidence should try, as Frederic Myers did nearly forty years ago in his Scheme of Vital Faculty (*Human Personality*, Vol. II, pp. 505–54), to construct 'a connected schedule or rational index of phenomena so disparate that the very possibility of their interdependence is even now constantly denied.' And that such an attempt should be made afresh is all the more to be desired because since Myers's death phenomena of a new type have been observed.

While, then, the authors of these small books recognize the need for some unifying theory, they have confined themselves to the less ambitious and less arduous task of marshalling a quantity of well-attested evidence for phenomena of many different kinds. For such views and comments as may be found in any of the books the individual writer, as has been stated above, is alone responsible.

CHAPTER I

THE purpose of this little book is to put before those who have not made a study of the subject some of the evidence which psychical research has been able to collect concerning the possibility of survival. It forms one of a series of such books, and is part of an attempt to gain a wider interest in the results of over fifty years of inquiry by members of the Society for Psychical Research.

Up till now the reading public has had, no doubt, a certain amount of rather vague and somewhat inexact knowledge of what the Society has done, but owing to the fact that the records of its work are contained, for the most part, in its *Proceedings* and *Journal*, which are not generally accessible, it is chiefly among its members that there exists any considerable acquaintance with the evidence which it has collected, and with the critical analyses and commentaries to which that evidence has been subjected. Moreover, the study of these records is, it must be admitted, a laborious task, and entails a great deal of very tedious reading, besides a not inconsiderable amount of special technical knowledge.

The Society as a body has no opinions, except that there are problems to be solved and that the critical method of approach may possibly lead to a solution. On the covers of the volumes of *Proceedings* is always to be found the following notice: 'The responsibility for both the facts and the reasonings in papers published in the *Proceedings* rests entirely with their authors.'

Thus it is that there is to be found among its members the widest divergence of opinion on most of the various topics which are discussed. There are those who are avowed Spiritualists, that is to say, who accept as a fact that the human personality persists after the death of the body and that it can, in certain favourable circumstances, communicate with those on earth; while there are others who hold the view that physical death entails the complete cessation of anything which could be called a personality.

These differences of opinion are, for the most part, concerned with the interpretation of facts and the inferences to be drawn from them, although in certain branches, more particularly in those dealing with physical phenomena, there is no general agreement as to the validity of the evidence; thus some believe that the evidence for the existence of physical phenomena, such as movements of objects without contact, known as telekinesis, materializations, or the production of visible or tangible forms, and so on, is sufficient in quality and quantity to carry a provisional conviction; while others are inclined to dismiss the whole thing as due to fraud, mal-observation, or some other normal cause.

In this book, however, we are not interested in physical phenomena, and the facts which constitute our evidence cannot be denied, as will be seen in the sequel. Various interpretations can, no doubt, be placed upon them and various causes assigned, but no one can dispute their reality except on the fantastic suggestion that a number of eminent scientists and scholars combined together to perpetrate a silly practical joke for the purpose of deceiving the readers of the Society's publications. Before embarking on my account of the phenomena, I should like to make a few further remarks concerning the scientific nature of the study.

In the ultimate resort all science depends on human testimony. It is true that in certain sciences, such as physics and chemistry, this testimony is reduced to its simplest form, and may be no more than the observation and recording of the movement of the needle of a galvanometer or similar instrument. There are, however, sciences where observation and testimony plays a larger part, notably those concerned with living things, such as biology in its many branches, and psychology.

In psychical research observation and testimony are of primary importance, for we must depend on them for most of our facts. Even where planned experimentation is employed, it is very rare that the necessary observation can be reduced to the level of pointer readings, that is to say, the recording of the movement of the indicator of a scientific instrument.

It is a truism that human testimony is unreliable; human memory is fallible and there is an innate tendency in most people to embroider and amplify. The courts of law, which have also to depend mainly on human testimony, reject hearsay evidence and will not listen to 'what the soldier said,' thus implicitly acknowledging the inherent weakness of the only available source from which knowledge of fact can be derived. The scope and accuracy of the powers of observation of the ordinary individual are far more restricted than is usually admitted. This has been tested by direct experiment by members of the Society.[1] A faked seance

[1] *Proc.*, S.P.R., Vol. XL, pp. 363–87.

was arranged, that is to say, the experimenter pretended
to be a medium producing physical phenomena under
the usual conditions of lighting and so on; the observers
knew that it was faked and were instructed to watch
carefully what happened. They recorded their impressions and these records were compared. It was found
that the correctness of the testimony of the sitters in
answer to a questionnaire of fifteen points concerning
what happened, varied from 5.9 to 61 per cent, averag-
ing 33.9 per cent. Only one sitter, out of the whole
forty-two, scored some success in reply to every question.
This weakness of observation is further plainly seen
when it is considered how much more is taken in by
the trained observer than by the untrained. Now it
cannot be said that anyone is really trained to observe
the type of fact which is of interest to psychical research,
for these facts are so various in character and cover the
whole range of human activity.

Where definite experimentation is undertaken, some
training in observation is possible, but unfortunately,
experiment plays a comparatively small part in supplying the psychical researcher with material. It is true
that efforts have been, and still are being made, to
extend the use of experimentation, but we still have to
rely for most of our evidence on ordinary observation. That herein lies one of the major causes of
difficulty in the subject was recognized by those directing the Society from the very outset, and they endeavoured to meet it by laying down rigid canons of
evidence, and refusing to publish any case which did not
comply therewith.

More than this could not have been done, and I think

that it may be said that on the whole these canons have been strictly observed.

But it follows that no conclusions arrived at from consideration of alleged phenomena can be held to be established with complete certainty. One must always insert some such clause as 'provided that the evidence can be accepted.' That the effect of such a qualification depends on the nature of the alleged facts is obvious. It would be, for example, far more important in cases where spontaneous phenomena, such as phantasms or hauntings were concerned, than in those which fall to be discussed in this book, that is to say, where the bulk of the material consists of writings done automatically. Here we have the advantage of dealing solely with documentary evidence—evidence, that is to say, which is objective and permanent, concerning which errors of observation and exaggeration cannot arise.

There is one further point which must be touched upon before we can get down to cases. In almost all sciences the element of personal feeling and predilection is, if not completely absent, at any rate of negligible proportions. Though scientists may have pet theories or a general bias towards one particular type of interpretation, these are not likely to exercise any compulsive influence over their conclusions. One cannot imagine an astronomer, for instance, being swayed in his judgment by his personal desires to the extent of refusing to accept plain facts or to draw plain inferences. He may, possibly, lay a greater stress on certain aspects of his problem because such are favourable to his pet theories, but I doubt whether the course of knowledge is materially influenced.

In psychical research, however, the position is very different and it is the common experience of most workers therein that divergent views are held, not merely with firmness, but also with something amounting to passionate resolve. In particular, in the matter of survival, one is apt to find that comparatively few students can maintain the attitude of dispassionate impartiality which is essential to the scientist. Of course, in a matter where human life and fate are involved, wherein man's most intimate hopes, fears and affections depend upon the answers to the questions, it is not reasonable to expect everybody to be cold and unemotional, yet any other attitude is prejudicial, if not actually fatal, to the scientific method.

It must be remembered that there are two sides to this question. It sometimes happens that the strong feelings involved have the effect of rendering an investigator hypercritical. A man may long to believe, yet, just because he is aware of the strength of his longing, he may become unduly sceptical for fear that his desire may warp his judgment.

The aim of the method is the discovery of hypotheses, not of absolute truth, and hypotheses are, or at any rate ought to be, constructed to withstand rough handling. If any hypothesis be so fragile as to crack under the strain of criticism, then it is worthless. It is surely unwise, therefore, to fix your heart on any hypothesis, for should criticism succeed in overthrowing it—and one never knows what may happen to even the most firmly rooted hypothesis—your heart may be broken in the fall.

All, then, that can be expected from scientific inquiry

is the ascertainment of the probability in favour of some particular hypothesis. In the case of psychical research these probabilities will not, as a rule, be very high by reason of the disabilities under which it labours, some of which I have pointed out. If, therefore, one turns to psychical research expecting to find a 'sure and certain hope' one is doomed to disappointment.

I do not deny that there may be other sources of knowledge besides scientific inquiry, and that these may yield a 'sure and certain hope.' I neither affirm nor deny it, it is quite outside my province.

There is, perhaps, one reflection in this connection which should be made. It has arisen from the fact that, as remarked above, our most intimate hopes, fears and affections, are concerned with the answers to the problems of psychical research, many people who have taken up the study have erected a religion upon it and that this has gone a long way towards confusing the issues and discrediting the purely scientific approach in the eyes, not only of the orthodox scientist, but also in those of the orthodox religionist of other persuasion.

CHAPTER II

FOR the benefit of those who have no previous knowledge of the results of psychical research, I propose to state briefly a few of the hypotheses for which a greater or less degree of probability has been established, but I shall touch only upon those which are relevant to the particular branch to be dealt with here.

The first, both in order of time and in magnitude of probability, is telepathy. This has been defined as 'the communication of impressions of any kind from one mind to another, independently of the recognized channels of sense' (Myers),[1] or 'the acquisition of the mental content of another without the intermediary of the organs of sense' (Driesch).[2]

Driesch divides it into two distinct kinds; first *pure telepathy*, wherein the agent, i.e. the person who normally possesses the knowledge, communicates it to the percipient, i.e. the person who supernormally acquires it; second, *thought reading*, wherein the percipient draws the knowledge from the mind of the agent. In pure telepathy the agent is the active party and the percipient passive, in thought reading the percipient is active and the agent passive.

[1] *Human Personality and Its Survival of Bodily Death*, by F. W. H. Myers. Vol. I, p. XXII.
[2] *Psychical Research*, by Hans Driesch (trans. Theodore Besterman), p. 71.

There may be also cases where both parties are active in varying degrees.

Now, although we can make these distinctions in theory, we have no certain grounds for holding that they actually exist in fact, the most that we can say in any case is that it looks more like one than the other.

There is a further possible alternative which has been suggested, though, from the nature of the facts, little or no objective evidence of its truth is obtainable; this is that the communication of impressions from one mind to another is carried out by means of the intervention of a third agency, such as a disembodied spirit. As we do not know for certain that disembodied spirits exist, nor, even if they do, whether they can communicate with embodied minds, this hypothesis cannot be taken as being much more than pure speculation.

The fact is, that although we have very good – some would say, conclusive – evidence, that impressions are communicated from one mind to another in this supernormal fashion, when we call it telepathy we are simply attaching a label to cover our ignorance. We know nothing of its real nature or of its *modus operandi*. Thus when the sceptic asserts, as he frequently does, that all supernormal mental phenomena can be covered by telepathy, he is simply explaining one mystery by another.

The next type of phenomenon to be mentioned is clairvoyance. Myers defined it as 'the faculty or act of perceiving, as though visually, with some coincidental truth, some distant scene.'[1] Clairaudience could be similarly defined by substituting hearing for sight. He

---

[1] *Human Personality*, Vol. I, p. XV.

preferred, however, the term telæsthesia to cover both clairvoyance and clairaudience.

Driesch defines clairvoyance as being 'the supernormal acquisition of knowledge about objective concrete situations.'[1]

Clairvoyance, or telæsthesia, may transcend the ordinary limitations of sense perception, both in the matter of space and of time. Thus the clairvoyant or seer may obtain knowledge of distant scenes, or some object which is normally inaccessible, such as the contents of a sealed envelope or a passage in a closed book. He may also acquire knowledge of past or even future events.

The evidence for clairvoyance, though considerable in amount, and high in point of quality, does not reach the level of that for telepathy; however, many students of the subject consider that it stands on a substantially firm foundation as regards its actuality.

As in the case of telepathy, we know practically nothing of its nature and *modus operandi.*

It is usually assumed that in clairvoyance the percipient or seer is the only person involved – no agent is necessary; but it must be borne in mind that many cases of apparent clairvoyance may be really telepathic, for, where the situation supernormally perceived by the seer is being, or has been, normally perceived by another person, the seer's knowledge may be derived from the mind of that person, either by pure telepathy or by thought reading.

Just as telepathy was subdivided, so we can form various sub-groups of clairvoyance; first, spatial clair-

---

[1] *Psychical Research,* p. 72.

voyance, where distant scenes or otherwise inaccessible objects are perceived; second, temporal clairvoyance, which could be further split up into retro-cognition and pre-cognition, i.e. supernormal knowledge of past and future events.

Clairvoyance and telepathy merge into one another apparently by imperceptible degrees, but until we understand more of their *modus operandi*, we cannot say whether they are actually different faculties or only different manifestations of one supernormal faculty of acquiring knowledge.

We must now consider some of the modes in which these two faculties, telepathy and clairvoyance, are shown, but I must first of all introduce the conception of the subliminal, or as some prefer to call it, the subconscious mind.

I cannot do better than quote from Myers' *Human Personality*, Vol I, p. 14: 'The idea of a threshold (limen, Schwelle) of consciousness; – of a level above which sensation or thought must rise before it can enter into our conscious life; – is a simple and familiar one. The word *subliminal* – meaning "beneath that threshold" – has already been used to define those sensations which are too feeble to be individually recognized. I propose to extend the meaning of the term, so as to make it cover *all* that takes place beneath the ordinary threshold or say, if preferred, outside the ordinary margin of consciousness. . . . Perceiving . . . that these submerged thoughts and emotions possess the characteristics which we associate with conscious life, I feel bound to speak of a *subliminal* or *ultra-marginal consciousness*. . . . I find it permissable and convenient to speak of subliminal selves, or more briefly of a subliminal self. I do not indeed by using this term assume that there are two correlative and parallel selves existing always within each of us. Rather I mean by the subliminal self that part of the Self which is commonly subliminal; and I conceive that there may be, – not only *co-operations* between these quasi-independent trains of thought – but also upheavals and alterations of personality of many kinds, so that what was once below the surface may for a time, or permanently, rise above it. And I conceive also that no Self of which we can here have cognisance, is in reality more than a fragment of a larger Self.'

I think that it is perhaps a pity that the prefix 'sub' has always been used in this connection, whether in subliminal or in subconscious, for it almost irresistibly brings in the idea of *beneath* consciousness, thus tending to make one think that the contents of the subliminal mind are lower or more rudimentary in character than those of normal or supra-liminal consciousness. This is not so, for the subliminal may, and frequently does, contain elements which are definitely higher or more advanced than our normal faculties.

The subliminal, it is true, is partly a rubbish dump, but it may also be a gold mine; it is littered with worn-out relics of other days, but it is the storehouse of forgotten memories; from it proceed dreams and delirium, but it may also be the fountain from which springs the inspiration of genius. It observes and records much that passes unnoticed by the supra-liminal. The subliminal is capable of carrying on an independent train of conscious process – I hesitate to call it thought, though, judging from the glimpses which we occasionally get, it is a process in many ways the same as our ordinary thought. Some writers, including Myers, as we have seen above, have boldly spoken of the subliminal self as distinguished from the supraliminal or manifested self of everyday life.

In normal circumstances there is a close relationship between the subliminal and the supraliminal, although the former does not intrude into view but remains more. or less active below the surface. There is a constant interchange between the two levels, parts of the content of the supraliminal consciousness sinking, as it were, into the subliminal, while occasionally the results of subliminal processes and activity force themselves to the surface.

In ordinary sleep the supraliminal is almost completely in abeyance, but the subliminal remains active, producing the material and weaving the patterns of our dreams.

But there are occasions when this close relationship is disturbed, and the subliminal takes to itself a greater degree of independence. This is usually known as dissociation.

It would be too great a digression to cite the evidence on which these views are based, I will, therefore, content myself with enumerating a few of the main types. They are the phenomena of multiple personality, of hypnosis, unconscious mentation, as, for example, when the solution of some problem which has baffled our ordinary thought springs suddenly into our minds.

There are good grounds for believing that the supernormal faculties exercised in telepathy and clairvoyance belong to the subliminal, and although it would perhaps be going too far to say that this is definitely established in all cases, I think that it is safe to say that it is generally true. Moreover, we may go further and say that in the majority of cases at any rate, these phenomena take place when there is a certain amount of dissociation between the subliminal and the supraliminal. The dissociation may be so slight as to be not noticeable, but I, personally, am inclined to think that it is always there.

Now as regards the modes in which telepathy and clairvoyance are commonly manifested, we have first, spontaneous telepathy between two individuals, as in cases when the same idea comes simultaneously into both minds. There is as a rule no conscious endeavour on the part of the agent to send a message, or on the part of the recipient to put himself into a state favourable to receive it. Dissociation, if it is present at all, is so slight that it can rarely be detected. Almost everyone, I imagine, has had personal experience of this phenomenon, with some people it is of everyday occurrence. In these cases it is usually impossible to say whether it is the agent or the percipient who is the active party. Spontaneous clairvoyance is usually accompanied by a more marked degree of dissociation; it occurs when a person suddenly acquires knowledge of a distant scene or a past or future event. It is much more rare than spontaneous telepathy and comparatively few people experience it.

Next come induced telepathy and clairvoyance. There are several methods which are commonly used. Thus two persons may deliberately try to obtain telepathic communication, one acting as agent and

thinking of a certain object or idea, the other as percipient endeavouring, by holding the mind blank, to
throw himself into a receptive state. Considerable
success, far beyond anything which could be attributed
to chance, has frequently been obtained in experiments
of this sort. Dissociation here may become quite
marked, particularly with the percipient. Then there
are those more advanced cases where trance is employed. A few peculiarly constituted individuals are
able to go into a trance state, more or less at will. In
such a state dissociation is very high and sometimes
the subject seems to be capable of becoming highly
receptive to telepathy, or of exercising thought reading
and clairvoyance with a considerable degree of success.

Such individuals are usually called 'Mediums.' The
term is a bad one, and I much prefer the synthetic
word 'Metagnome.'

It is somewhat unfortunate that psychical research
is encumbered with terms which implicitly assume
some sort of spiritistic hypothesis; thus the term
'medium' suggests a medium of exchange or transmission, a mediator between two parties; the term
communicator, again, implies a personal identity.

I do not say that the spiritistic hypothesis is untenable,
but it is clearly undesirable that terms which beg the
question in respect of any hypothesis whatsoever should
be used.

However, they have the sanction of custom; moreover, they are for the most part convenient in avoiding
cumbrous circumlocutions. I shall therefore continue
to speak of mediums, communicators, controls, spirits,
messages, and the 'other side,' but I want to make it

perfectly clear that in doing so I imply no acceptance of any explanatory hypothesis whatsoever.

In what follows when I speak of a medium I shall mean exclusively one who produces the so-called mental phenomena, i.e. speech, writing or communications by any other method, such as table-tilting. In most instances when this term is used it will be of a person who produces these phenomena in trance, when there is no trance I prefer the term 'automatist.'

Generally speaking, trance mediums have what is called a 'control.' This purports to be a disembodied spirit who, as a rule, claims identity with a deceased human being, very commonly of a rather exotic extraction, such as a Red Indian Chief, or, as in the case of Mrs. Osborne Leonard's control, Feda, an Indian girl; the control frequently adopts a childish manner of speech or uses broken English.

In the case of Mrs. Piper, the one medium, as distinguished from automatist, here concerned, the controls were a group of rather enigmatic personages known as Rector, Prudens, Imperator and Doctor. They were not, so to speak, 'all her own invention,' but were taken over, or at least their names were, from Stainton Moses, a clergyman, who had manifested remarkable mediumistic powers and was well known both in spiritualist circles and among those interested in psychical research.

I shall have more to say about these controls, but should mention here that in their case the manner of speech was by no means childish, it was, in fact, extremely dignified.

It must also be said that the claim that they were

the same set of individuals who had controlled Stainton Moses cannot be admitted as being established.

Although these claims have never been substantiated, and in some cases have been proved to be almost certainly false, so much so that many students hold that the control is only a kind of secondary personality of the medium, it must be admitted that they maintain a consistency of character and behave as though they were separate individuals. As one might say, the dramatic personation is good.

The function of the control is to direct proceedings 'from the other side,' to arrange the methods and manner in which the sittings are held, and to receive the messages from other purporting communicators, i.e. from what claim to be the surviving spirits of deceased human beings desirous of communicating with those remaining on earth. The control then delivers the message through the medium, or acts as an amanuensis.

The scene which is portrayed may be thought of somewhat as follows. The medium may be likened to a telephone with a loud-speaker to which the sitter listens and through which he may speak to the control. At the other end is the control who converses with the communicators and relays the messages through the telephone. Occasionally the sitter may catch fragments of conversations going on between the control and the communicators, also the communicator may sometimes oust the control, and speak directly through the telephone.

This is, of course, a fanciful picture, and must not be taken too seriously: whether it really represents what actually takes place need not be considered here, all that we are concerned with is the content and meaning of the messages. Sometimes, even with a trance medium, the messages are written instead of being spoken. If the messages are veridical, that is to say, truth-telling, and if the knowledge contained in them should be such that it cannot be ascribed to the medium's consciousness, then we must find some hypothesis to account for it.

Besides trance mediumship there are other methods whereby sensitive persons may render themselves receptive to supernormal influences.

There is, first, crystal-gazing or 'scrying.' This practice is of ancient origin, we have records of its employment in very early times. Sometimes a ball of crystal or glass is used, sometimes a pool of some liquid, occasionally the polished thumb-nail. It does not seem to matter what is used, the *modus operandi* is always the same. The scryer concentrates attention and gazes fixedly at the object, and gradually scenes appear on its surface, or, if a crystal is used, in its interior; these scenes may be simply a kind of externalized dream, but sometimes they are veridical, that is to say, they convey information not known normally to the scryer.

The function of the crystal or pool of liquid appears to be simply to induce a state of dissociation, thus rendering the emergence of subliminal impressions easier; the fact that the scenes appear to be in the crystal is due to externalization of the subliminal impression, it is a form of induced hallucination.

There are also several forms of what is technically called 'automatism.' One of the most common of these is automatic writing, which may be performed with or without a planchette. The planchette, as most people know, is a small heart-shaped board with a pencil, point downwards at one corner, and two little wheels or castors at the others, so that it can move easily over the paper, causing the pencil to leave marks. The operator, or operators, rest a finger lightly upon it, taking care not to direct its movement consciously.

In some cases, however, the automatic writing is done simply by holding a pen or pencil, and allowing the hand to move as it were by its own volition. Quite a large number of people can do this with a little practice.

In other cases, though the hand does not move automatically, the automatist does not know the meaning of what is being written. He or she may know what word is being actually written, but does not connect the words up into sentences.

In still other cases the automatist writes down words and sentences which come into the mind from the outside, as it were. It is as though the words were being taken down from dictation.

There is probably always a certain amount of dissociation when automatic writing is being performed, but it is frequently imperceptible.

As a very large proportion of the evidence to be discussed here comes through automatic writing, I shall describe, in some detail, the methods employed by two or three of the principal automatists. I reserve a description of Mrs. Piper's methods until later.

The first to be mentioned is Mrs. Verrall. She was a lecturer in classics at Newnham, and wife of Dr. A. W. Verrall, the well-known Cambridge classical scholar.

She was also a member of the Council of the Society for Psychical Research. In a paper on her automatic writing, published in *Proceedings*, S.P.R., Vol. XX, October, 1906, she says: 'Whether I write in light or dark, I do not look at the paper. I perceive a word or two, but never understand whether it makes sense with what goes before. Under these circumstances, it will be seen that though I am aware at the moment of writing what language my hand is using, when the script is finished I often cannot say, till I read it, what language has been used, as the recollection of the words passes away with extreme rapidity.

'I have tried more than once to reproduce from memory what has just been written, but I have never been able to give more than a word or two and I have no impression as to the general sense, if there has been any.[1]

'I usually write when I am alone, and I prefer not to have a bright light; it is desirable also to write at a time of day or under circumstances when I am not likely to be interrupted. But none of these conditions is essential.[2]

'It is quite common for me to write in a railway-carriage with other travellers present.[2]

'My left hand writes automatically as well as my right; I should say that I normally can write with both hands, and use the left when the right is incapacitated by writer's cramp.[2]

'I am sometimes exceedingly sleepy during the production of the writing, and more than once I

---

[1] Op. cit., p. 12.   [2] Op. cit., p. 13.

have momentarily lost consciousness of my surroundings.'[1]

It will be observed from what Mrs. Verrall says about getting sleepy while writing, that some degree, often considerable, of dissociation was present.

A large part of her script consists of purported communications from Mr. F. W. H. Myers, poet, classical scholar, and one of the founders of the Society for Psychical Research. He was the author of *Human Personality and Its Survival of Bodily Death*, from which I have already quoted, as well as volumes of poems, essays, etc. He died on January 17th, 1901.

The next to be described is the lady who is known as Mrs. Holland. She was at first not personally acquainted with any of the officers or members of the Society, but corresponded with Miss Alice Johnson, the Secretary. She lived at the time in India, but came home for a year or so in April, 1904. She met Miss Johnson for the first time in October, 1905, and Mrs. Verrall in the November following.

She began automatic writing for her own amusement in 1893.

The bulk of her script at the period for the first ten years, consisted of verse. In a letter to Miss Johnson, dated September 14th, 1903, she says: 'The verses, though often childishly simple in wording and jingling in rhyme, are rarely trivial in subject. Their striking feature is the rapidity with which they come. I once wrote down fourteen poems in little over an hour. . . . When I write original verse I do so slowly and carefully, with frequent erasures: automatic verse is always as

[1] Op. cit., p. 14.

if swiftly dictated and there are never any erasures. I am always fully conscious, but my hand moves so rapidly that I seldom know what words it is forming.[1]

'I have been asked if automatic writing has ever stated facts previously unknown to me, which were afterwards proved to be correct.' She then quotes a poem written automatically, which ran as follows:

'Under the orange tree
Who is it lies?
Baby hair that is flaxen fair,
Shines when the dew on the grass is wet,
Under the iris and violet.
'Neath the orange-tree
Where the dead leaves be,
Look at the dead child's eyes!'

'This is very curious,' said my friend, 'there is a tradition that a child is buried in the garden here, but I know that you have never heard it.'[2]

She mentioned a few other instances wherein her script seemed to contain information unknown to her, and says: 'Since then I have felt on three occasions that some unseen but very present personality was striving to transmit a message through me to a well-beloved.'[3]

In June, 1903, Mrs. Holland read Myers' great work, *Human Personality*. This led to her getting into correspondence with Miss Johnson, also, apparently, to a change in the character of her script; at any rate whether or not there was any connection with her reading the book, a marked change in the script fol-

[1] *Proc.*, S.P.R., Vol. XXI, p. 171.   [2] Ibid., p. 173.   [3] Ibid., p. 174.

lowed immediately. Instead of poems, which presumably were the work of her subliminal mind (she is widely read in the English poets, and as her letter above quoted mentions, writes original verse herself) her automatic writing from this period purports to be inspired chiefly by Fred Myers, but also, to a lesser extent, by Edmund Gurney (died June 22nd, 1888), and Prof. Hy. Sidgwick (died August 28th, 1900), the two friends to whom Myers had dedicated his book, and with whom he had been associated in life in the work of psychical research.

These may be described as being almost controls in the sense described above (p. 16). The Myers control preferred to write with a pen, while the Gurney control used a pencil. Miss Johnson says: 'As usual in automatic writing, there are various different indications of which "control" is purporting to be present. Occasionally, but not very often, the "control" uses a signature – either in full, or in initials. Often the contents of the writing leave no doubt as to who it is. And, as usual, varieties of handwriting are associated with the different controls, though they are not always used consistently for the same one.'[1]

That the automatic writing took place in a state of partial dissociation is clearly seen from the fact that at one time Mrs. Holland was much troubled because of a strong tendency to go into trance when writing automatically; she sought Miss Johnson's advice as to the best way to counteract it. Miss Johnson advised the use of auto-suggestion, and this was completely successful in preventing actual trance, but I think that there is

[1] *Proc.*, S.P.R., Vol. XXI, p. 180.

no doubt that a state of partial dissociation continued to prevail.

The third automatist whom I propose to describe was known as Mrs. Willett. In a paper published in *Proceedings*, Vol. XLIII, May, 1935, Lord Balfour discusses the psychological aspects of Mrs. Willett's mediumship. With the bulk of the contents of this paper we are not now concerned, but I draw upon it for a description of the *modus operandi* of Mrs. Willett's automatism.

Lord Balfour says: 'In her early girlhood Mrs. Willett discovered that she possessed the power of automatic writing, but, having no one to guide or advise her, she soon gave up the practice of it.

'In the second half of 1908 circumstances into which I need not enter led to a renewal of her interest in the subject.[1]

'During the first stage the communications reach the automatist when she is alone, and in a condition normal or hardly to be distinguished from the normal. They take the form of automatic script in a hand different from Mrs. Willett's ordinary handwriting. But it does not appear that the act of writing is fully automatic in the sense that the hand seems to be moved for her by some external influence and without her co-operation – though something of the kind did apparently occur on one unique occasion. According to her own account the words seem to form in her brain "a hair's-breadth" before she sets them down; but this does not mean that her mind anticipates the sense of what is coming, but only each individual word as it comes. As to her

[1] Op. cit., p. 49.

recollection, when the script is finished, of what she has written, it is not easy to form any precise estimate, and probably the extent of it varies considerably.'[1]

A second stage, introducing a fresh method, occurred in 1909.

Mrs. Willett began to receive impressions mentally. In a letter to Mrs. Verrall she says: 'I heard nothing with my ears, but the words came from outside into my mind as they do when one is reading a book to oneself. I do not remember exact words, but the first sentence was: "Can you hear what I am saying?" '[2]

In a subsequent letter she says: 'I got no impression of *appearance*, only character, and in some way voice or pronunciation.'[2]

Mrs. Willett wrote down the communications which came to her in this manner in her ordinary way.

A third stage developed when it became customary in September, 1910, for someone to sit with Mrs. Willett. Lord Balfour says of it: 'Its course is a progress towards deeper and deeper trance.'[3]

In this stage Mrs. Willett, though she continues to produce automatic writing as formerly, speaks a considerable part of the communications. It is as though she were listening to and reporting the words of some one who was invisible and inaudible to the sitter.

The controls are the same group as for Mrs. Verrall and Mrs. Holland, viz. Myers, Gurney and Sidgwick, with occasional interventions from one or two more of this group of friends.

There were, besides these three ladies, several other automatists who played a part. I will, however, make

[1] Op. cit., p. 50.   [2] Op. cit., p. 52.   [3] Op. cit., p. 56.

no attempt to describe their individual methods as to do so would occupy much space and add little of value. Their names were Mrs. Forbes (pseudonym), Miss Helen Verrall (daughter of Mrs. Verrall), a brother and sisters known as the 'Macs' and one or two more. Last, and by no means the least, the famous trance medium, Mrs. Piper, of Boston, U.S.A. Mrs. Piper, probably the most remarkable trance medium known, had been working for members of the Society for a considerable number of years, and had, during the period November, 1906, to June, 1907, paid a visit to England for the purpose of giving sittings.

With a professional medium it is necessary to take precautions and to institute investigations which might be deemed superfluous if applied to a private non-professional automatist. With the latter the question of fraud can hardly arise; no reasonable person could suggest that a group of ladies of the culture and intelligence of those here involved, would combine together to carry out a scheme of concerted cheating – a conspiracy of fraud, and persist in the practice for over thirty years. Moreover, it is hard to assign any motive for such conduct: had it been for the sake of a practical joke, it was surely a strange sense of humour which could derive satisfaction from anything so cumbrous and prolonged; had it been for the sake of 'showing up' the investigators, the scheme missed fire for the plot was never divulged.

However, the investigators took what precautions were possible to avoid leakage of information from one automatist to another, also investigation into their knowledge of facts, both supraliminal and subliminal, was, of course, undertaken. It should be stated here that in every case the automatists gave the fullest assistance to the investigators, and frequently furnished information which led to the discovery of a normal source from which the knowledge might have been derived.

They also, in some cases, voluntarily submitted themselves to restrictions in the matter of reading, abstaining from looking at books and other publications, the reading of which might invalidate the evidence. Thus, Mrs. Holland, for example, preferred to be kept in ignorance of the success, or otherwise, of the investigations while they were being carried out.[1]

A further argument against the suggestion of collusion, were one needed, may be derived from the fact that the 'Myers' of Mrs. Holland's scripts is so totally unlike that of Mrs. Verrall's; in fact, in many respects incredible. Had the automatists conspired together in a plot, Mrs. Verrall, who knew Myers, would have seen to it that the personation in the scripts of the other automatists was at least plausible.

With professional mediums, however, one must always bear in mind the possibility of conscious or unconscious fraud. The investigation concerning Mrs. Piper in this respect was most searching and thorough-going, she was even watched by private detectives in case she should be making surreptitious inquiries for the purpose of obtaining information which might later be retailed as being supernormally acquired. The result of this investigation was completely satisfactory; not the smallest indication of anything underhanded or dis-

[1] *Proc.*, S.P.R., Vol. XXI, p. 175.

honest was found. Everyone who has had any dealings with her has been completely satisfied as to her bona fides.

As has been mentioned above, the controls in Mrs. Piper's case at the time, were personages known as Rector, Imperator and Prudens. Whether they were actually, as they claimed to be, the surviving spirits of persons deceased long ago, it is not necessary to discuss. They were distinguishable personalities, even if they were no more than secondary personalities of Mrs. Piper herself. Rector acted as amanuensis for a large part of the proceedings, and purported to write through Mrs. Piper's hand messages which he received from other ostensible communicators. These communicators included Myers and his group, also Dr. Richard Hodgson who had himself been prominent in the investigation of Mrs. Piper's mediumship, and a communicator known as George Pelham (pseudonym), usually spoken of as G.P.

Mr. Piddington, one of the investigators, describes Mrs. Piper's trance as follows: 'Mrs. Piper sits at a table with a pile of cushions in front of her, and composes herself to go into trance. After an interval varying from two or three to ten minutes her head drops on the cushions with the face turned to the left and the eyes closed, her right hand falling at the same time on to a small table placed at her right side. A pencil is put between her fingers, and the hand proceeds to write. The writing being done without the aid of sight and with the arm in a more or less strained position is often difficult to decipher, at least without practice; but in spite of its not being easy to read, it is remarkably consistent in character, so that, its peculiarities once grasped, the correct interpretation of all but a few words is not a matter of conjecture. The coming out of trance is a longer process than the going into trance. After the hand has ceased to write the medium remains quiescent for a few minutes. She then raises herself slowly, and often with difficulty, from the cushions. When her body is erect, she begins to speak. Her utterance at first is usually indistinct, but as she gradually regains her normal condition it becomes clearer.[1] The trance-script was always kept out of Mrs. Piper's sight and taken away at the end of the sitting, so that she never saw it or had access to it at any time. In her normal condition she neither asked for nor received any information whatever about what had happened at the sittings, except that she was occasionally told that the results were considered interesting and promising, and that they were of a different nature from what had previously been obtained. Since there is strong ground for believing that in her normal state she remembers absolutely nothing of what has occurred in the trance state, it would seem impossible that in the intervals between the sittings she could have got up any information bearing on them, even had she wished to do so.'[2]

Thus, besides what was written while Mrs. Piper was in trance, there were spoken messages in what was called the 'waking stage.' These referred to, and sometimes amplified, the information given in the written messages; sometimes fresh topics were initiated in the waking stage.

[1] *Proc.*, S.P.R., Vol. XXII, p. 24.   [2] ibid., p. 25.

Finally, I must mention the investigators. It was usual for the automatists to send their script immediately after its production to a particular investigator who studied it and compared it with scripts from other automatists; thus Mrs. Verrall first sent hers to Sir Oliver Lodge, later to Mr. Piddington, while Mrs. Holland posted hers to Miss Johnson.

The chief investigators were Mr. J. G. Piddington, the Rt. Hon. Gerald Wm. Balfour (now Earl of Balfour), Sir Oliver Lodge, Mrs. Sidgwick, and Miss Alice Johnson, Secretary of the S.P.R. Mrs. Verrall filled the dual role of automatist and investigator.

It so happens that most of these were well versed in the classics and were thus able to appreciate the many classical allusions and literary puzzles based on classical authors which abound in the scripts. As I have already mentioned, Fred Myers was a classical scholar.

Such is the *mise en scène* of the series of cases which I now turn to discuss.

CHAPTER III

THE unique and peculiarly interesting feature of this series is that they purported to be experiments invented and arranged on 'the other side.'

On January 17th, 1901, Fred Myers died. He had, during his life, played a leading part in scientific psychical research and had an intense desire to discover objective evidence of survival such as would establish high logical probability, in fact, what would be considered as proof in any science of observation. He, himself, fully believed in survival, although he knew that the evidence available was not sufficient to compel general belief. In the communications which purport to come from him through automatic writing we can see again and again the passionate longing to prove his continued existence, and to convince his friends on earth of his identity. For example, in Mrs. Holland's script of January 12th, 1904, Myers, purporting to communicate, writes: *If it were possible for the soul to die back into earth life again I should die from sheer yearning to reach you to tell you that all that we imagined is not half wonderful enough for the truth,*[1] and through Mrs. Piper, *I am trying with all the forces . . . together to prove that I am Myers,*[2] and again through Mrs. Holland, *Oh, I am feeble with eagerness – how can I best be identified.*[3]

[1] *Proc.*, S.P.R., Vol. XXI, p. 233.
[2] *Proc.*, S.P.R., Vol. XXII, p. 105.
[3] *Proc.*, S.P.R., Vol. XXI, p. 234.

Now Myers, as an experienced psychical researcher, was fully aware of the difficulty of eliminating the possibility of explaining away evidential messages by telepathy or clairvoyance. The matter stands thus. The very large bulk of those cases wherein evidence of a supernormal kind is put forward as proving personal survival, consists of communications of knowledge which is not in the possession of any living person concerned, but was, or could have been, possessed by the individual from whose surviving spirit the messages purport to come.

Now, it is clear that for such communications to be of any value as evidence, the information conveyed must be capable of verification, and this implies that some living person must know the facts or else that some record exists or some circumstances from which the facts may be inferred.

But if this be so, it is always possible to hold that the information was conveyed telepathically to the mind of the medium from the living person who knew the facts, or else that the medium clairvoyantly became aware of the record or circumstances in which it is embodied. We have to bear in mind that it is not only the ordinary supraliminal knowledge of living persons which is available, but also the subliminal; further that a telepathic impression may be received and lie dormant in sub-liminal mind of the percipient, emerging into ordinary consciousness only after a lapse of time, sometimes of quite considerable length.

In these circumstances it is hard to imagine any possible evidence which could bring unequivocal proof of survival. Now Myers, as I have said, was fully aware

of all this, and what makes these experiments so peculiarly interesting is that, if we take the statements of the
communicators at their face value, it looks as though his
surviving spirit had invented a means of getting over
the difficulty and had endeavoured to carry it out.

I must, however, lay stress on the words 'at their face
value.' Whether this represents a true picture of what
actually occurred and whether the spirit of Fred Myers
survived his bodily death and carried over into his new
mode of existence his memories, affections and interest
in psychical research, must be decided on the evidence
itself.

When reading the reports of the cases and the scripts
of the various automatists, one can hardly help feeling
that it was indeed Myers, Gurney, Sidgwick and the
rest, who once had lived on earth and worked enthu-
siastically for psychical research, continuing their
labours from the other side, and making strenuous
endeavours to prove their identity.

But feelings are not enough, in fact, they should be
sternly put aside by those who seek scientific knowledge.
I shall have to speak of the dramatic personation later
and try to assess its evidential value, but until it has
been subjected to severe criticism its persuasive
influence must be discounted.

Briefly, the plan which purports to have been devised
by Myers and his associates on the other side is as
follows.

Suppose a message in cryptic terms be transmitted
through one automatist, and another message, equally
incomprehensible, through a second at about the same
time, and suppose that each automatist was ignorant

of what the other was writing, we have then two meaningless messages entirely disconnected with each other.

Now, if a third automatist were to produce a script which, while meaningless taken by itself, acts as a clue to the other two, so that the whole set could be brought together into one whole, and then show a single purpose and meaning, we should have good evidence that they all originated from a single source.

It may be looked at like this. Two people are each given one piece of a jigsaw puzzle, taken separately each piece is meaningless, nor will they fit each other. A third person is then given a third piece, and when the pieces are all brought together, it is found that they not only fit each other, but that when fitted they exhibit a coherent picture showing evidence of design and purpose.

It is quite obvious that telepathy between the automatists, in so far as their supraliminal knowledge is concerned, would not explain these facts, for none of them is able to understand the meaning of their own particular fragment, and so could not possibly convey to the other automatists the knowledge required to supply the missing portions. In most cases the puzzle – for the very essence of the whole thing is that they are puzzles – has been solved by an independent investigator, in fact, frequently the automatists themselves have remained in ignorance of any scripts but their own.

It is true that this independent source might possibly be the subliminal mind of one of the automatists, or that of some living person. We can only form a tentative decision on this point when we have studied the actual cases as we have to rely entirely on internal evidence, i.e. the nature and characteristics of the messages.

A case such as this where three automatists are concerned would be the ideal type of Cross Correspondence, as they are called, and it must be admitted that up to the present no perfect example has been found.

A less convincing form of cross correspondence would be where two automatists independently produce scripts which, taken separately, are meaningless, but when put together are found to be complementary and mutually explanatory. Of this type we have several good examples.

Besides these cross correspondences there are a large number of instances where the script of two or more automatists has references to the same subject at about the same time. In such cases the complementariness is reduced to simple reference to a single topic, and, in the absence of other evidence, we should have no hesitation in explaining them, provisionally at least – for all explanations are provisional at the present stage of our knowledge – as being due to telepathy between the automatists.

That telepathy does occur I have little doubt, but the cases seem to form a series of ascending complexity until we reach a point at which the hypothesis of simple telepathy fails. Where the line should be drawn it is impossible to say.

This, then, is the scheme or plan which, by their own account, was invented by the communicators on the other side, and we have passages in the scripts to bear this out. For example, the automatist is sometimes exhorted 'to weave together' and told that singly they can do little. In Mrs. Verrall's script we find: *Record the bits and when fitted they will make the whole;*[1] again, *I will give the words between you neither alone can read but together they will give the clue he wants.*[2]

Moreover, there occurs in several instances instructions to the automatist to send her script, either to one of the other automatists, or else to one of the investigators, in fact, it was on account of such instructions that in one or two cases the automatists were first brought together.

I will conclude these preliminary explanations by quoting a few passages from a paper by Miss Alice Johnson, *Proceedings*, Vol. XXI, June, 1908, wherein the theory of Cross Correspondences is fully discussed for the first time. On page 375, she says: 'The characteristic of these cases – or at least of some of them – is that we do not get in the writing of one automatist anything like a mechanical verbatim reproduction of phrases in the other; we do not even get the same idea expressed in different ways – as well might result from direct telepathy between them. What we get is a fragmentary utterance in one script, which seems to have no particular point or meaning, and another fragmentary utterance in the other, of an equally pointless character; but when we put the two together, we see that they supplement one another, and that there is apparently one coherent idea underlying both, but only partially expressed in each.' On page 377, she writes: 'Now, granted the possibility of communication, it may be supposed that within the last few years a certain

[1] *Proc.*, S.P.R., Vol. XXI, p. 385.   [2] ibid., p. 382.

group of persons have been trying to communicate with us, who are sufficiently well instructed to know all the objections that reasonable sceptics have urged against the previous evidence, and sufficiently intelligent to realize to the full all the force of these objections. It may be supposed that these persons have invented a new plan – the plan of cross-correspondences – to meet the sceptic's objections. . . .

'We have reason to believe . . . that the idea of making a statement in one script *complementary* of a statement in another had not occurred to Mr. Myers in his lifetime, for there is no reference to it in any of his written utterances on the subject that I have been able to discover. . . . Neither did those who have been investigating automatic script since his death invent this plan, if plan it be. It was not the automatists that detected it, but a student of the scripts; it has every appearance of being an element imported from outside; it suggests an independent invention, an active intelligence constantly at work in the present, not a mere echo or remnant of individualities of the past.' And on page 389, 'Assuming that the controls are actually trying to communicate some definite idea by means of two different automatists, whom at the same time they were trying to prevent from communicating telepathically with one another, what the controls have to do is to express the factors of the idea in so veiled a form that each writer indites her own share without understanding it. Yet the expression must be so definite that, when once the clue is found, no room is left for doubt as to the proper interpretation.

'It will be seen that, *ex hypothesi*, the idea must be

prevented from reaching the subliminal consciousness of the automatists; yet we cannot be certain in any case that it has been so prevented, as we can only interrogate their supraliminal consciousnesses. It is conceivable, however, that the controls are more capable than living persons of manipulating their own telepathic faculties. Just as we in ordinary conversation can say what we like and abstain from saying what we wish not to say; so it is possible that the controls can telepathically convey certain things to the automatists, stopping short at whatever point they choose, and thus excluding subliminal comprehension of the underlying ideas.'

CHAPTER IV

I NOW propose to give a selection from the large mass of evidence which is contained in the Volumes of *Proceedings* of the S.P.R., from about 1906 until 1917.

I shall be able to give only very condensed summaries of the cases, the original reports being in many instances very long; moreover, I shall quote only some half a dozen or so of each class. It has been a difficult task to condense these reports so as to present a fairly adequate picture; many of them are extremely complicated, most involve reference to classical and literary topics and in some instances the evidential value turns upon some subtle point of classical scholarship or literary criticism, so that it may be doubted whether the full strength can be appreciated by the reader who is not versed in these subjects. However, the investigators have explained fully their reasons for the conclusions at which they have arrived, in language which makes it possible for the ordinary reader to understand, even if he may not fully appreciate. He may not be able to judge from his own knowledge whether these reasons be good or not, that must be left to the experts.

Still, apart from these difficult points of classical erudition, there is a very large mass of facts concerning which the ordinary reader can pass judgment. If an impartial consideration of these facts should tend to support the findings of the investigators, then it may reasonably be held that the interpretation which they

have put upon the obscure passages – an interpretation
which is in accord with those findings – gains considerably in plausibility.

As regards the omission of the great number of the
cases from the account given here, I do not think that
this need in any way prejudice the reader in forming
his judgment. I have selected what I consider to be a
fair representative sample and have included those
cases which throw light on some special points, such
as *modus operandi*.

To repeat the same thing over and over again would
not help in any way unless we should accept the canon
of evidence laid down by Lewis Carroll in *Hunting the
Snark*, 'What I say three times is true.'

If a sufficient number of actual cases is cited to give
the reader a thorough knowledge of the general
characteristics, and if he knows that these cases are only
a few out of many similar ones, he is just as well able
to form a judgment as he would be if he had waded
through the entire series. When an expert judges a
cargo of wheat he does not examine each bag but takes
a representative sample and decides on that.

I shall first give a selection of incidents which tend to
show, on the face of them, that some telepathic exchange,
whether it was pure telepathy or thought reading, takes
place between the automatists, or that one automatist,
by clairvoyance, obtained knowledge concerning
another's script.

I must repeat here that in postulating telepathy or
clairvoyance we are simply giving names to phenomena
which we do not in the least understand; we have not,
in the strict sense, explained them. But as there is a

very large mass of first-class evidence which goes to show that transference of impressions and acquisition of knowledge does occur by means other than the normal senses, we are compelled by the rules of scientific procedure to class together all cases which can be brought under these headings rather than to assume that they belong to a different type which involves the co-operation of an additional factor external to the percipient and the agent.

But I think that we shall see, as we go along, that the cases get more and more complex, and that the difficulty of accounting for the facts by the supernormal transference of information, or by the supernormal acquisition of knowledge by the automatist without external assistance, grows progessively greater.

In my opinion we soon reach a point where the hypotheses of simple telepathy and clairvoyance become so strained that they are untenable, provided that some other not too intrinsically improbable explanation can be found.

The next class of cases are those of simple cross correspondence; these are those where in the scripts of two or more automatists there occurs the same word or phrase, or else two phrases so similar as to be clearly interconnected.

Of course, it is obvious that these words or phrases must be in some way marked out as being intended to be cross-correspondences, the mere occurrence of two phrases in common use in the scripts of two automatists would be of no evidential value whatsoever, it must frequently happen by chance.

As with the first class of cases, we shall see that these

grow progressively more complex, and that the dividing line between them and the succeeding class cannot be drawn with any degree of certainty.

This succeeding class is that of complex cross correspondences: these are cases where the topic or topics are not directly mentioned, but referred to in an indirect and allusive way. As a general rule these references are made by means of quotations from classical or literary sources, or else by mention of some other topic which is connected by association with the one originally given.

I will give a fanciful example of what is meant by a complex cross correspondence. Suppose that the topic chosen was 'Time.' Automatist A, might start the ball rolling by a quotation from the hymn, 'Like an ever-rolling stream.' Automatist B might follow on with a quotation from *Alice in Wonderland* dealing with the discussion concerning Time at the Mad Hatter's tea-table, e.g. 'He won't stand beating,' or, 'We quarrelled last March – just before he went mad, you know' and then, Automatist C gives the clue with 'Time and tide wait for no man.' If the investigator were to recognize the source of these quotations, he would see that there was a common idea in all of them, viz. Time. This would, of course, be an extremely simple example, but it may serve to make the underlying idea clear. Most of the actual cases are far more subtle and it was not until after much research that the connections were discovered. It is probable that even now a good many have been overlooked.

To solve puzzles devised by a scholar such as Myers, required investigators endowed with considerable

knowledge, even if they were not all of them com-
parable with him in scholarship.

Dr. Verrall was a classical scholar of a high order,
and although he was not, strictly speaking, one of the
investigators, he gave advice and assistance. Mrs.
Verrall was, as has been mentioned, lecturer in classics
at Newnham, and among the others were some whose
knowledge of classical literature was extensive.

In what follows I shall adopt the methods of terminology of the original reports. The writers of the
automatic scripts are termed automatists, and this
name is also applied to Mrs. Piper, who, although a
trance medium, produces the bulk of her material in
writing. As has already been explained, she speaks
while coming out of trance, and anything taken
from what is then said will be referred to as 'waking
stage.'

Script is the word usually used for the writing of the
automatists, and this includes the drawings which are
frequently made in the same automatic fashion.

Those personalities, or rather, one should say, those
purporting personalities who inspire or produce the
script through the hands of the automatists, are usually
spoken of as communicators. Where it is possible to
distinguish one communicator from another and to
identify him, he will be called by the name which he
claims to bear with a suffix letter. Thus Myers$_P$ stands
for that, whatever it is, which inspires those scripts
of Mrs. Piper which purport to be the work of the
surviving spirit of Fred Myers; similarly, Myers$_V$ stands
for the author of similar communications through
Mrs. Verrall. The suffixes H.V stands for Miss Helen

Verrall's communicators, H for Mrs. Holland's and W for Mrs. Willett's.

When the name Fred Myers or Myers alone is used, it must be understood that the living man of that name is being referred to. The other communicators, Hodgson, Gurney, Sidgwick and the rest, are treated in the same way.

It must be clearly understood that this terminology is adopted solely for the sake of convenience and brevity. It does not imply any acceptance of the hypothesis that the scripts originate from, or are inspired by, the surviving personalities which are named or, indeed, from any personality external to the mind of the automatist.

That they are so inspired is the constant claim made by the scripts themselves, but this cannot be accepted prior to investigation of the evidence, in fact, it is solely to test this claim that the whole investigation was undertaken.

Thus, though we may speak of Myers$_P$ or any other communicator saying or writing so and so, it is always with the definite reservation that no such personality may exist at all as a separate entity.

To adopt any other terminology would, however, entail such ponderous and tiresome circumlocutions that the reader would soon become wearied of reading over and over again the same set of conditioning clauses.

The identification of the communicator is frequently easily made, because the scripts are signed, or else the name is given; when in Mrs. Willett's scripts Myers purports to communicate, the name Myers will appear sometimes three or four times in one paragraph. There is also in some cases a difference in handwriting, though there is not always any resemblance with the actual handwriting of the communicator when living. With Mrs. Holland, Myers$_H$ usually prefers a pencil, while Gurney$_H$ uses a pen.

Identification can also be made with a fair degree of certainty in many instances from the general characteristics of the script. The dramatic characterization is sometimes very high, and there is, on the whole, great consistency throughout the scripts of one automatist, though it must be admitted that the characterization of Myers$_V$, for example, does not always tally with that of Myers$_H$ or Myers$_W$, nor is it always a true portrayal of the man himself as he was known by his friends in life.

I shall discuss this point at some length in my concluding chapter.

I will commence by giving extracts from a script of Mrs. Holland, November 7th, 1903,[1] purporting to come from Myers. (It should be remembered that Mrs. Holland had read *Human Personality* for the first time in June, 1903.) It begins with a scrawl ending with the initial F (Myers frequently signed himself in this way). Mrs. Holland then wrote in her own hand, a question to the communicator. *My hand feels very shaky – shall I let it scrawl?* Myers$_H$ replied: *Yes let it go quite freely just exactly as it likes,* and then goes on, *My Dear Mrs. Verrall I am very anxious to speak to some of the old friends – Miss J. – and to A. W.* (Miss Johnson and Dr. A. W. Verrall are meant). Then followed a long description of a man

[1] *Proc.,* S.P.R., Vol. XXI, p. 186.

which was in the main accurate of Dr. Verrall, and an address, 5, Selwyn Gardens, Cambridge. After some matter, which need not be repeated here, the address is given again, and finally came the words: *Send this to Mrs. Verrall, 5, Selwyn Gardens, Cambridge.*

Mrs. Holland knew the name Mrs. Verrall, as it occurs in *Human Personality*, but beyond that she had no knowledge of her. She certainly did not know her address, or even if there were such a place as Selwyn Gardens, Cambridge. She had never been in Cambridge.

It was this script which led to the association between Mrs. Holland and Mrs. Verrall, an association from which there arose many cross correspondences.

Now Fred Myers had lived in Cambridge and was an intimate friend of the Verralls. If, therefore, he survived death and retained his interest in psychical research, it is quite understandable that he should have endeavoured to bring about this association so that he might put into practice the scheme of cross correspondences which he and his group had devised, and to do this what better or more straightforward way could have been chosen than to instruct one of the automatists to send her script to the other, giving both name and address?

If the knowledge of the address did not come from the surviving spirit of Myers, an alternative must be found.

Mrs. Holland had been in communication with Miss Alice Johnson on the subject of automatic writing, and Miss Johnson, of course, knew Mrs. Verrall very well as another automatist, so it was possible that the information was conveyed telepathically by her. It is not likely that it came from Mrs. Verrall direct, as she had not heard of Mrs. Holland at that time.

If it was not telepathy from Miss Johnson, we can only suggest that it was either telepathy from some unknown person, or else that Mrs. Holland somehow or other perceived the address by clairvoyance.

A few weeks previously to this, Mrs. Holland's script contained a detailed description of a room which she was unable to recognize.[1] Miss Johnson, to whom the script was sent, was equally at a loss. However, some two years later Mrs. Verrall happened to be reading it and at once recognized the room described as being her dining-room. The description was correct in every respect but one, viz., that there was a bust on a pedestal; it was curious that a friend of Mrs. Verrall's on being told of this description, said: 'But there is a bust in your dining-room.' He had apparently mistaken a filter, which stood in a dark corner of the room, for a bust.

Now, if this knowledge was acquired clairvoyantly by Mrs. Holland, and if clairvoyance be somehow or other analogous to ordinary vision, it seems quite possible that she had made the same mistake. On the other hand, the message purports to come from Myers, so it might be that the mistake was his.

On January 5th, 1904, Myers$_H$ described in the script a woman in some detail.[2] On March 22nd following, Mrs. Holland had an impression which corresponded very nearly with the description, but contained other details.[3] Both these were sent to Miss Johnson who

[1] *Proc.*, S.P.R., Vol. XXI, p. 194.   [2] ibid., p. 212.   [3] ibid., p. 257.

recognized them as mainly correct of Mrs. Verrall, with which opinion Mrs. Verrall herself agreed.

It must be remembered that at this time Mrs. Holland had not met Mrs. Verrall, and only knew of her through having seen her name mentioned in *Human Personality*, and from Miss Johnson's letters.

In subsequent scripts there were several instances of supernormal knowledge of Mrs. Verrall and her doings. It is not necessary to quote all these in full. I will give just one instance.

On March 28th, 1906,[1] the script contained the words, *A new dress not a black one this time*. Mrs. Verrall notes on this (April 10th, 1906): 'Some time ago, I think on February 2nd, I called on my dressmaker to arrange for an evening dress, which I intended should be black. She, however, insisted on a colour, and I eventually agreed. About March 11th, I appointed March 31st to be fitted.'

All these incidents can be explained on the hypothesis of telepathy between Mrs. Holland and Mrs. Verrall, or clairvoyance on the part of Mrs. Holland, and had they stood alone, we should have been compelled, by the canons of scientific procedure, to accept that explanation provisionally.

If, however, we find other incidents in the scripts which would necessitate a considerable stretching of the hypothesis to make it cover the facts, it will throw some doubt upon it as a valid explanation.

Here is another incident which looks, on the face of it, like simple telepathy.[2] Mrs. Forbes had tried, as an

---

[1] *Proc.*, S.P.R., Vol. XXI, p. 339.
[2] *Proc.*, S.P.R., Vol. XX, p. 256, *et seq.*

experiment, to impress Mrs. Verrall with the idea of lilies and this had failed. About a month later Miss Verrall, who knew nothing about the experiment, had the following in her script. *If you had seen her picking lilies you would have understood,* and, *the house is large and there is a belt of rhododendrons. In the north you have seen it. Not you, I mean, but Mrs. Forbes.* In reply to questions, Mrs. Forbes said : 'I looked at the lilies and cut some, and mentally asked if it would be possible to tell our friends at Cambridge (the Verralls) about them. We have been planting a belt of rhododendrons to the north of the garden.' Both Mrs. and Miss Verrall were ignorant of this latter fact.

In the next case the hypothesis of telepathy becomes a little strained.[1] On April 10th, 1903, Mrs. Forbes wrote automatically : *Will you be so good as to write – to arrive to-morrow – to tell Mrs. Verrall our letter must be read with one word corrected, which means more. E.G.* (Edmund Gurney). *A grower of flowers one year will be a sower of seed. Send the message.* Then followed instructions for Miss Verrall to write with planchette. Neither Mrs. Forbes nor Mrs. Verrall could make any sense of this message, but Miss Verrall explained it at once. She had been staying with a friend who was a professional gardener and during her stay there was much discussion over a suggestion made by her friend's new head man, that certain plants should be grown from seed instead of from cuttings as hitherto. The new man was particularly skilled in raising plants from seed.

If this was due to telepathy, it was not between Mrs.

[1] *Proc.*, S.P.R., Vol. XX, p. 254.

Verrall and Mrs. Forbes, but the agent was presumably Miss Verrall.

I am not keeping to the chronological order in giving these examples, but rather picking out those incidents which will illustrate the point which I am wishing to make, viz., the difficulty of explaining the information shown in the scripts on the hypothesis of simple telepathy.

Beginning in March, 1901,[1] Mrs. Verrall's script contained what she took to be references to Mrs. Forbes; on March 21st it contained the Latin words, *Ne falle rogatricem* (Do not fail (?) her who asks). On March 24th, Mrs. Forbes writing with planchette with another person had, *Tell Mrs. Verrall to send you her last writing.* There is, therefore, a possible connection between the two scripts.

On August 28th Mrs. Verrall wrote automatically, words in Latin, of which the translation is: *Sign with the seal. The fir-tree that has already been planted in the garden gives its own portent.* Then followed some scrawls and drawings of a sword and a suspended bugle.

The suspended bugle is part of the badge of the regiment to which Talbot Forbes, Mrs. Forbes's deceased son, who purported to communicate through her, belonged. Mrs. Forbes had in her garden four or five fir-trees grown from seed which had been sent her by her son, and were called by her Talbot's trees. This was unknown to Mrs. Verrall.

On the same day Mrs. Forbes's script contained the statement that her son was looking for a 'sensitive' who wrote automatically so that he might obtain corroboration of her writing. Thus, though the same subject was

[1] *Proc.*, S.P.R., Vol. XX, p. 222, *et seq.*

not mentioned in both scripts, there appears to be a connection between them.

The next case[1] which I shall quote, is of a more advanced type, and for it we must introduce Mrs. Piper for the first time.

On January 31st, 1902, Mrs. Verrall wrote, automatically: *Panopticon,* then in Greek characters, *sphairas atitallei syndegma mystikon ti ouk edidos.* (Latin) *volatile ferrum – pro telo impinget.* The whole quasi-Greek sentence appears to mean something like 'universal seeing of a sphere fosters the mystic joint reception.' Volatile ferrum = flying iron, and is used in Virgil for 'spear,' 'pro telo' = for a weapon, 'impinget' = will hit.

The whole thing seemed nonsense to Mrs. Verrall, and she was unable to make anything out of it.

Mrs. Piper was at this time at Boston, U.S.A., and at a sitting with Dr. Hodgson on January 28th, 1902, he suggested to the control that he should try to appear to Miss Verrall holding a spear in his hand. The control evidently misunderstood, for he asked: 'Why a sphere?' Dr. Hodgson repeated the word 'spear' and the control said that the experiment should be tried for a week.

On February 4th, at the next sitting, the control claimed to have been successful, but he spelled the word 'sphear.' It was evident that the misunderstanding still persisted to some extent. Although the claim to have appeared was false, it seems to be much beyond chance that Mrs. Verrall should have in her script, only three days later, both the Greek word for sphere and a Latin phrase meaning spear.

[1] *Proc.,* S.P.R., Vol. XX, p. 213, *et seq.*

Here the hypothesis of simple telepathy requires very considerable stretching to make it cover the facts. First, the message reaches Mrs. Verrall instead of Miss Verrall. I do not think that any stress can be laid on this, for the same thing frequently happened; it seemed as though the communicators were either indifferent, which of the two automatists they used, simply taking whichever was available, or else that they were actually not always able to distinguish. In any case, telepathic messages do sometimes miss their proper targets and hit another; until we know more of the conditions in which it occurs, no explanation of the reason for this can be suggested.

A far more formidable objection to the telepathic hypothesis rests on the form in which the message was received. Mrs. Piper knows no Greek or Latin, Dr. Hodgson might have known the Greek for sphere and Virgil's use of 'volatile ferrum' for spear, but the message which he would have intended to send would have been of spear alone. It is true that the confusion between the words which Mrs. Piper's control had made might have been transferred to his mind, but it does not seem very likely; moreover, there appears to be no reason why he should use Greek and Latin instead of English, the more so as the impression which it was desired to convey was a visual and not a verbal one.

As regards the percipient, it might have been that the translation into Greek and Latin was performed by her subliminal mind, but it is curious that such translation should have resulted in what appeared to her as mere nonsense. I do not say that it is impossible, or even highly improbable, only that it is curious and involves an added difficulty to the telepathic hypothesis. If, on the other hand, one considers the view suggested by the communicators, the whole thing appears to be more reasonable. Myers undoubtedly had the necessary knowledge of Greek and Latin and if he desired, in accordance with the scheme of cross correspondences, to convey the message in an indirect and allusive form, he certainly succeeded in doing so, although I cannot see any reason why he should have made it into nonsense; anyone equipped with the classical and literary erudition of Fred Myers would, one would imagine, have made a much neater job of it.

In studying these scripts one comes constantly up against this difficulty, viz., that so much consists of disjointed fragmentary sort of matter. It is true that with most of the automatists we do get long coherent passages sometimes, showing high intellectual power and a comprehension of the difficulties of the problem, but there is also a great amount of apparent nonsense, and it is in this part that we find most of the evidential matter.

I do not think that it can be said of the automatists, with the exception of Mrs. Piper, that the intellectual level of the scripts was ever higher than could be attributed to them, they were all cultured and well-read women, so that it is not beyond the bounds of possibility that the source from which these portions of the script were drawn was the subliminal mind of the automatist.

Moreover, when we consider the case of Mrs. Piper and those passages which show intellectual attainment beyond her reach, it must be remembered that the sitters were in nearly every case persons of culture and learning, so that if we concede the possibility of telepathic exchange between medium and sitter, we can account for the phenomena by regarding the subliminal mind of the sitter as the source of the knowledge shown.

We are, therefore, in something of a dilemma. If the source of the scripts were really the surviving personalities of Myers and his friends, how was it that they were able to transmit through the automatists clear and logical disquisitions on the theoretical side of the subject, yet when it came to getting through the more important evidential matter, they were able to make only what, in my opinion, must be considered a rather poor job?

In this connection I quote here a passage from an early script of Mrs. Holland[1] wherein Myers$_H$ describes the conditions under which he labours. He writes: *The nearest simile I can find to express the difficulties of sending a message – is that I appear to be standing behind a sheet of frosted glass which blurs sight and deadens sounds – dictating feebly to a reluctant and somewhat obtuse secretary.'*

There are several such passages in these scripts: both Myers$_H$ and Gurney$_H$ exhibit a tendency to scold the automatist most unmercifully, and I think that it is great tribute to Mrs. Holland that she accepted it all in good part and continued to carry on in spite of these scoldings.

But, it may be said, if the secretary can receive these long discourses without confusion, in spite of 'the frosted glass,' why is it that the evidential parts are so

[1] *Proc.*, S.P.R., Vol. XXI, p. 230.

scrappy and muddled? Suppose that, on the other hand, we ascribe the non-evidential parts of the script to the subliminal mind of the automatist – and it is not impossible that even the scoldings came from thence – we are left with the problem of accounting for the cross correspondences.

It may be, of course, that there are two sources from which the messages come which operate in alternation, or else are somehow mingled.

It has been suggested – and there are fairly good grounds for the suggestion – that the communicators are limited by the normal contents of the mind of the automatist; thus, while Greek and Latin quotations are freely given through Mrs. and Miss Verrall, who are thoroughly conversant with those languages, it is very rare to find them with Mrs. Holland and Mrs. Willett, who normally know very little of the classics. It must be looked upon as being partly a process of selection from already available material, rather than the introduction of entirely fresh matter from the outside. We may think of the communicator surveying, as it were, the contents of the mind of the automatist and picking out such things as will best suit his purpose to weave into the pattern he desires.

On this view, perhaps, we may gain a partial understanding and a possible explanation of the peculiar character of the scripts. It is true that we do sometimes find in the scripts evidence of knowledge which was not normally in the possession of the automatist, but we cannot ever exclude the possibility of its being conveyed telepathically to her subliminal mind from some living person.

There is quite a good example of this in a script of Mrs. Holland's, January 7th, 1904.[1] Myers$_H$ writes therein: *I want to make it thoroughly clear to you that the eidolon is not the spirit, only the simulacrum.* He was discussing the question of apparitions and the views expressed were similar to those held by Fred Myers, as were given fully in a chapter on 'Phantasms of the Dead' in *Human Personality.* As Mrs. Holland had read this book, we may suppose that her memory of it was the source from which this script was derived, except for the combined use of the words 'eidolon' and 'simulacrum,' which does not occur in that chapter. Mrs. Verrall, on reading the script, pointed out that these words were used in a correct and scholarly style, such as would not normally be expected from one who, like Mrs. Holland, is not a classical scholar. But this usage would have been appropriate for Myers himself, familiar as he was with Homer and Lucretius wherein they occur.

The next incident which I shall summarize, introduces a fresh type of puzzle. On March 7th, 1906, Mrs. Verrall's script[2] contained an original poem, commencing with the words:

Tintagel and the sea that moaned in pain.

When Miss Johnson read this she was struck with its similarity with a poem by Roden Noel, entitled 'Tintadgel,' which, to the best of her recollection, Mrs. Verrall had never read.

On March 11th, 1906, Mrs. Holland's script contained: *This is for A. W. Ask him what the date May 26th, 1894, meant to him – to me – and to F. W. H. M. I do not*

---

[1] *Proc.,* S.P.R., Vol. XXI, p. 215, *et seq.*   [2] ibid ., p. 317, *et seq.*

think that they will find it hard to recall, but if so – let them ask Nora.

The date given, which conveyed nothing to Mrs. Holland, is that of the death of Roden Noel; the initials A. W. refer to Dr. Verrall, F. W. H. M. is, of course, Myers, both of whom knew Noel, though not intimately. Nora means Mrs. Sidgwick and the instruction to ask her is singularly appropriate as Noel was an intimate friend of Dr. Sidgwick.

On March 14th, 1906, before any of these facts were known to Mrs. Holland, she wrote, automatically: *Eighteen, fifteen, four, five, fourteen, Fourteen, fifteen, five, twelve. Not to be taken as they stand. See Rev. 13, 18, but only the central eight words, not the whole passage.*

Mrs. Holland did not look up the text, and the whole thing was quite meaningless to her. But Miss Johnson did do so, and found that the central eight words were: 'for it is the number of a man.' Acting on this hint, she translated the numbers given in the script into letters of the alphabet, and found that they spelled Roden Noel, R being the eighteenth letter, and so on.

It should be said, however, that in a script of February 9th, 1906,[1] i.e. about a month earlier Mrs. Holland had written another list of numbers which had, in the same way, given the name of Richard Hodgson,[2] and that this had been pointed out to her by Miss Johnson, so that it is possible that while the Roden Noel message meant nothing to her normally, it was understood subliminally.

[1] *Proc.*, S.P.R., Vol. XXI, p. 304.
[2] Dr. Richard Hodgson, died December 20th, 1905.

There was a further reference to Roden Noel in her script of March 21st, 1906, and in Mrs. Verrall's of March 26th, 1906. On March 28th, 1906, Mrs. Holland's script contained the name Roden Noel written out in full, a reference to Cornwall which was appropriate for him, and a description of him which was partially correct.

I must not occupy much further space with these cases of simple cross correspondence, but will conclude this section by summarizing briefly, a further two or three characteristic cases. The first is on the word 'Arrow' and can be summarized best by the following table, which gives all the necessary facts in brief.[1]

Feb. 11th, 1907 -- Mrs. Verrall's script has a drawing of three converging arrows, followed by the words: 'Tria convergentia in unum.'

Feb. 12th – Hodgson$_P$ says he has given 'Arrow' to Mrs. Verrall.

Feb. 13th – Mr. Piddington sees Mrs. Verrall's script of February 11th.

Feb. 17th – Miss Verrall's script has a drawing of an arrow, followed by the words 'many together.'

Feb. 18th about 11.15 a.m. – Mrs. Verrall's script has several words beginning with 'a' and 'ar' such as 'architrave,' 'arch,' etc.

Feb. 18th, about 11.30 a.m. – Hodgson$_P$ reminds Mr. Piddington to 'watch for arrow.'

Feb. 19th, 10.55 a.m. – Mr. Piddington sees Mrs. Verrall's script of 18th and Miss Verrall's of 17th.

Feb. 19th, 11.20 a.m. – Hodgson$_P$ says Mrs. Verrall wrote 'ar' and 'w.'

Feb. 20th – Mr. Piddington tells Hodgson$_P$ that Mrs. Verrall has written several words beginning with 'ar.'

[1] *Proc.*, S.P.R., Vol. XXII, p. *77*, *et seq.*

Feb. 25th – Hodgson_P asks: 'Got arrow yet?' Mr. Piddington says Mrs. Verrall has not written the word, but has drawn an arrow. Hodgson_P says he will make a further attempt to make Mrs. Verrall write 'arrow.'

Mar. 18th – Mrs. Verrall's script has a drawing of a bow and arrow, an arrow, and a target.

June 4th – Mrs. Verrall learns for the first time that 'arrow' has been the subject of a cross-correspondence experiment.

Laurel and laurel wreath form the subject of a simple cross correspondence.[1] On February 26th, 1907, in the waking stage of Mrs. Piper's trance, the word 'laurel' was repeated several times, and *I gave her that for laurel* said. (When 'I gave her' is thus used it refers to Mrs. Verrall.) On February 27th, Myers_P said: *I gave Mrs. Verrall laurel wreath*. On February 6th, Mrs. Verrall's script had: *Laura and another. There is a great obstruction this morning* (probably referring to the automatic writing). *Apollo's laurel bough* (twice given), *Laureatus* (Latin = laurelled), *A laurel wreath*, then a drawing representing a laurel wreath, *corona laureata* (Latin = laurel crown), *With laurel wreath his brow serene was crowned*, and *a laurel crown*.

Neither the word 'laurel' nor 'wreath' occurs elsewhere in Mrs. Verrall's scripts of this period.

On March 17th, Miss Verrall's script contained the words: *Laurel leaves are emblem. Laurel for the victor's brow.*

This is the only occurrence of the word 'laurel' in her scripts of this period.

Some of these passages are included in another cross-correspondence, viz., the 'Medici Tombs' case, which I shall summarize later.

[1] *Proc.*, S.P.R., Vol. XXII, p. 94, *et seq.*

Thanatos.[1]   In the waking stage of Mrs. Piper's trance on April 17th, 1907, a word was spoken which was at first heard as *Sanatos,* and then repeated as *Tanatos.* Mrs. Sidgwick, the sitter, inserted a note on the record to the effect that 'Thanatos' was probably meant. On April 23rd, again in the waking stage, it was correctly pronounced as 'Thanatos,' on April 30th it was said three times and on May 7th, *I want to say Thanatos* came again in the waking stage.

Thanatos is a Greek word meaning 'Death.'

Repetition of a word in this disconnected fashion is usually a sign that it has been used for a cross correspondence.

On April 16th, 1907, Mrs. Holland, in India, had in her script: *Maurice Morris Mors. And with that the shadow of death fell upon his limbs.*

'Maurice Morris' are probably first attempts to get the Latin word 'Mors' which, of course, means 'Death,' the occurrence of the English word 'death' in the next sentence points to this.

Mrs. Verrall's script of April 29th, 1907, had: *Warmed both hands before the fire of life. It fades and I am ready to depart,* then a drawing of a triangle or else the Greek letter delta; then, *Manibus date lilia plenis* (Latin for 'Give lilies with full hands'), a little later: *Come away, Come away, Pallida mors* (Latin = pale death) occurs in a sentence, and finally: *You have got the word plainly written all along in your own writing. Look back.*

Mrs. Verrall had always taken the Greek letter 'delta' as a sign for death. 'Manibus date lilia plenis' is a quotation from the Aeneid where Anchises foretells

[1] *Proc.,* S.P.R., Vol. XXII, p. 295, *et seq.*

the early death of Marcellus. 'Come away, come away' is, of course, from Shakespeare, and the next word in the song is 'death.'

Thus we have the keyword given by three automatists, and in three different languages, besides allusive references.

If the coincidence of the idea were due to direct telepathy, we should hardly expect to find it take this form.

The word 'death' only occurs once in Mrs. Verrall's script of this period, and four times in Mrs. Holland's.

Finally, the 'Laus Deo' case.[1] In the waking stage of Mrs. Piper's trance of April 17th, 1907, the word *Lausteo* was spoken, and then *Laus Deo*, the first word being obviously an attempt at the latter.

It is quite clear that the communicators or controls sometimes have to have two or three shots at a word before getting it right, frequently one can see them feeling their way by closer and closer approximations (See 'sanatos,' 'tanatos' and 'Maurice, Morris, Mors.')

If one takes at their face value the accounts given by the communicators of the conditions under which they work, it is clear that they do not always know exactly what has been got through, although they sometimes seem to be aware that a shot has missed its mark.

On November 16th, 1906, Mrs. Verrall's script had: *Laus in aeternum, Deo Laus et Gratia.* The cross correspondence is obvious, though the time interval is somewhat long. The words appear only this once in Mrs. Piper's trance and once in Mrs. Verrall's script of the period.

[1] *Proc.*, S.P.R., Vol. XXII, p. 304, *et seq.*

CHAPTER V

IN this chapter I propose to summarize, very briefly, some half a dozen or so of the more complex and highly developed cases. In some of those which I have given under the heading of simple cross correspondences it will have been noticed that the communicators go beyond the mere repetition of a word or phrase through two or more automatists, and approach the more elaborate and complicated puzzles with which we have now to deal. It is quite obvious that mere repetition would not be evidence of anything beyond pure telepathy or mind reading on the part of one or other of the automatists concerned, but where the idea is suggested by allusions, or conveyed in a disguised form, then the telepathic hypothesis becomes more difficult to sustain.

The original reports of the cases which I am about to mention occupy many hundreds of pages in *Proceedings*, and to appreciate fully all the various points brought out by the investigators requires, not only lengthy and close study, but also some considerable knowledge of classical literature. It is quite certain, therefore, that in the summaries to which the exigencies of space confine me, a good deal of the evidential value has been lost. In a way this may not be altogether a bad thing, for it can be fairly said that I have not overstated my case.

The first incident[1] to which I refer is, strictly speaking, not a cross correspondence, but an experiment in telepathy.

In April, 1901, Dr. A. W. Verrall decided to try an experiment in telepathy with his wife, who had just then begun automatic writing. Mrs. Verrall knew nothing of his intentions or even that an experiment was being tried.

He wrote down three Greek words which he tried to convey to her telepathically, thinking that, should he succeed in doing so, they might appear in her script. These words were 'monopolon es ao.' This comes from the 'Orestes' of Euripides, and is usually taken to mean 'to the one-horsed dawn,' the phrase 'one-horsed' referring to the one-horsed car of the dawn, as distinguished from the four-horsed chariot of the sun in Greek mythology. Dr. Verrall, however, was inclined to translate the word 'monopolon' as 'solitarily wandering.' It had occurred in a passage which was set in a translation paper at an examination for the Cambridge classical Tripos in which he was concerned many years before. In June, 1901, Mrs. Verrall's script had a reference to the East, i.e. the quarter of the dawn. In July, a Latin sentence describing an old man and containing the Greek word '*monochitonos*,' meaning 'with a single garment,' appeared, it also contained the Latin word *alba*, used in the sense 'white.' In the Greek word we may see an attempt at 'monopolon,' the first part being correct, while the word 'alba' is a late Latin word for 'dawn.' References to this old

[1] *Proc.*, S.P.R., Vol. XX, p. 156, *et seq.* See also Vol. XXX, p. 175, *et seq.*

man in a white robe appeared in many of the subsequent scripts, but space forbids me to quote them.

On August 13th, there was a possible allusion in a 'crowing cock,' and a motto about dawn, and in the next few scripts the idea was constantly cropping up. On August 29th the Greek letters *es* were given, and on September 2nd, *es to*, evidently an attempt at 'es ao,' this was followed by *monostolos, monochitonos, monos . . . but I want the final word.*

On September 7th *mol es to* came in, and on September 9th, the cryptic sentence, *Pye is also a bird but not ours*, and again, on September 12th, *Pye gives one clue but there is another.* The first attempt at 'monopolon' on September 2nd, was very nearly correct, except that 'st' stood in place of 'p' or rather the Greek π called 'pi.'

The sentences about 'pye' may, therefore, be looked upon either as a kind of punning reference to this error or else to a dreamlike association between the missing letter and a bird; in either case it shows a recognition of the letter wanted to complete the desired word.

In all the above scripts we can see repeated attempts to get through either the meaning, the sound, or the spelling of the words, and the communicating agency, whatever it may have been, seems perfectly aware that it had failed. In many of the scripts these attempts are accompanied by instructions to *show them to A. W.*, or else it is stated that *A. W. will understand*, or *A. W. must be satisfied.* Dr. Verrall was familiarly known as A. W. by many of his undergraduate friends.

Before giving it up in despair another line of approach is tried.

On September 9th, the following was written: *Find the herb MOLY that will help, it is a guide*, then in Greek: *Seek and you will find at last.* This conveyed no meaning at first, although it was recognized that a reference was made to a passage in Milton's *Comus*, running as follows:

'And yet more med'cinal it is than that moly
Which Hermes once to wise Ulysses gave.'

It was only after some years that it was discovered that the passage from Milton had been set as the subject for Latin hexameters in the same Tripos examination in which the phrase 'monopolon es ao' was included.

When it is considered that the subjects in these examinations can be drawn from the whole range of literature, it is obvious that this association in the scripts of the word 'moly' with the test phrase could hardly have been due to chance.

But the matter did not end there. It was not until 1918 that Mr. Piddington published a paper[1] giving the results of his study of the case. He identified the old man in white with Oedipus of the Greek tragedies by Sophocles, and he claimed to show a consistent and intelligible plan running through the whole.

He adduces very strong arguments, based on the actual words used in the scripts, to show that these refer to a footnote in Sir Richard Jebb's edition of the *Oedipus Tyrannus*, and he argues that it is hard to suppose that all this arose from the mind of Dr. Verrall, who was concerned only with the transmission by telepathy of a sentence of three words, and he

[1] *Proc.*, S.P.R., Vol. XXX, p. 175, *et seq.*

suggests that the Myers group of communicators took over, as it were, the management of the experiment, and adapted it to their own purposes.

His argument is too long and too subtle to be summarized here, involving, as it does, recondite points of classical scholarship. Even apart from Mr. Piddington's theories, it is difficult to attribute this case to simple telepathy, the constant shifting of the ground and variation of expedient seems inconsistent with that view.

I am painfully aware that the account here given is woefully inadequate, and must seem to the reader to be 'a bald and unconvincing narrative,' but the case is so involved that nothing short of a prolonged and careful study of the original reports can give anything like an adequate appreciation of its value.

The next is called the 'Hope, Star and Browning' case.[1] This is a very complex case, involving Mrs. and Miss Verrall, as well as Mrs. Piper.

In Mrs. Verrall's script of January 23rd, 1907, there appeared: *an anagram would be better. Tell him that – rats, star, tars and so on . . . or again, tears, stare.* Then follows an anagram which Mrs. Verrall subsequently remembered as having been made by Myers, her husband and Sir Richard Jebb.

On January 28th, her script starts, *Aster* (Latin = star) *Teras* (in Greek characters, meaning wonder or a sign). *The world's wonder. And all a wonder and a wild desire. The very wings of her. A WINGED DESIRE. Upopteros eros* (Greek = winged love). *Then there is*

---

[1] *Proc.*, S.P.R., Vol. XXII, p. 59, *et seq.*, and Vol. XXVII, p. 28, *et seq.*

Blake. And mocked my loss of liberty. But it is all the same thing – the winged desire. Eros potheinos (Greek = love — the much desired) *the hope that leaves the earth for the sky – Abt Vogler for earth too hard that found itself or lost itself – in the sky. That is what I want. On earth the broken sounds – threads – In the sky, the perfect arc. The C major of this life. But your recollection is at fault.* Then followed drawings

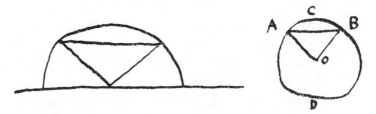

A D B is the part that unseen completes the arc.

Mrs. Verrall's note at the time was, 'January 29/07. 'Is the enclosed attempt at *Bird?* "winged" upopteros, and Abt Vogler (Vogel) suggests it. The later part is all quotations from R.B.'s *Abt Vogler* and earlier from the Ring and the Book. "Oh Lyric Love, etc."'

On February 3rd, Miss Verrall, who knew nothing of Mrs. Verrall's scripts, wrote, among other things: *A green jerkin and hose and doublet where the song birds pipe their tune in the early morning therapeutikos ek exoticon* (a healer from aliens). Then followed a monogram and drawings of a star and a crescent moon, with the words: *A monogram, the crescent moon, remember that, and the star.* After some other words, which I need not give, there came a drawing of a bird.

On February 11th, Mr. Piddington was sitting with Mrs. Piper and Myers$_P$ wrote: *Did she* (Mrs. Verrall) *receive the word Evangelical?* Mr. Piddington replied that he did not know, and Myers_P went on: *I referred also to Browning again. I referred to Hope and Browning . . . I also said Star.*

In a later sitting it was made clear that the word 'Evangelical' had been distorted in transmission, and had been intended for 'Evelyn Hope,' the title of a poem of Browning's.

On February 15th, Mrs. Verrall told her daughter that a cross correspondence had been made, but in order that her script should not be influenced, gave the words as 'Planet Mars,' 'Virtue' and 'Keats,' instead of 'Hope, star and Browning.'

On February 17th, Miss Verrall's script contained a drawing of a star, then: *That was the sign she will understand when she sees it. . . . No arts avail . . . and a star above it all rats everywhere in Hamelin town.*

On March 6th Myers_P told Mr. Piddington that he had given Mrs. Verrall a circle, and then attempts at drawing a triangle were made, and he said: *It did not appear.* He also said, in reply to a question by Mr. Piddington, that he also wrote something about Bird when he gave the circle.

Now Mr. Piddington had asked Myers_P on January 16th, 1907, if he would mark attempts at cross correspondences in some way, say by drawing a circle with a triangle inside, as a sign that one was being attempted.

Myers_P was evidently referring to Mrs. Verrall's script of January 28th, quoted above, but was incorrect in stating that the triangle had not appeared, he had succeeded better than he knew.

The anagrams must first be explained. There is a possible use for anagrams in automatic writing, for they form a disguise for the word and thus prevent the mind of the automatist from understanding immediately what is being written. In this case, however, there may be another explanation. Mr. Piddington, when going through Dr. Richard Hodgson's papers, after his death, came across a good many scraps of paper on which anagrams had been worked out. He remembered this when he read Mrs. Verrall's script and requested Hodgson's executors to let him have these scraps. On one of them he found the anagram, 'Arts, star, etc.,' as well as the other anagram in the script.

He found, also, correspondence with Myers which showed that he had been exchanging anagrams with Hodgson for at least five or six years. Among this was a post card dated 1896 on which Myers had written: 'As many more anagrammatic epigrams as you like. F. W. H. M.' When it is remembered that Richard Hodgson was one of the group of communicators with Myers, the coincidence is, at least, suggestive.

The employment of this device of using anagrams to conceal the meaning of what was being written from the automatist would seem to come quite naturally from both Myers and Hodgson, whereas it is not one which would have normally occurred to Mrs. Verrall, who was not particularly interested in them.

There is an obvious cross correspondence in these scripts. Mrs. Verrall's first contains the word 'star,' her second, 'aster,' the Latin for star, also a quotation from Browning's poem 'Abt Vogler,' containing the word 'hope,' which, by the way, is a misquotation, for it should be 'passion.' (It has been suggested that this misquotation was deliberately done so as to draw attention to the word. There are several other apparent instances of the same thing in other scripts.) In Miss Verrall's first script a star is drawn, and 'remember the star' is written. In her second it is again drawn with the words, 'that is the sign she will understand,' thus corresponding with the Greek word, 'teras' in Mrs. Verrall's script. ('Teras' is sometimes used in the plural for a constellation), it is also an anagram for the Latin word for star, 'aster.' The word 'arts' corresponds with Mrs. Verrall's anagram for star. Then, 'a star above it all,' and finally, 'rats everywhere in Hamelin town,' brings in another of the anagram words besides Browning, the author of the poem.

From Mrs. Piper we have the word 'Evangelical,' later stated to have been a mistake for 'Evelyn Hope,' which brings in the word 'hope' as well as the author of the poem, Browning, also the direct statement by Myers$_P$: 'I referred to Hope and Browning, I also said "Star." '

There are also some other less direct correspondences, for example, in Miss Verrall's first script, the words 'a healer from aliens' might have been a reference to the Pied Piper, who obviously complies with this description, moreover, there occurs in the previous sentence the word 'pipe.'

In Mrs. Verrall's second script there are many references to wings, e.g., 'the very wings of her,' 'a winged desire,' etc., so much so, that she asks in her note: 'Is enclosed attempt at Bird?' In Miss Verrall's script there is a drawing of a bird, followed by the word 'bird.'

Then there is the drawing of the circle and triangle in Mrs. Verrall's script, with its reference to Browning's poem 'Abt Vogler,' 'In heaven the perfect arc, etc.', and Myers$_P$ statement that he had given the circle and said 'Bird' at the same time.

At a further sitting with Mrs. Piper on March 13th, 1907, Myers$_P$ repeats that he drew a circle for Mrs. Verrall, then he drew a circle and triangle, and a little later said: *But it suggested a poem to my mind, hence* $\begin{smallmatrix} B \\ H \\ S \end{smallmatrix}$ (i.e., Browning, Hope, Star).

Finally, on April 8th, Mrs. Sidgwick had a sitting with Mrs. Piper, whereat Myers$_P$ again repeats that he drew a circle, and adds that he drew, or tried to draw, a star, and finally says, 'also a crescent,' all of which statements were correct, except that the star and crescent were drawn for Miss Verrall and not for Mrs. Verrall.

This case seems to fulfil the requirements for an ideal cross correspondence pretty nearly. We have a complex set of references made allusively and by implication in the scripts of two automatists, so that, taken by themselves, they are quite meaningless. In the third, Mrs. Piper's, the words are given outright and thus disclose the clue by means of which the whole puzzle is made clear.

Although exact calculations cannot be made, it seems pretty obvious that this result could not have been due to chance alone.

I pause here in my account of the evidence to consider briefly what implications can be seen to follow from this case. I think that it is indisputable that the various scripts are interconnected, so that we must suppose either that there was collusion between the three automatists, or else that some directing agency inspired them all. That there was collusion is so fantastic an idea that it requires no discussion. What then was the directing agency? If it were one of the automatists, the most plausible suggestion is that Mrs. Verrall was the one responsible. Her scripts come first in the point of time and initiate the whole thing. Yet, as is shown by her note of January 29th, she had not, at least in her supraliminal mind, recognized all the topics involved, she took the chief reference to be to 'Bird,' which actually was only subordinate. It was not until after the clue had been given in Mrs. Piper's sitting of February 11th that she recognized the 'Hope, star, Browning' motif.

We must, therefore, suppose that her subliminal mind devised the complicated puzzle and carried it out by incorporating parts in her own script, and telepathically influencing her daughter to write other parts, and Mrs. Piper to give the clue, while all the time her normal consciousness remained in ignorance.

If it were not Mrs. Verrall who was responsible, we must ascribe the authorship to some external intelligence. It might have been, at least in theory, the subliminal mind of some one living, but I venture to think that it would be a difficult task to suggest any plausible candidate for the office. If, however, we accept the possibility of the continued activity of the minds of deceased human beings, the explanation that the scripts were inspired by Myers, or by him and other members of his group, seems to cover all the facts.

In assessing the relative probabilities of these alternatives we must bear in mind the use of the anagram device. This, as has been said, would have been quite natural for Myers and Hodgson, but, to say the least, unexpected from Mrs. Verrall.

Autos ouranos akumon.[1] This incident also is an extraordinarily complicated one. Mr. Piddington's original report covers some sixty-five printed pages, while a second by Miss Johnson, takes another fifty.

It all started with an idea of Mrs. Verrall's. It occurred to her to put a test question to Myers$_P$, and she laid down the following conditions.

(1) It must be unintelligible to Mrs. Piper.

(2) It must be short.

(3) It must concern some subject with which Fred Myers had been thoroughly familiar.

(4) The answer must be complex and require allusions to several associations.

(5) It must be proved to have been known to Fred Myers.

(6) Both question and answer must be connected with subjects already mentioned by Myers$_V$.

She finally hit upon the Greek phrase 'autos ouranos akumon.' This is a quotation from the Neo-Platonist philosopher, Plotinus, and means, 'The very heavens waveless.' Plotinus, in describing the conditions necessary for the attainment of ecstasy or communion with the Divine, says that the individual soul 'must be freed from deception and every kind of beguilement,

[1] *Proc.*, S.P.R., Vol. XXII, p. 107, *et seq.*, and *Proc.*, Vol. XXVII, p. 77, *et seq.*

and be in a state of peace, also that the earth must be calm, the sea calm, and the air, and the very heaven waveless.'

Mrs. Verrall chose it because the passage had been used by Fred Myers as a motto for his poem on Tennyson, also a translation of it occurs in the second volume of *Human Personality*,[1] further, that it seemed to be connected with a phrase that had occurred in one of her scripts, viz. 'Celestial halcyon days.'

On January 29th, 1907, Mrs. Verrall, sitting with Mrs. Piper, put the question to Myers$_P$ and spelled over each word. On the next day Myers$_P$ mentioned 'larches' and 'laburnum' together. As it happened this association brought Tennyson to Mrs. Verrall's mind, both trees being mentioned in 'In Memoriam' in striking passages.

It is, perhaps, significant that the verse in which 'larches' occurs, ends with the line: 'The sea-blue bird of March,' i.e., the kingfisher or halcyon.

Shortly after this numerous references to Tennyson's works appeared in Mrs. Verrall's script, containing allusions to calm and serene spaces, thus, on February 12th *Avilion where blows not any wind* is quoted. This was associated in the script with *faery lands forlorn*, which, besides being a quotation from Keats, is the title of a poem by Myers, in which the words, 'that heaven high vault serene' occur.

In this script several of Tennyson's poems are referred to, viz., 'Voyage of Maeldune,' 'Merlin and the Gleam,' 'The Passing of Arthur' and 'Lucretius.'

Fred Myers, in his lifetime, was an intimate friend

---

[1] *Human Personality*, Vol. II, p. 291.

and great admirer of Tennyson, and was well acquainted with his works. It was not until five years afterwards that Mr. Piddington noticed that two of the quotations in the script are derived from two different passages in the 'Odyssey.'

On February 25th, there came another quotation from Tennyson. *The lucid interspace of world and world.*

On February 26th, *Autos ouranos akumon* was written in Greek characters, followed by, *I think I have made him* (probably the control, Rector) *understand but the best references will be made elsewhere, not Mrs. Piper at all.* Of course, this may have come from Mrs. Verrall's own mind, and is not at all evidential in itself. It was followed by: *And may there be no moaning of the bar – my pilot face to face,* and the names of Tennyson and Browning were given with comments on them, including the words: *After the earthquake and the fire and the wind, in the stillness comes the voice that can be heard,* alluding, obviously, to Elijah on Mount Horeb.

On March 6th came the words, *the calm, the heavenly and earthly calm,* and a quotation from 'In Memoriam,' *And in my heart, if calm at all. If any calm, a calm despair.*

Finally, on March 11th her script combined allusions to Plato and Tennyson, with phrases about *unseen and half-seen companionship – voiceless communings – unseen presence felt.*

These continual references to Tennyson's 'In Memoriam' led Mrs. Verrall to suspect a more definite connection between that poem and Plotinus, a connection which she finally traced, and concerning which she published a paper in the *Modern Languages Review,* July, 1907.

Now Myers was well aware of the influence of Plotinus on Tennyson, as is shown in his essay on 'Tennyson as a Prophet,' in which stress is laid on the affinity between them. In a footnote in another book Myers says that that essay was based partly upon Tennyson's own conversation.

It will be seen how all these references, not only contain the idea of heavenly calm, which is, of course, the meaning of the Greek phrase, but also, in the case of 'In Memoriam,' go even closer, for that poem has definite connections with Plotinus; moreover, calm is mentioned therein in connection with the poet's trance when he seeks communion with his dead friend, thus forming an exact parallel with the context of the Greek words.

It should be observed that, although Mrs. Verrall knew of the connection which the quotation from Plotinus had with Tennyson through Myers, having used it as a motto for his poem, she did not suspect the much closer link which the scripts themselves led her to discover. Fred Myers, however, was fully aware of it.

We must now turn to the other side, viz. Mrs. Piper's trance.

On March 6th, 1907, Myers$_P$ gave, without explanation, these words: *Cloudless sky horizon*, followed by *a cloudless sky beyond the horizon*; in the waking stage following came the words: *moaning at the bar when I put out to sea*, also *Arthur Hallam, Goodbye. Margaret.* (Mrs. Verrall's name is Margaret.)

The question of cross correspondences had been under discussion at this sitting.

On March 13th Myers$_P$ said: *I saw Mrs. Verrall and*

gave her a sign like this – then followed a rough drawing – *and said I have crossed it.* He explained, on being questioned, that the drawing represented a bar.

Up to this time Mr. Piddington, the sitter with Mrs. Piper, had no knowledge of Mrs. Verrall's scripts concerning this matter, except one referring to 'crossing the bar,' and a quotation from 'In Memoriam,' which he did not recognize. He had not read 'Plotinus,' nor Myers' poem on Tennyson, nor, although he read Greek, did he know the exact meaning of the rare word 'akumon': it seems highly unlikely, therefore, that the knowledge displayed in Mrs. Piper's trance was derived from his mind.

As regards Mrs. Verrall, it must be noted that she had not grasped the significance of the combination of quotations from 'In Memoriam' and 'Crossing the Bar' until after this sitting with Mrs. Piper, so that if the knowledge were derived from her mind, we must suppose that she had subliminally seen the connection before she discovered it normally.

Mrs. Verrall, herself, had a sitting with Mrs. Piper on April 29th, and the words *Azure and blue sea* were given, which were taken to be an association with 'halcyon days.'

At the end of the sitting there was a disconnected reference to Swedenborg, St. Paul and Dante. Next day Myers$_P$ claimed to have answered the question about the Greek quotation, saying that it had reminded him of Socrates and Homer's *Iliad*.

The references to these names seemed at first to be simply nonsense. But on May 1st Mrs. Verrall's script contained the words: *Eagle soaring over the tomb of*

Plato; this is a phrase descriptive of Plotinus quoted in Myers' *Human Personality*.[1]

This led her to investigate further, and she found that in the Epilogue of that book the vision of Plotinus is described, and is prefixed by a quotation from Plato's *Krito*, in which the story of Socrates' vision of a fair, white-robed woman is given. This woman speaks a line from Homer's *Iliad*. Thus Plotinus had been associated by Myers in his life with Socrates and Homer, an association very unlikely to have been made by anyone but a Greek scholar such as he was.

But a further, and even more significant discovery was made. On the same page that contains the phrase 'eagle soaring over the tomb of Plato,' there is a list of 'the strong souls who have claimed to feel it' (ecstasy) and among these, after Plotinus and before Tennyson occur Swedenborg, St. Paul and Dante. We thus see in the scripts and trance utterances a number of unusual associations which had been made by Myers in his lifetime.

And to conclude the business, on May 6th Mrs. Sidgwick, sitting with Mrs. Piper, had intended to ask Myers_P again for the name of the author of the Greek quotation, but he forestalled her by saying: *Will you say to Mrs. V. Plotinus?* She asked: 'What is that?' and Myers_P replied: *My answer to autos ouranos akumon.*

I have devoted a great deal of space to describing this highly complex incident, because it seems to me to be one of the best examples which we have of the complex type of cross correspondence. The knowledge shown in the Piper sittings was completely outside Mrs.

[1] Op. cit., Vol. II, p. 261.

Piper's own range, also was unknown to the sitter, Mr. Piddington and to Mrs. Verrall, but it had been in the possession of Fred Myers and was characteristic of him.

The answers given were allusive and indirect, and thus avoided the possibility of explanation by direct telepathy, moreover, on more than one occasion the scripts themselves gave guidance to the investigators by supplying the necessary clues which led them to discover the associations, as, for example, when the phrase 'eagle soaring over the tomb of Plato' directed Mrs. Verrall's attention to that part of *Human Personality* where she found the unlikely associations between Plotinus, Socrates, Homer, Swedenborg, etc.

The next case which I shall summarize is far less complex, it is the Euripides case.[1]

On March 4th, 1907, in Mrs. Verrall's script, appeared, *Hercules Furens* ('The Mad Hercules,' a play by Euripides). This was followed by a message to Dr. Verrall about the play. Then: *Ask elsewhere for the Bound Hercules* (an incident in the play is the binding of Hercules to a pillar).

On March 25th, Mrs. Verrall's script had: *The Hercules story comes in there and the clue is in the Euripides play if you could only see it. Bound to the pillar.*

In Mrs. Holland's script of April 16th, there was: *Lucus. Margaret. To fly to find Euripides. Philemon.*

Now Browning translated the 'Hercules Furens' of Euripides and this translation appears in a poem, entitled 'Aristophanes' Apology.' One of the characters in the 'Hercules Furens' is Lukos or Lukus, and in

[1] *Proc.*, S.P.R., Vol. **XXII**, p. 210, *et seq.*

Browning's poem another is Philemon, who is made to say: 'I'd hang myself to see Euripides.' There is thus a clear reference to this Browning poem in the script, a poem which is mainly concerned with Euripides. The name Margaret refers to Mrs. Verrall.

In the meantime, on April 8th, at Mrs. Piper's sitting with Mrs. Sidgwick, Myers$_P$ mentioned several words and phrases which he claimed had been given as cross-correspondences, among these is Euripides.

Mrs. Piper had no knowledge of the classics and Mrs. Holland although she was familiar with the English poets, did not read Greek, and her direct acquaintance with the works of classical authors was slight. She stated definitely, in reply to Miss Johnson, that she had not read 'Aristophanes' Apology' – 'it was one of the peaks in the Browning range which I still wait to scale.'

Mrs. Verrall was, of course, quite familiar with the 'Hercules Furens' in the original Greek.

If the source of these allusions in the three scripts were the same, it is possible to see why that which came through the subliminal mind of Mrs. Verrall should be couched in classical terms and refer directly to the original play, while through Mrs. Holland the quotations should be from a translation by an author with whom she was familiar, though she had not read this particular work. Mrs. Piper, on the other hand, had very likely never heard of the 'Hercules Furens,' and it is very doubtful whether she had read *any* Browning translations, so that all we get through her is the simple word 'Euripides.' Classical references are rare in Mrs. Piper's and Mrs. Holland's scripts.

The next is again fairly simple, but exhibits certain

instructive and interesting features. I call it the Spirit – Angel case.[1]

In Mrs. Verrall's script of March 25th, 1907, there was: *But let Piddington know when you get a message about shadows*, then followed various classical quotations in which the Latin word for 'shades' and the Greek for 'shadow of a shade' occur. Shade or shades in this sense mean the ghost or spirit of the dead.

On March 27th Mrs. Holland had in her script the word *tenebrae* (Latin for shadows) also the word *shadow* in English.

On April 8th with Mrs. Piper, Myers[P] says: *Spirit and angel. I gave both*, and, *Nearly all the words I have written to-day are with reference to messages I am trying to give through Mrs. V.*

To complete the case, I give in full the script of Mrs. Verrall of April 3rd.

Write three words – something about their serried ranks – the avenging flame – the troop triumphant –
no not quite that
flaming swords – no
flammantia moenia mundi (Latin = flaming walls of the world). *But wings or feathered wings come in somewhere.*
And with twain he covered his face
Try pinions of desire
The Wings of Icarus
(Then a drawing of a wing with feathers.)
long pointed rainbow wings. But you keep going round the ideas instead of giving three plain words
LOST PARADISE REGAINED
Of man's first disobedience – no that is something else

[1] *Proc.*, S.P.R. Vol. XXII, p. 220, *et seq.*

a fluttering faint desire. Triumphant hosts in long array the wings point upwards behind the marshalled hosts.

It is a picture can you not see it? with sweeping stationary wings, not used in flight, but making a great aureole behind the central group. The hosts of heaven. (Scribbles.) *No, I can't get it at all.*

Leave it to-day
his flame-clad messengers
        (Then a drawing of an angel with wings.)
that is better
F.W.H.M. has sent the message through – at last!

I have quoted this in full because, besides showing the cross correspondence for 'angel,' it exhibits clearly how the two factors – if there really be two – which go to make up the script interact with each other. These two factors are the subliminal mind of the automatist, and the external source which introduces the topics; this hypothetical external source utilizes the contents of the subliminal memory, selecting those things which will serve to introduce the topic to which it is desired to refer. But occasionally the subliminal of the automatist seems to take charge and to wander away on associations of its own. Thus *Lost Paradise Regained* sets it off on reminiscences of Milton's poem, and the next words are a quotation from him, having no bearing on the topic desired.

Then the external source interposes: 'No, that is something else,' and brings back the original topic of angels and wings with the word 'fluttering.' One can almost see the fumbling endeavours to get the idea through a refractory medium and the despair: 'No, I can't get it at all.' Then one more attempt which finally succeeds in giving a drawing of an angel with wings, and the final expression of triumph and relief. 'That is better. F.W.H.M. has sent the message through at last.'

There is one further significant point. The words, 'flammantia moenia mundi' are quoted from Lucretius i, 73, and Myers wrote a poem, entitled, 'The Passing of Youth,' the last lines of which are a paraphrase of the passage from Lucretius from which this quotation is taken. But Myers added in his paraphrase, 'with wings unfurled,' whereas 'wings' does not enter into the lines of Lucretius. It seems likely, therefore, that the association would be more natural to the mind of Myers than to that of the automatist who did not discover the connection between the Myers' poem and Lucretius until some months later.

Light in the West.[1] I have found it quite impossible to summarize this case; it is highly complex and involves so many references and subtle associations that no condensed account could give an adequate picture of the whole.

Those concerned were Mrs. Verrall, Mrs. Holland, Mrs. Piper and Miss Verrall. The main idea is the union of the East and the West, and this is conveyed by the Latin word 'claviger' which appeared in Mrs. Verrall's script. It means 'club-bearer,' also 'key-bearer.'

The three personages to whom it has been applied are Hercules, the club-bearer; Janus, the key-bearer, and St. Peter, also a key-bearer. 'The Myth of

[1] *Proc.*, S.P.R., Vol. XXII, p. 241, *et seq.*, and Vol. XXVII, p. 127, *et seq.*

Hercules,' though belonging to the West, probably had part of its origin in the East; Janus, the two-faced Roman deity, is essentially western, but stands for the union of the West and the East, as he is able, with his two faces, to look in both directions at once. St. Peter, an Oriental, became the head of the Western church.

There are secondary references to the same topic, e.g. bridging of the Hellespont whereby East and West were joined; also in some quotations from Tennyson's 'Maud.'

Arising from this main stem are other cross correspondences involving quotations from Dante, in particular referring to the monster Geryon, on which Dante and Virgil were carried, connected with Geryon or Geryones, the monster slain by Hercules and mentioned in Euripides' play, 'Hercules Furens.' From Dante again comes the idea of identification of opposites, which is, of course, involved in the main topic. This is given in Mrs. Holland's script where the words, *Martha became as Mary – and Leah as Rachel* occur.

Martha and Leah are given by Dante as exemplars of the active type, while Mary and Rachel are contemplative. That this is connected with the main topic is clearly shown by the words which immediately precede, *made the East as beautiful and as richly coloured as the West*. Mrs. Holland had not read Dante, and knew practically nothing about the 'Divina Commedia.'

Arising further out of these associations, came others which formed subordinate cross correspondences, such as Aphrodite, Cytherea, Daffodils (Tennyson), and Daffodils (Wordsworth), and from thence to the Wordsworth country.

The entire case is a complicated web of cross correspondences, one leading out of the other.

Mr. Piddington, in his original report, exercises a great deal of ingenuity and classical erudition in making out the pattern, and he succeeds in putting up a persuasive case for the view that it all resulted from a preconceived design on the part of someone, most probably the communicator, Myers and his group. His arguments are subtle and rather finely spun, frequently they depend on fine points of classical scholarship. I do not, however, feel quite happy about it all, as it seems possible to me that the main design which Mr. Piddington traces had its origin in his own mind. Possibly the arguments would appeal with greater force to a classical scholar than to one like myself, who is not versed in that lore.

Nevertheless, there is unquestionably an intricate mass of cross correspondences which are evidential in themselves, even if they do not form parts of a larger pattern as Mr. Piddington claims. To those interested in the subject I would recommend a careful study of the original report, which will repay any labour expended on it.

Ave Roma Immortalis.[1] In Mrs. Verrall's script of March 2nd, 1906, there occurred the Latin words, *primus inter pares*, meaning 'first among his peers,' also a statement that she would receive a message *through another woman.* On March 4th her script contained: *Pagan and Pope, the Stoic persecutor and the Christian. Gregory not Basil's friend ought to be a clue. . . . Pagan and*

---

[1] *Proc.*, S.P.R., Vol. XXI, p. 297, *et seq.*, and Vol. XXVII, p. 11, *et seq.*

Pope and Reformer all enemies as you think. Then in Latin: *The cross has a meaning. The cross bearer who is one day borne.*

Dr. Verrall, on reading this first script, identified 'primus inter pares' as the Pope, and possibly this accounted for the references to Popes in the second script. He did not say so at the time, but he was reminded by this second script of Raphael's picture in the Vatican of Pope Leo I meeting Attila and turning him back from sacking Rome. The Stoic persecutor was identified by Dr. and Mrs. Verrall as Marcus Aurelius.

It was quite clear that events in the history of Rome were being referred to.

On March 7th Mrs. Holland's script contained the words: *Ave Roma Immortalis. How could I make it any clearer without giving her the clue?*

There is an obvious cross correspondence here, unless we attribute the simultaneous reference to Rome to chance, but in that case the words: 'How could I make it any clearer, etc.,' would have no meaning.

Miss Johnson, with much labour and ingenuity, traced a number of other points in Mrs. Verrall's script which showed that Rome was the subject to which reference was being made, but it is not necessary to quote them here.

I include this case for the reason that the investigators, Miss Johnson in particular, expended on it a very large amount of research, and appeared to think that it was an outstanding example of the complex type of cross correspondence. I must confess, however, that I personally do not feel inclined to attach so much importance to it. It appears to me to be one of those cases where the explanation by simple telepathy between the automatists is quite plausible.

The Medici Tombs case.[1] Beginning in November, 1906, there commenced to appear in Mrs. Holland's scripts, references to shadows, death and sleep, dawn, evening and morning, and in two cases the name Margaret was written, signifying a cross correspondence with Mrs. Verrall. On January 21st, 1907, in Mrs. Verrall's script, laurels and laurel wreath were mentioned several times.

The following is from the waking stage of Mrs. Piper's trance of February 26th, 1907,[2] at which Mr. Piddington was the sitter.

Morehead(?)

J.G.P.: 'Morehead'?

Morehead (?) (or some such name or word) – laurel for laurel.

J.G.P. Say that again.

for laurel. I say I gave her that for laurel. Good bye.

A few moments later Mrs. Piper looked at Mr. Piddington with an expression of disgust and alarm, and said:

There are – a nigger. Oh dear. You go out.

I don't like you at all.

(Rub hands together.) *Dead.*

Later on came:

Well, I think it was something about laurel wreaths.

At a sitting on the next day it was stated:

I gave Mrs. V. laurel wreaths.

---

[1] *Proc.*, S.P.R., Vol. XXVII, p. 50, *et seq.*
[2] See also *Proc.*, S.P.R., Vol. XXII, pp. 94–5.

On March 17th, Miss Verrall's script had: *Alexander's tomb . . . laurel leaves, are emblem laurels for the victor's brow.*

On March 27th Mrs. Holland had: *Darkness, light and shadow, Alexander Moor's head.*

On October 7th, 1908, the Mac script contained: *Dig a grave among the laurels.*

Thus we have a set of topics interconnected together, but with little apparent meaning. Light and shadow, death and sleep might be associated normally, but laurels, Morehead or Moor's head, and Alexander did not seem to fit at all.

Then, after the lapse of nearly two years, the clue came through a different automatist, Mrs. Willett. On June 10th, 1910, her script contained the words: *Laurentian tombs, Dawn and Twilight.*

On July 8th, 1910, in Mrs. Piper's trance, the subject was again referred to in the words: *Meditation, sleeping dead, laurels.*

It was not until 1912 that the riddle was solved, when it was seen that the whole series of references pointed to the Medici tombs. The laurel was the special emblem of Lorenzo, the Magnificient.

On the tomb of Lorenzo, Duke of Urbino, there is a figure known as Il Pensieroso (vide, 'Meditation' in Mrs. Piper's script) of which Elizabeth Barrett Browning wrote, 'with everlasting shadow on his face'; also, two recumbent figures representing Dawn and Twilight, or Morning and Evening: on that of Giuliano, Duc de Nemours, two figures representing Day and Night.

Alessandro de Medici, the most infamous of the family, was murdered and his body secretly placed in the tomb of Lorenzo, Duke of Urbino. This tomb may therefore be called Alexander's tomb. He was son of Clement VII and a mulatto slave, and is shown in his portrait as having woolly hair, thick lips and generally a negro-like appearance. He was known as Il Moro (the Moor). It is, therefore, quite correct for him to be called Alexander, Moor's Head.

Miss Verrall, at this time, had never been to Florence, and though she knew of the existence of the tombs, had no other knowledge concerning them. To the best of her belief she had never heard of Alexander de Medici, and took the words 'Alexander's tomb' in her script to refer to Alexander the Great.

Mrs. Holland, however, knew the tombs; moreover, her script had had references previously to Diamond Island where the Lodge-Muirhead system of wireless-telegraphy was being tried in which she took an interest. It seems probable, therefore, that 'Alexander Moor's head' in her script was derived from the name of Dr. Alexander Muirhead, and this view is strengthened by the fact that the words are connected with a drawing of masts, and the words: 'The tall mast, but this one is not at sea.' But there is in the same script a quotation from *Othello* which goes to show that there was an association with Moors.

However, even if this explanation of the occurrence of the name be accepted, it does not bar out the possibility that there was a double reference intended. As has been mentioned before, the communicators seem sometimes to be able to seize upon normal memories in the mind of the automatist, and to use them for their special purposes.

It is not unreasonable to suppose that, if these scripts are really due to the inspiration of a source external to the mind of the automatist, it is somehow easier for the communicator to cause that mind to function along its accustomed lines; thus the use of Greek and Latin words in Mrs. and Miss Verrall's scripts, and the comparative absence of those languages from those of the other automatists. This view is strongly supported by a consideration of the Piper contribution in the sitting of February 26th.

Some weeks earlier, Mrs. Piper had a sitting with Professor J. H. Muirhead. It was not until the summer of 1936 that Mr. Piddington learned that Professor Muirhead had been introduced to Mrs. Piper by name, and he tells me that he believes that what he heard as 'Morehead,' was a mispronunciation or mishearing of the name 'Muirhead.'

But the view that this was spoken with a double reference is supported by the following words: 'I gave her that for laurel'; 'that' evidently referring to the name just spoken. Now 'laurel' is the keyword in this Medici case, laurels being the special emblem of the Medicis. There is further confirmation in the mention of the word 'nigger' a few moments later. There is no possible association between the name Muirhead, laurel and nigger, but there is a very close connection if the name was intended to convey 'Moor's head' through Alessandro de Medici, Il Moro.

The last case which I have selected to be summarized, is the Lethe case.[1]

[1] *Proc.*, S.P.R., Vol. XXV, p. 113, *et seq.* See also Vol. XXIV, p. 86, *et seq.* and pp. 327–8.

In March, 1908, Mrs. Piper, being back again in Boston, U.S.A., had been having sittings with Mr. Dorr, and Myers$_P$ had been asked what the word 'Lethe' suggested to him.

It occurred to Sir Oliver Lodge that it would be a good thing if the Myers communicator, who purported to write through Mrs. Willett, were asked the same question, so in September, 1909, he wrote the following letter, to be read by Mrs. Willett to Myers$_W$.

'My dear Myers, I want to ask you a question – not an idle one. WHAT DOES THE WORD LETHE SUG-GEST TO YOU?

'It may be that you will choose to answer piece-meal and at leisure. There is no hurry about it. OLIVER LODGE.'

I will summarize here some remarks which Sir Oliver Lodge makes in his report on this incident.[1] He says that he does not regard the various Myers personalities which come through Mrs. Piper, Mrs. Willett, Mrs. Verrall and Mrs. Holland, as being all exactly the same. The utmost assumption is that each contains something of the real Myers. The personalities would probably differ, because in no case is the Myers element pure and undiluted. It must surely be influenced by the material channel through which it conveys its intelligence. In the case of an entranced medium it might be anticipated that the control would be more complete, and that the effect of the 'dilution' less than with a medium not entranced, such as Mrs. Verrall.

He says further: 'It is becoming clear to me that when communications are being sent in such cases as

[1] Op. cit., pp. 118–9.

those of Mrs. Verrall, Mrs. Holland and Mrs. Willett the process consists in a kind of selection rather than in creation and origination.'

Myers_W himself seems to recognize this, for he says in script, February 10th, 1910: *That I have to use different scribes, means that I must show different aspects of thought, underlying which, unity is to be found;* and in a later script: June 5th, 1910: *Write the word 'Selection.' Who selects, my friend Piddington? I address this question to Piddington. Who selects?*[1]

On February 4th, Mrs. Willett sat for script, and the following was written: *Myers yes I am here. I am ready now to deal with the question from Lodge. Before you open the envelope reread his letter to you the one that accompanied the letter to me.*

Mrs. Willett then opened the envelope, and read the letter to Myers twice. The script then began at once: *Myers the Will again to live the Will again to live the River of forgetfulness not reincarnation Once only does the soul descend the way that leads to incarnation the blending of the Essence with the instrument Myers tu Marcellus Eris you know the line you* (Mrs. Willett) *I mean. . . . Write it nevertheless, and add Henry Sidgwicks In Valle Reducta. . . . Add too the Doves and the Golden Bough amid the Shadows add too Go not to Lethe . . . Myers. . . . There was a door to which I found no key . . . and Haggi Babba too. This is disconnected but not meaningless the shining souls shining by the river brim. The pain forgotten but there is another meaning another more intimate link and connection that now I cannot give it does not escape me I see the bearing Rose fluttering rose leaves blown like ghosts from an enchanter fleeing Myers and*

[1] Op. cit., p. 128.

Love Love the essential essence not spilt like water on the ground far off forgotten pain not here (A break and pause here.) *Darien the peak . . . in Darien the Peak . . . Peak PEAK* (another pause.) *mMyers I have not done yet to Lodge this may have meaning to Lodge this may have meaning Let him remember the occasion Myers I am not vague I am not vague I want an answer to this . . . to this Script from Lodge Myers tell him I want an answer Does he recognize my recognition Does he recognize my recognition Myers pause* (did so) *Let Lodge speak* (?) *speak let him speak Myers enough for to-day Myers let Lodge speak. F.*

The next day, in the evening, while looking at *The Times*, Mrs. Willett felt an overpowering urge to write, and although other people were in the room, sat down and obtained the following script, which she describes as the most untidy which she has ever had. There was some scribbling, but the rest was clearly written. It was as follows.

You felt the call it I it is I who write Myers I need urgently to say this tell Lodge this word Myers Myers get the word I will spell it (scribbles) *Myers yes the word*(?) *is DORR*

We (?) *H* (scribbles, perhaps M) *Myers the word is* (scribbles) *D DORR Myers enough F.*

Mrs. Willett could make nothing of this, except that she knew the name Dorr as that of an American who had had sittings with Mrs. Piper. She knew nothing of his connection with the 'Lethe' question.

As regards the script of March 4th, the allusions to Lethe are obvious. 'The will again to live' is a quotation from a translation of Virgil made by Myers himself, and refers to the souls mustering on the banks of Lethe, waiting to drink the waters of forgetfulness, and thus will again to live on earth. 'The blending of the essence with the instrument,' is a paraphrase of a passage in Virgil's *Aeneid* where Anchises explains to Aeneas concerning the Lethean spirits. 'Tu Marcellus eris' is a quotation from the *Aeneid*, but Mrs. Willett had seen it recently quoted in *Proceedings*. It is, therefore, not evidential except that it is doubtful whether she knew its connection with Lethe. 'In valle reducta' is the opening phrase of Virgil's description of the River of Lethe. Mrs. Willett had seen these words in a report on the Mac scripts, where they were represented as having come from Henry Sidgwick. The memory of this may have accounted for the mention of his name here.

The doves and the golden bough are further references to Virgil's account of the journey of Aeneas to the infernal regions. He had to obtain the bough before he could reach the River Lethe, and it was the doves who guided him to it in the woods round Avernus.

The subject is then changed, and a quotation from Omar Khayyám is given which has no obvious connection with Lethe, also the name, Haggi Babba.

Some month later, Myers$_W$ says that he made a pun somewhere: 'I, Myers, made a pun, I got in a word I wanted by wrapping it up in a quotation.'

Sir Oliver Lodge interpreted this as referring to the word 'door' in the Omar Khayyám quotation as a pun on the name Dorr, the American who put the Lethe question to Myers through Mrs. Piper. Haggi Babba he thinks is meant for Ali Baba and is brought in because of his connection with the door of the robber's cave which opened only to the words 'Open Sesame.' This door might clearly be described as 'a door to which I found no key.' From the fact that the name Dorr was given spontaneously on the following day this interpretation seems justifiable.

Moreover, at about this time Mrs. Forbes' script contained allusions to Sir Oliver Lodge and opening doors. The Mac script had a similar reference to 'key and door,' but as this occurred some eighteen months earlier, it can hardly be considered as having any connection; there was, however, a simple cross correspondence with Mrs. Holland's script of about that date, which contained a drawing of a key.

In the remainder of the script there are other indirect references to Lethe, but those which I have quoted will suffice to show that whoever or whatever it was which inspired the script, was conversant with Virgil and his account of Aeneas' visit to Lethe, also that there was a connection between this topic and the name Dorr.

Though Mrs. Willett knew practically no classics, she had read Church's *Stories from Virgil*, but a study of that book convinced Sir Oliver Lodge that she could not have derived the knowledge shown from that source. He states that at the time he was not familiar with the Sixth Book of the *Aeneid*, which is the one concerned. Myers, however, was in his lifetime, a great student of Virgil.

Myers$_W$ evidently understood what was being done, for he says in a script of February 10th: *Dorr's scheme excellent. That I have different scribes* (automatists) *means that I must show different aspects of thoughts underlying which unity is to be found* and *I know what Lodge wants. He wants me to prove that I have access to knowledge shown elsewhere.*

I think that it may be fairly said that Myers$_W$, whatever he may have been, succeeded, if not in proving this conclusively, at least in giving evidence of considerable weight in support.

In later scripts he shows himself possessed of wide classical knowledge, completely beyond anything which could be attributed to Mrs. Willett.

Sir Oliver Lodge, commenting on this, says:[1] 'The way in which these allusions are combined or put together, and their connection with each other indicated, is the striking thing – it seems to me as much beyond the capacity of Mrs. Willett as it would be beyond my own capacity. I believe that if the matter is seriously studied, and if Mrs. Willett's assertions concerning her conscious knowledge and supraliminal procedure are believed, this will be the opinion of critics also; they will realize, as I do, that we are tapping the reminiscences not of an ordinarily educated person but of a scholar – no matter how fragmentary and confused some of the reproductions are.'

Besides these cases which I have summarized, there are a number of others, some of which were treated at great length by the investigators. I have abstained from attempting to give any summary of them, partly because of their complexity and the difficulty of giving any adequate account in a form condensed to the degree that is here necessary, and partly because I do not wish to weary my readers.

To those who are sufficiently interested in this matter

[1] Op. cit., p. 172–3.

of cross correspondences, I would recommend a careful study of the original reports in the volumes of the *Proceedings* of the Society for Psychical Research, and I have put in an Appendix a full list of those volumes in which reports bearing on the matter may be found.

CHAPTER VI

In this chapter I propose to summarize two cases which, though not strictly speaking cross correspondences, may logically be included in the series, seeing that the evidence was the production of one of the leading automatists, Mrs. Willett, and that one of the communicators was Dr. Verrall who had been concerned, though indirectly, with the earlier experiments, and that the object was the same, viz. proving identity.

They were investigated by the Rt. Hon. Gerald W. Balfour (now Earl of Balfour), and reported in two papers published in *Proceedings*, Volumes XXVII and XXIX. The first is known as the 'Statius,' the second, as the 'Ear of Dionysius' case.

I will take the Statius case first.[1]

On July 6th, 1912, a few weeks after the death of Dr. A. W. Verrall (June 18th, 1912), Mrs. Willett's script contained the following: *Does she remember the passage in which there's a reference to a river? A traveller looks across it, and sees the inn where he wishes to be; and he sees the torrent and is torn both ways, half disliking to battle with the current, and yet desiring to be at his destination.*

Should it be possible to identify this passage, the matter would prove interesting.

What the passage does not say I draw from my own mind to make the connection clear.

---

[1] *Proc.*, S.P.R., Vol. XXVII, p. 221, *et seq.* See also Vol. XXVII, pp. 244-9 and 458-74.

The passage is not from Christina Rossetti; but I want to say that too:

> *Yea, beds for all that come –*
> *You cannot miss that Inn.*

The passage referred to was not traced, and the matter fell into abeyance until on August 13th, 1913, the following appeared in her script: *Some one indignant at the delay calls out*

HAS THE PASSAGE

been identified about the traveller looking across a stream; dips his staff in, fears to wade, takes a run, heart misgives him. (Here Mrs. Willett said out loud: 'Someone is laughing so.'—NOTE BY SITTER) *longs to be over and done with*

> *Faith and*
> *Hair*
> *in a Temple*

(Drawing of a wheel) *Wheel.*
Pilgrim.
There was a reason for the CHOICE, if you find the passage alluded to, it will be clear.

Have this seen to, for he swears he will not here exercise any patience whatsoever. Not even about

> *Lavender or Lub.*

Another reference was made on August 17th, 1913, as follows:

But it is of another one I want to write. I said Pilgrim. Now write this –

Not a one-horsed dawn, but a two horsed chariot, though one-horsed in a way might fit, because as compared to another charioteer's exploits, his were but a one-horsed affair. It is a poem I am alluding to.

*A man who drove two horses in a less ambitious manner.
His predecessor –*
Does God exact day labour, light denied?
That ought to make it clear.

Hair in a temple was said.
And again on September 8th, 1913.
*He of the little patience demands now this third time whether
the Pilgrim has been understood.*
*Now if I say Passionate Pilgrim, I know all sorts of con-
notations will be dragged in. But think of the passages twice
inserted.*
The River and he who would be across.
Letting I would not wait upon I would.
That seems jumbled up somehow, never mind.
A passionate Pilgrim but

NOT H.S's

one
*What moves the stars and all the heavenly bodies? Dante
makes it clear.*
*Then again I repeat and will continue to repeat until you are
all sick and tired of the subject*

HAIR IN A TEMPLE

That belongs
The investigators formed the conclusion that the
scripts were somehow connected with Dr. Verrall, and
the statement that 'Dante makes it clear,' gave them
the clue. In the spring of 1913 a volume of essays by
Dr. Verrall was published, one of which, entitled:
'Dante on the Baptism of Statius,' had appeared
originally in the *Albany Review* of 1908. Mrs. Willett
had never heard of the *Albany Review*, and although she

had received a copy of the volume of essays in May, 1913, she had not read any of them. Anyhow, as the volume was not published until after the date of the first script, it could not have been the source of the information contained therein.

Statius, a Latin poet of the second half of the first century A.D., was an imitator of Virgil. His principal work, *The Thebaid*, described the legendary war against Thebes. He was inclined to be rather long-winded and dilatory, and some authorities think that the name Statius = the 'Stayer,' was given him as a nickname on this account.

In the *Purgatorio* Dante describes how he and Virgil met the soul of Statius who, having just completed his purgatorial expiation, was free to accompany them on their journey. Statius, having been in Purgatory, must therefore have been a Christian, and Dante, according to Dr. Verrall, had 'the audacity to date the baptism by a particular passage in the *Thebaid*.'

Dante makes Statius say: 'I had received baptism before, as a poet, I had brought the Greeks to the rivers of Thebes.'

Dr. Verrall, in his essay, then discusses the meaning of the passage in Dante where Statius is represented as making this statement, and shows how he describes himself as lingering on the other side of the river of baptism, but before he brought the Greeks in his poem to the Theban River, he, himself, had made the passage.

The actual words which Dante puts into his mouth are: 'Ere in my poem I had brought the Greeks to Thebes' river, I received baptism, but through fear I was a secret Christian, long time pretending paganism.'

The passage in the first script clearly describes a traveller hesitating to cross a river, and is obviously apposite to Statius.

That this was the actual reference intended is confirmed by the words: 'What the passage does not say I draw from my own mind to make the connection clear,' which is a paraphrase of the opening sentence of the speech of Statius, and by the statement in the last script that 'Dante makes it clear.'

If this identification of the passage be admitted, we have to account for its appearance somehow. Mrs. Willett could not have possessed the knowledge normally, so that we are compelled to adopt either the hypothesis of chance, or that of supernormal acquisition. It is clear, I think, that all four scripts refer to the same topic, and exhibit a coherence and design of a sort.

The first script sets the puzzle, and in those following we see a semi-humorous impatience, and in each fresh clues given. When at last the solution is found the matter is dropped.

I doubt whether this could reasonably be ascribed to mere chance, the concordance is too great. If it were due to supernormal acquisition, Mrs. Willett could have acquired the information either by clairvoyance or telepathy. If the former, we must assume that she perceived clairvoyantly a copy of the *Albany Review* of 1908, a review which had a very narrow circulation and short life, and one of which she had never even heard; or else she perceived the unpublished volume of essays.

Then from this source, she elaborated the puzzle in

her subliminal mind, and later devised all the fresh clues given in the subsequent scripts, some of which were drawn from other sources. Such an elaboration would entail minute study of the essay, and I find it difficult to suppose that her subliminal mind could have carried it out. In my opinion the hypothesis of clairvoyance, though abstractly possible, is practically untenable and fantastic.

If it were due to telepathy, there appear to be two alternatives, i.e. telepathy from some living person, and telepathy from the surviving consciousness of a deceased human being.

Suppose it were telepathy from some living person, the most plausible, in fact, one may say, the only plausible suggestion, is that it was derived from Mrs. or Miss Verrall. They were in possession of the knowledge, and they were both capable of elaborating such a puzzle. But it must have come from their subliminal minds, for, until they learned of the solution proposed by Lord Balfour, they were unable to make anything of it. It is possible that this elaborate scheme might have been devised by the subliminal mind of one or other of them, and yet left the supraliminal in complete ignorance, but on the whole I think that it is rather unlikely.[1]

If it were telepathy from a deceased person, all the evidence points to that person being Dr. Verrall.

The reader must decide for himself which of these alternatives is preferable. As I said at the outset, complete proof cannot be obtained, all we can hope for is probability.

[1] See op. cit., p. 235, for Lord Balfour's comments on this point.

There are a few subsidiary points in the later scripts and these I will shortly describe.

In all three 'Hair in a Temple' is emphatically mentioned.

Lord Balfour, in commenting on this, states that it conveys to him a definite and evidential meaning. There are, he says, only two passages in classical literature to which it can be referred, one a poem by Catullus called, 'The Hair of Berenice,' the other a poem by Statius himself. If it were the latter it is surely suggestive, but he considered that the weight of evidence was in favour of the former. It may well have been, of course, that there was here a double reference, and that Dr. Verrall, supposing his mind to have been the source, utilized this as giving added cogency to the evidence. He had undoubtedly been familiar with both passages.

Unfortunately, the reason for ascribing the reference to the Catullus poem cannot be given, and, as Lord Balfour says: 'I must ask you to accept from me that there *is* a connection, but one which I have to leave unexplained, because it involves a reference to private matters which I am not at liberty to disclose.'

I think that no one will have any difficulty in accepting Lord Balfour's assurance on this point.

The next item is 'Pilgrim,' or 'the passionate Pilgrim.'

The word 'Pilgrim' is, of course, a clear association with the traveller hesitating to cross the river. A clue to the meaning of all this part of the scripts may be found in the words, 'A passionate Pilgrim, but not H.S.'s one.' H.S. stands for Henry Sidgwick, and in an early script of Mrs. Verrall's 'the passionate pilgrim' occurs in a passage which was afterwards connected by her with Professor Sidgwick. This passage had been published and read by Mrs. Willett. Lord Balfour suggested a further explanation, but I need not give any summary of it here.

The reference to 'one-horsed dawn' is, of course, to the experiment in telepathy known by that name, which was instituted by Dr. Verrall. I have summarized it on page 63. This is most ingeniously connected with a poem by Gray, entitled 'The Progress of Poesy, a Pindaric Ode,' wherein Dryden is compared with Milton, and the simile of a two-horsed charioteer is used. The words in the script: 'Does God exact day labour, light denied?' are a quotation from Milton's sonnet on his blindness. In Gray's poem reference is made to Milton's blindness. The last work on which Dr. Verrall was engaged before his death was a set of lectures on Dryden, in the course of which this passage from Gray's ode was quoted.

The last point is the cryptic phrase, 'Lavender or Lub.' These words had appeared in a script of Mrs. Verrall's on January 13th, 1908, and had been read by Mrs. Willett. Lord Balfour had also seen this script and knew that the original source of the words was a poem in *Punch* wherein several variations on the alternative names of the fish, Chavender or Chub, were made. What neither of them knew was that these lines had been exceedingly familiar to Dr. Verrall, and had become a standing family joke. Mrs. Verrall wrote in answer to Lord Balfour's inquiry: 'During many years,

for instance, the mention of bathing invariably produced the lines:

> And when I take my Tavender
> My Tavender or Tub.'

It appears quite obvious that all these passages point
unmistakably to Dr. Verrall, so much so, that if the
source was not in his mind, they must have come from
someone who was most intimately connected with him,
that is to say, Mrs. or Miss Verrall. I have already
discussed the question of their authorship in regard to
the Statius passages, and it seems to me that these
further points of identification go a long way to reinforce the unlikelihood of ascribing it to either of them.
The final case of which I shall treat is 'the Ear of
Dionysius.'[1]

Here again the automatist was Mrs. Willett, and the
investigator Lord Balfour.

The first mention of the topic was on August 26th,
1910, when the following words were spoken. (It must
be remembered that in the more advanced stage of
Mrs. Willett's mediumship, spoken as well as written
messages were given) *Dionysius' Ear, the lobe.*

The name was given the Italian pronunciation. The
reference was entirely disconnected, and nothing was
made of it by Mrs. Verrall, who was sitting with Mrs.
Willett.

The 'Ear of Dionysius' is a kind of grotto in the
quarries at Syracuse, in Sicily. These quarries had
been used for a prison for the Athenian prisoners of

---

[1] *Proc.*, S.P.R., Vol. XXIX, p. 197, *et seq.* See also pp. 260–9 and
270–86.

war after the failure of the siege of Syracuse, and later were again used for other prisoners by the elder Dionysius, Tyrant of Syracuse. The grotto is supposed to have the properties of a whispering gallery, and it is partly for this reason and partly on account of its shape, that it came to be known as 'the Ear of Dionysius,' though the name dates only from the sixteenth century.

Mrs. Willett had spent some time in Italy and knows Italian, but had never been to Sicily. She may, however, have heard of the grotto, as it is one of the show places of Syracuse.

Nothing more was heard of this topic until January 10th, 1914, when the following script was written: *Do you remember you did not know and I complained of your classical ignorance IGNORANCE. It concerned a place where slaves were kept – and Audition belongs, also Acoustics.*

Think of the Whispering Gally [sic].

To toil, a slave, the Tyrant – and it was called Orecchio – that's near

One Ear, a one-eared place, not a one-horsed dawn (here the automatist laughed slightly), *a one-eared place – You did not know (or remember) about it when it came up in conversation, and I said Well what is the use of a classical education –*

Where were the fields of Enna

(Drawing of an ear.)

an ear ly [sic] *pipe could be heard*

To sail for Syracuse

Who beat the loud-sounding wave, who smote the moving furrows

The heel of the Boot

Dy Dy and then you think of Diana Dimorphism

To fly to find Euripides
not the Pauline Philemon
This sort of thing is more difficult to do than it looked

Sir Oliver Lodge was the sitter at this sitting, but the message appears to have been addressed to Mrs. Verrall who had been the sitter on the earlier occasion. She had made a note shortly after that sitting (i.e. in August, 1910, nearly two years before his death) to the effect that she had asked her husband what was meant by the words, 'Ear of Dionysius,' and she afterwards remembered that he had expressed surprise at her ignorance. He had explained that it was the name of a place at Syracuse where Dionysius could overhear conversations. This is clearly reflected in the opening sentences of this script. Unfortunately, Lord Balfour was unable to say whether he had mentioned this conversation between Dr. and Mrs. Verrall to Mrs. Willett. He had a dim recollection of having done so, but Mrs. Willett, herself, remembered nothing of it. This is a pity, as an otherwise good piece of evidence is spoiled.

Mrs. Willett gave the Italian word for ear, viz., 'orecchio,' which recalls her use of the Italian pronunciation of Dionysius on the first occasion.

Our old friend, the one-horsed dawn, is again brought in, but this by itself is not evidential as the phrase was familiar both to Mrs. Willett and to the sitter, Sir Oliver Lodge.

Enna, which is next mentioned, is a town in Sicily and the fields of Enna were famous as the scene of the rape of Proserpine.

'An *ear*-ly pipe' is a reminiscence from Tennyson,

being brought up, presumably, by the punning association with 'ear.'[1]

The next sentences, 'To sail for Syracuse,' 'Who beat
the sounding wave, etc.,' and 'the heel of the boot,'
evidently refer to the Athenian expedition against
Syracuse and to the Athenian prisoners of war who
were confined in the quarries. Some of the words here
are again reminiscent of Tennyson.

Then comes an attempt at the name Dionysius.

'To fly to find Euripides' is a phrase which had
appeared in a script of Mrs. Holland's (see page 79)
which Mrs. Willett had read; it refers to Browning's
poem, 'Aristophanes' Apology.' In this poem Balaustion
tells Philemon that she had sent the original tablets of
Euripides' play, 'Hercules Furens,' which he had given
to her as a parting gift, to Dionysius, Tyrant of Syracuse. Mrs. Willett had not read this poem, but she had
seen references to it in the reports of the 'Euripides'

---

[1] Mr. Piddington has pointed out to me that there may also be an
association of ears of corn with Demeter and Proserpine.

This would connect up with 'the fields of Enna' and he quotes two
verses from Swinburne's poem, 'The Garden of Proserpine.'

Although the fields of Enna are not mentioned in this poem, there
is an implicit connection, for they were famous as the scene of the Rape
of Proserpine. These verses, which moreover make contact with the
script at other points, are as follows:

> Here life has death for neighbour
> And far from eye and ear
> Wan waves and wet winds labour

And

> Pale, without name or number,
> In fruitless fields of corn
> They bow themselves to slumber.

The points of contact are obvious; death, slumber, eye or ear, and
waves.

Two lines from this poem of Swinburne's are quoted in the next script,
a fact which lends confirmation to Mr. Piddington's suggestion.

cross correspondence in *Proceedings*, so it is just possible that she may have known of the connection with Dionysius, though it does not seem likely as this point was not mentioned in the earlier reports.

The next script from which an extract is quoted is that of February 28th, 1914, Lord Balfour being the sitter.

Some confusion may appear in the matter transmitted, but there is now being started an experiment not a new experiment but a new subject and not exactly that but a new line which joins with a subject already got through

a little anatomy if you please

Add one to one

One Ear X [sic] *one eye*

(Then a drawing of an ear and an eye in a circle)

the one eyed Kingdom

no, in the K of the Blind the 1 eyed man is King

It is about a 1 eyed man (Man was crossed out in the original)

1 eyed

The entrance to the cave Arethusa

Arethusa is only to indicate it does not belong to the 1 eyed

A Fountain on the Hill Side

(Then a drawing of a volcano or smoking mountain)

What about Baulastion [sic]

(Then a drawing of a boot)

(Laughs) *Supposed to be a Wellington Boot*

12 little nigger boys thinking not of Styx

Some were eaten up and then there were Six   Six

(At this point Mrs. Willett ceased to write and began dictating to the sitter)

Some one said – Oh I'll try, I'll try.   Oh Someone's showing me a picture and talking at the same time.

Someone said to me Homer. . . .

> *Nor sights nor sounds diurnal*
> *Here where all winds are quiet*
> (Swinburne, 'The Garden of Proserpine')

. . . It's about a cave, and a group of men. Somebody then – a trident, rather like a toasting fork I think.

Poseidon, Poseidon

Who was it said, It may be that the gulfs will wash us down – find the great Achilles that we knew (Tennyson's *Ulysses*)

He's got a flaming torch in his hand. And then some one said to me, Can't you think of Noah and the grapes?

Optics – Oh! that, you know (putting a finger to her eye)

. . . Somebody said to me, Don't forget about Henry Sidgwick, that he pleased not himself. Do you know he used to work when he hated working. I mean sometimes he had to grind along without enjoying what he was doing. That's what I'm trying to do now. Do you know that man with the glittering eyes I once saw? He hit me with one word now (Note by Lord Balfour: Here Mrs. Willett traced a word with one finger along the margin of the paper. I failed to make it out and handed the pencil to her, whereupon she wrote)

Aristotle

(Dictation resumed) *And Poetry, the language of the Gods. Somebody killed a President once and called out – something in Latin, and I only heard one word of it, Tironus, Tiranus, Tiranius – something about sic.* (Note by Lord Balfour: 'Sic semper tyrannis' – uttered by Booth when he murdered Lincoln. . . .)

What is a tyrant?

Lots of wars – A Siege I hear the sound of chipping. Its on stone. . . .

Fin and something gleba. Find – Oh it's got to do with the serf. It's about that man who said it was better – Oh! a shade among the shades. Better to be a slave among the living, he said.

Oh, the toil – Woe to the vanquished.

That one eye has got something to do with the one ear. That's what they wanted me to say There's such a mass of things, you see, rushing through my mind that I can't catch anything.

(A pause and then sobbing) *He was turned into a fountain that sort of Stephen man, he was turned into a fountain. WHY? that's the point: WHY?*

Oh dear me! Now I seem to be walking about a school, and I meet a dark boy, and – it's the name of a Field Marshall I'm trying to get, a German name. And then something says, All this is only memories revived: it's got nothing to do with the purely literary – There are two people in that literary thing, chiefly concerned in it. They're very close friends – they've thought it all out together.

Somebody said something about Father Cam walking arm in arm – with the Canongate? What does that mean?

Enough for this time. There is sense in that which has been got through though some disentanglement is needed. A Literary Association of ideas pointing to the influence of two discarnate minds.

Most of the topics of the previous script are again mentioned; these need not be further discussed, but may be briefly enumerated. They are:

The Ear of Dionysius.

The stone quarries in which the vanquished Athenians worked.

Enna (indirectly suggested by a quotation from 'The Garden of Proserpine').

Syracuse (Wars – a Siege, and Arethusa).
The heel of Italy (Wellington boot).
The Adventures of Balaustion.

It was further said that an experiment was being tried, and in a part which I have not quoted, it is expressly enjoined that May (Mrs. Verrall whose name is Margaret, but who was always called May) is to hear nothing of it. It is also stated that it is the work of two friends who were no longer in the flesh. They are indicated as being Professor Butcher and Dr. Verrall. The 'man with the glittering eyes I once saw,' refers to Professor Butcher. Mrs. Willett had seen a vision of him a few weeks after his death: in her record of it, made the following day, she says: 'Last night after I had blown out my candle and was just going to sleep, I became aware of the presence of a man, a stranger, and – almost at the same moment – knew it was Henry Butcher. I felt his personality very living, clear, strong, sweetness and strength combined. A piercing glance. He made no introduction, and said nothing. So I said to him: "Are you Henry Butcher?" He said: "No, I am Henry Butcher's ghost." I was rather shocked at his saying this, and said: "Oh, very well, I'm not at all afraid of ghosts or of the dead." He said: "Ask Verrall if he remembers our last conversation, and say the word to him: Ek e tee." '

This last was apparently meant for 'Hecate' which had a significance for Dr. Verrall. Professor Butcher had written a work on Aristotle. So the name 'Aristotle' written by Mrs. Willett after Lord Balfour had failed to understand the letters traced on the table, serves as an additional point of identification.

The references to the school, dark boy, etc., concern Dr. Verrall, of whom they were veridical. 'Father Cam walking arm in arm with the Canongate' signifies the association between the two friends. Dr. Verrall, was, of course, a Cambridge man, while Professor Butcher was professor of Greek at Edinburgh, hence 'the Canongate.' He was also a highly distinguished Cambridge man and was member of Parliament for the University.

Mrs. Willett had met Dr. Verrall two or three times, but not Professor Butcher, though she knew the latter by name.

Besides the topics already mentioned there are two additional subjects which are introduced into this script; they are the stories of Polyphemus and Ulysses from Homer, and of Acis and Galatea from Ovid. The first story recounts how Ulysses was driven by storm to the lands of the Cyclopes, how he and twelve of his comrades sheltered in the cave of one of them, Polyphemus, the one-eyed son of the sea-god Poseidon. Polyphemus imprisons them in the cave and proceeds to devour them two at a time. Ulysses and his remaining companions, having made Polyphemus dead drunk with wine which they had brought from the ship, burn out his single eye with the glowing point of an olive stake which they had thrust into the embers. Next morning they escape from the cave, concealed under the bellies of the sheep which had been herded there for the night.

Ancient tradition located the cave in Sicily, though Homer is silent on the matter.

The references in the script to this story are obvious

once we have the clue, e.g. '12 little nigger boys, etc.,' mention of Homer, a cave, Poseidon, the flaming torch, of Noah and the grapes, etc.

The second story also brings in Polyphemus: Acis, a shepherd dwelling at the foot of Mount Etna, loves Galatea, a sea nymph. She is also beloved by Polyphemus, but rejects his suit. He, mad with jealousy, hurls a rock at Acis and crushes him to death. Galatea gives her dead lover a kind of immortality by changing him into a stream which issues as a fountain from the rock which killed him. The references to this story are, 'a fountain on the hill-side,' the drawing of a volcano, and 'he was turned into a fountain that sort of Stephen man.' The reference to Stephen being, of course, on account of the similarity of the manner in which St. Stephen and Acis were killed, i.e. by stoning.

The next script in the series, on March 2nd, 1914, was as follows.

The Aristotelian to the Hegelian friend greeting. Also the Rationalist to the Hegelian friend greeting. (The Aristotelian is Professor Butcher, who had written about Aristotle, the Rationalist, Dr. Verrall, with a side allusion to his book, *Euripides the Rationalist.* The Hegelian is Lord Balfour, the sitter.)

These twain be about a particular task and now proceed with it

(Then came a drawing of a Zither.)

a Zither that belongs the sound also stones, the tool of prisoners and captives beneath the Tyrant's rod

The Stag not Stag, do go on

Stagyr write rite

(Here Mrs. Willett ceased writing, and proceeded to dictate)

Somebody said to me Mousike.

Do you know, it's an odd thing, I can see Edmund [i.e. Edmund Gurney] *as if he were working something; and the thing he is working is me. It isn't really me, you know; it's only a sort of asleep me that I can look at. He is very intent – and those two men I don't know. One's very big and tall, with a black beard. The other man I don't see so well. But he holds up a book to me.*

Oh! Somebody wrote a book about something, and this man, who's holding up the book, wrote a book about him. And the reference he wants isn't just now to what he wrote, but to what this person he wrote about wrote.

What does Ars Poetica mean?

Edmund said to me Juvenal also wrote satires – and then he laughed and said, Good shot.

The pen is mightier than the sword. Oh, it's so confusing – stones belong, and so does the pen. Oh!

Somebody said, Try her with the David story. She might get it that way. The man he sent to battle hoping he'd get killed, because he wanted him out of the way.

A green-eyed monster.

Now, all of a sudden I had it. Jealousy, that first infirmity of petty minds.

What does Sicilian Artemis mean?

Such an odd old human story of long ago.

He that hath an ear to hear, let him hear.

What is an ear made for?

Oh, this old bothersome rubbish is so tiresome.

(Here Mrs. Willett commenced writing again, and first drew an ear and a circle)

Find the centre. (Here she added an eye in the circle)

Not to you to Golden numbers golden numbers, but add 1 to 1 two singles, dissimilar things, but both found normally in pairs in human anatomy – Good.

Gurney says she has done enough now, but there is more, much more, later. Until the effort is completed the portions as they come are not to be seen by any other AUTOMATIST. E.G.

The passages, 'Try her with the David story, etc.,' 'A green-eyed monster' and Jealousy, etc.,' are answers to the question asked in the previous script, viz. why Acis was changed into a fountain. Zither, Mousike, Stagyr and Ars Poetica are references to Aristotle, the Stagyrite, and thus indirectly to Professor Butcher, who wrote a treatise on Aristotle's *Poetics*;[1] there is also a further association from the subject of *Poetics* to Satire, one of the classical forms of poetry. This is reinforced by the mention of Juvenal, the classical satirist.

To recapitulate, we have now the following list of topics.

The Ear of Dionysius.
The stone quarries of Syracuse.
The story of Polyphemus and Ulysses.
The story of Acis and Galatea.
Jealousy.
Music.
Something to be found in Aristotle's *Poetics*.
Satire.

So far there seems to be very little to connect up the various pieces, but in August, 1915, a further script, contained the following passages; Mrs. Verrall was the sitter.

---

[1] Horace's *Ars Poetica* is referred to at least three times in Professor Butcher's book, *Aristotle's Theory of Poetry and Fine Art.*

Someone speaks a tall broad figure with a dark beard and eyes that emit light with him stands the man who said I am Henry Butcher's ghost do you remember?

Ecate

. . . . . .

The Aural instruction was I think understood Aural appertaining to the Ear

and now he asks HAS the Satire satire been identified

Surely you have had my messages concerning it [*it*] *belongs to the Ear and comes in*

It has a thread. Did they not tell you of references to a Cave

The mild eyed melancholy Lotus Eaters came

That belongs to the passage immediately before the one I am now trying to speak of. men in a cave herds

listen don't talk (Mrs. Verrall had repeated two words, half aloud.)

herds and a great load of firewood and the EYE

olive wood staff,

(then a drawing something like an arrow head)

the man clung to the fleece of a Ram and so passed out surely that is plain

well conjoin that with Cythera and the Ear-man

The Roseman said Aristotle then Poetics The incident was chosen as being evidential of identity and it arose out of the Ear train of thought.

There is a Satire

write Cyclopean Masonry, why do you say masonry I said Cyclopean

Philox He laboured in the stone quarries and drew upon the earlier writer for material for his Satire Jealousy

The story is quite clear to me and I think it should be identified

a musical instrument comes in something like a mandoline thrumming thrumming that is the sense of the word
  He wrote in those stone quarries belonging to the Tyrant
  Is any of this clear?
(Drawing of an ear)
You have to put Homer with another and the Ear theme is in it too. The pen dipped in vitriol that is what resulted and S H knows the passage in Aristotle which also comes in. There's a fine tangle for your unravelling and he of the impatience will
  Let her wait try again Edmund
  Sicily
He says when you have identified the classical allusions he would like to be told.

It will be seen that the same subjects were again mentioned with but little extra added, but that little extra gave the key to the puzzle.

The important words were, 'Cythera,' 'Cyclopean,' 'Philox,' 'He laboured in the stone quarries and drew upon the earlier writer for material for his Satire.' 'Jealousy.'

Now Philoxenus of Cythera was a poet of some repute in antiquity, but very little is known of him nowadays except to specialists in classical literature, as only a few lines of his work have been preserved.

His story is as follows. He was a writer of dithy-rambs, a kind of poetry which combined music with verse in which a Kithara or Zither was generally employed. He spent some time at the court of Diony-sius of Syracuse, and ultimately quarrelled with his patron and was imprisoned in the quarries. Accounts differ as to the cause of the quarrel. According to some Dionysius was offended because Philoxenus refused to praise his poems, another version is that the quarrel was on account of the poet's 'too close intimacy with the Tyrant's mistress, Galateia.'

The most famous poem of Philoxenus was one entitled, 'Cyclops or Galatea,' and was a burlesque on the love of Cyclops for the Nymph; it was written to avenge himself on Dionysius who was wholly or partially blind in one eye. In it he represents the Tyrant as Polyphemus and himself as Odysseus. It may therefore be described as a satire.

These facts are very little known and are drawn from Lempriere's *Classical Dictionary* and Dr. Herbert Weir Smyth's *Greek Melic Poets*, neither of which works were known to Mrs. Willett.

It is evident that all the leading topics as enumerated in the lists given above, are combined into one whole in this narrative.

The scene – the stone quarries and the 'Ear of Dionysius,' Polyphemus and Ulysses from one story, supply two of the characters of the satirical poem of Philoxenus, Galatea from the other story supplies the third character. Jealousy, the motive. Music and Zither come in as being the accompaniment of the particular form in which the poem was cast, viz. the dithyramb. Satire, the character of the poem.

The references to Aristotle link up with both Professor Butcher and with Aristotle's *Poetics*, in which the dithyramb is described, not only so but this actual poem of Philoxenus is cited as a specimen of satirical poem.

The final script which closes the incident, seems to make it clear that the solution found is correct, it came on August 19th, 1915. Lord Balfour being the sitter; the following is an extract.

(Sitter: First of all, Gurney, I want to tell you that all the classical allusions recently given to Mrs. Verrall are now completely understood.)

Good – at last!

(Sitter: We think the whole combination extremely ingenious and successful.)

and A W ish –

(Sitter: What is the word after 'A.W.'?)

A W-ish

(Sitter: Yes)

Also S H – ish

A. W. and S. H. are, of course, Dr. Verrall and Professor Butcher.

All the facts were normally unknown to Mrs. Willett, the books from which they might have been derived were such as were most unlikely to have come under her notice, being of interest only to specialists. None of the group of investigators knew anything about Philoxenus of Cythera and his work, until the occurrence of the name 'Philox' in the script led Mrs. Verrall to make a search. It was only a ripe scholar who could have devised this literary puzzle, and even among scholars there are comparatively few who could be credited with the requisite knowledge.

Among these, however, was Dr. Verrall in his lifetime. Dr. Smyth's book, which contains the fullest account, was in his possession and had been used by him in connection with some of his lectures.

That it was not derived telepathically from the mind of someone living, cannot be disproved, but at the same time it was found impossible to suggest any person who could have filled the role. It seems unlikely that a scholar, entirely unconnected with the group of experimenters, and probably unaware of their existence as such, should, without any apparent motive or interest, intervene subconsciously in the experiment and foist upon the investigators a complicated and subtle literary puzzle under false names.

Moreover, the positive indications that the source is to be found in the minds of Dr. Verrall and Professor Butcher, are, to say the least, significant.

The reminder in the first script to Mrs. Verrall of his surprise at her ignorance concerning the 'Ear of Dionysius' would have been very striking, but unfortunately this point is vitiated by Lord Balfour's inability to say with any certainty whether he had mentioned it to Mrs. Willett or not. He, himself, believes that he did not mention it, and Mrs. Willett had no recollection of having ever heard of it.

The characteristic traits and mannerisms of Dr. Verrall which were so strongly shown in the 'Statius' case, are not so apparent here but are not wholly absent.

I think that the conclusion to be drawn may be fairly stated thus.

While there is not positive proof that the operating mind was that of Dr. Verrall, assisted by Professor Butcher, as is specifically claimed in the scripts, there is strong evidence in support of that view, and to accept any other alternative would require a stretching of hypothesis and an unlikely combination of circumstances.

Moreover, if we accept the statement explicitly made

in the scripts, that a complex puzzle had been deliberately set and that the various quotations and allusions were given as parts of that puzzle and aids to solving it, then the view that other 'Communications, some of which have been summarized earlier in this book, bear the same character, receives considerable support.

The fragmentary, enigmatic and allusive nature of these communications is intentional, and their obscurity is due not solely to the deficiencies of the investigators. Puzzles which are too easily solved fail of their purpose.

CHAPTER VII

WE must now address ourselves to the task of summing up the evidence and arguments on both sides.

I should first, perhaps, explain what I consider to be my position in the matter. I could have approached it from the standpoint of an advocate briefed to argue in support of one particular view – say the hypothesis that the scripts were inspired by, and the information contained therein derived from, the surviving personalities of Myers, Gurney, Verrall, and the others. Had this been so, I should have tried to present the evidence in the light most favourable to that view, although I should not have suppressed any that was unfavourable. As regards the arguments, I should have felt it permissible to put forward only those which supported my case, leaving those against it to 'counsel' on the other side. If I mentioned hostile arguments at all, it would have been only when I considered that I was able to refute them.

But I do not conceive that my duty lies in this direction; my function is more that of a judge who has to sum up the evidence and arguments on both sides, leaving it to the jury to decide.

The judge may indicate his own personal opinion, but if he be truly impartial, he should lay as much stress on those points which tell against it as on those which support it.

In speaking of a jury, I mean, of course, the readers

of this book (with my usual caution, I feel bound to put in the proviso, 'if there be any') but the analogy is not quite exact.

A jury in an English Court has to find one way or the other, in a Scottish Court there is a third alternative, viz. 'Not proven,' but the juryman here is not called upon to do this; the utmost that can be expected of him is that he should decide on the relative probabilities of the alternative hypotheses, of which there may, of course, be more than two. It is not at all likely that he will in any case be able to assess these probabilities at a definite figure, and thus give a mathematically exact verdict, the most that he will be able to say is that such and such a view is highly probable. It will be lucky if he can go even as far as this, most likely he will have to be content with finding that the balance of probability lies in a particular direction.

As I said at the very outset, the scientific method cannot yield certainty, and in this matter, as in many others, we have to be, and are, content to act upon probable hypotheses.

The first point to be noticed is that the cases which I have cited are only a sample of a considerably larger number. I think that this sample is fairly representative of the whole, and I have included in it some which appear to me to be of a lesser evidential value than was assigned to them by the original investigators.

I have been most anxious not to overstate the case.

The sample is, in my opinion, sufficiently large to enable the reader to form his judgment, and I doubt whether he would have been aided in doing so had the whole number been put before him, as those which have been omitted do not contain any facts of a different type.

To repeat evidence over and over again increases its weight in one respect only, though this respect is of great importance, viz. as against chance. Were we to find in the scripts of several automatists one or two scattered cases of cross correspondence, we might reasonably attribute them to chance coincidence, but should they occur in large numbers, the tenability of that hypothesis is much lessened. Further, when this large number of cross correspondences is accompanied by definite indications of intention, and indeed, by explicit statements in the scripts that they are parts of a planned experiment, then explanation by chance alone can be confidently rejected.

That the number of cross correspondences which occurred in the scripts of this period is sufficient to exclude chance, is a matter which the jury must decide, and in making their decision they must bear in mind quality as well as quantity.

When the topic mentioned is highly specific and not a mere commonplace, the possibility of chance coincidence is much lessened; thus, though two automatists might very likely make references to the works of some poet, say Tennyson, in their scripts of a particular short period, that they should both refer, not only to the same poem, but also to one particular passage or subject in the poem, is much more unlikely. This, as we have seen, is precisely what happened.

In my opinion the chance hypothesis has very little to recommend it, though it is, of course, abstractly possible. I have little doubt that the jury will be nearly unanimous in their verdict against it. However, it is for each individual juryman to decide for himself.

The next hypothesis is that of collusion or fraud.

Here we are, I think, on even firmer ground. Precautions to avoid any of the automatists acquiring knowledge of the contents of the scripts of others were taken. Where, in any particular case, an automatist was in possession of such knowledge, the fact has been mentioned and allowance made. The reader will doubtless call to mind several instances of this.

But apart from this, the character of those engaged affords an amply sufficient refutation of the hypothesis. I cannot imagine that anyone would seriously suggest that all those engaged in the experiment deliberately set out to deceive. I do not think that I need add anything to the comments which I have already made on this point (see page 26).

In my opinion the hypothesis of fraud is so fantastic that it need only be mentioned to be dismissed. Of course, anyone is entitled to believe what absurdities he pleases, but there are consequences entailed by doing so; one of these consequences is that no attention need be paid to the judgment of a person who seriously entertains ridiculous beliefs.

The next point to be considered, is the nature of the evidence and the possibility of mistake in reporting. This possibility, which presents a very real difficulty in most spontaneous cases, hardly arises here. When we are dealing with eye-witness accounts of alleged supernormal happenings, there is always a possibility of mal-observation, and—even more important – of bad reporting, exaggeration, lapse of memory, and so on.

But with the scripts of automatists none of these possibilities exists; there is the permanent objective evidence of the documents themselves. They can be examined and studied at leisure. It is true that in a few instances, particularly with Mrs. Piper, there was some uncertainty in reading a word here and there, and, in the spoken matter of the waking stage, difficulty of hearing, but these form a very small proportion of the whole and wherever they occurred they were noted and allowance made.

Thus, it is that, from the point of view of the evidence itself, these cross-correspondence cases stand at a far higher level than the bulk of the material with which psychical research has to deal. The scripts are there for anyone to examine, the only question is their interpretation, and to this question we must now turn.

Even if, in face of the assertions of the automatists themselves, it is denied that they were automatically written in the sense described on page 19, we still have to account for the concordance between them. Conscious collusion would have been fraudulent, and this we have ruled out, chance coincidence we have already discussed; it remains, therefore, to find another hypothesis.

In the case of Mrs. Piper the writing was done in conditions which rendered it practically impossible for her to have known what was being written; with the other automatists I do not think that any reasonable person would doubt their word. I am not, of course, suggesting that Mrs. Piper's word is in any sense untrustworthy, but the professional medium must be prepared to be subject to a type of criticism which is not levelled against the non-professional.

As a matter of personal opinion, I fully accept the statements of all the automatists; whether this opinion be shared by my readers is for them to decide, but even if they disagree it does not materially affect the issue.

The main task is, therefore, to explain how the concordance between the scripts of the different automatists arose.

The first hypotheses to be tested are those of clairvoyance and direct telepathy, or mind reading.

We have other evidence that these phenomena occur, and if it can be shown that either of these hypotheses, or a combination of both taken together, can be made to account for the facts, then, by the canons of scientific method, we must accept that explanation provisionally.

Further, we must be prepared to allow some stretching of the ordinary conception of clairvoyance and telepathy; we know so little of the conditions in which they occur and of their *modus operandi*, that we cannot lay down any hard and fast limits. Whether the stretching which is required is reasonable or not is a question for the jury to answer.

Clairvoyance has been defined as 'the supernormal acquisition of knowledge about objective concrete situations (page 10).

Let us see what would be entailed by supposing that the cross correspondences were due to the exercise of this faculty by one or other of the automatists. Automatist A writes a script – that is an objective concrete situation – Automatist B clairvoyantly becomes aware of that script and is thus able to make references in her own script to some topic contained therein. Of course this all takes place subliminally.

Moreover, it is quite possible that the script of Automatist B might make the reference oblique and allusive, such a thing is not beyond the powers of the subliminal mind.

To take a specific instance: in the 'Ave Roma Immortalis' case, Mrs. Holland might have become clairvoyantly aware of Mrs. Verrall's scripts, and recognized them as having reference to Roman history; her own script comments thereon as one might say: 'Hullo!–Rome.' The succeedings words: 'How could I make it any clearer without giving her the clue,' are, perhaps, more difficult to account for, but it is not beyond possibility that they arose from subliminal invention, particularly if the writer had knowledge of the cross-correspondence idea.

But when one comes to apply the hypothesis to the more complex cases, difficulties rapidly increase. Clairvoyance would give knowledge only of what had actually been written, so that if the concordance between the scripts is not merely one of identity or simple reference to the same topic, some further amplification of the hypothesis must be made. Where the concordance consists of appropriate complementary quotations, the question whether the clairvoyant automatist had normal knowledge of their source immediately arises. Where this was so we might suppose that the elaboration was performed by her subliminal mind, but when no normal knowledge was possessed, as, for example, in Mrs. Holland's scripts, which appeared to derive from Browning's 'Aristophanes' Apology,' a poem which she had not read, we should have to suppose that a further act of clairvoyance was performed to give her supernormal knowledge of that poem. But in that case, how did she know where the words which she clairvoyantly perceived in the script of the first automatist came from? To recognize the quotation implies some knowledge of the source.

It is quite true to say that actual concrete records, such as books and documents, were in existence in almost all cases, and thus might, in the abstract, be available to clairvoyant perception, but the difficulty is to account for that perception being turned in the proper direction.

Where there are several scripts concerned, or in cases where the cross correspondence involves more than two automatists, a further crop of difficulties arises.

Until we can lay down with some certainty the limits of possible clairvoyance, we cannot say definitely that explanation by that hypothesis is impossible, but if we have to make a large number of unsupported assumptions which ascribe to the faculty powers far exceeding anything of which we have independent evidence, then its plausibility becomes much weaker and we are compelled to test other hypotheses.

If we can find one which covers the facts without entailing similar assumptions, or which involves a smaller number, we must accept it provisionally, provided that its antecedent improbability is not so great as to outweigh its advantages in this respect. Let us, therefore, test the hypothesis of telepathy between the automatists. On this hypothesis simple correspondence is easily explicable, but in the more complex cases, where the corresponding reference in the second script is indirect and allusive, we must suppose that the matter had been previously elaborated in the subliminal mind of the agent automatist, i.e. the one who sends the message. This, in itself, is not impossible, nor, in fact, too improbable to be accepted in most of the cases, and were it not for one or two facts which appear to be incompatible with it, it is the explanation which I, personally, should be inclined to accept.

But these facts must be covered somehow, they cannot be ignored.

For example, in the 'autos ouranos akumon' case, Mrs. Verrall was led by the scripts to discover a connection between Tennyson's 'In Memoriam' and Plotinus, which she had not before suspected. Can we assume that her subliminal mind knew of this connection before, as the result of some study and research, she became supraliminally aware of it? In the 'One-horsed dawn' case, she was normally ignorant of the fact that 'herb moly' had any connection until a long time after it had appeared in the script.

In the 'Lethe' case the appropriateness of the conjunction of the names of Dante, Swedenborg and St. Paul was not recognized until the clue given in the script directed Mrs. Verrall's research.

There is one point on which I have already touched, but perhaps insufficiently stressed. The suggestion that the puzzles were devised and the communications inspired by the subliminal mind of some one living involves the ascription of intent to deceive. We must assume, therefore, that this campaign of deception was carried on consistently over a period exceeding twenty years, during which the personnel of the group of automatists changed from time to time as fresh recruits came in or members dropped out. Several of the recruits were unknown to the members of the group before joining it, and in some cases they never became personally acquainted. Yet the plan of cross correspondences was consistently carried on.

It is true that if it were within the power of an hypothetical disembodied mind, or group of minds, to initiate and carry out the plan, it is, so far as we can see, equally within the power of an embodied mind. There is no reason to suppose that the enfranchisement from the prison of the flesh endows the surviving mind with added powers of telepathy. It may be so, but in the absence of any evidence, we must not assume it.

The point is that the embodied mind must have had the intention to deceive, and it is hard to suppose that this intention would persist over so long a period covering so many changes.

Even more significant, perhaps, than the fact that changes in the group of automatists produced so little change in the character of the communications, is the striking change which followed the death of Dr. Verrall. He had, in his lifetime, taken no very active part in the business, he was interested and gave advice, but was neither an automatist nor an investigator, properly speaking.

But immediately after his death we have two important cases, the 'Statius' and the 'Ear of Dionysius,' wherein he purports to appear as communicator, and in these cases there is exhibited a manifest difference in style which differentiaties them sharply from those which purport to come from the Myers group.

On the other hand, the death in 1916 of Mrs. Verrall,

one of the principal automatists, made very little difference in the character of the communications.

While these facts are not conclusive as against the telepathic hypothesis, for it is possible that if the sub-liminal mind of someone living were responsible for the phenomena, that mind might have appreciated the point, and utilized it as an aid in its plan of deception, they seem to me to render that hypothesis considerably less plausible.

Further, some of the most characteristic individual possessions of the human mind are the associations which it makes between ideas. These associations are the result of past history and are as clear an indication of psychical individuality as finger-prints are of physical. No two persons will make exactly the same associations between ideas, because no two persons have ever had exactly the same history.

If, then, we come across peculiar and unusual associations which we subsequently discover to have been made by some particular individual, there is good reason to ascribe to that individual's mind some share in their origin.

In many cases we find associations which had been made by Myers in his lifetime, and were thus normal for him, but which were unlikely to have been made by the automatist; so that unless we can show that they could have been derived from the latter's knowledge of Myers' works or history, it is difficult to avoid the conclusion that his mind was somehow responsible for their appearance in the script.

In the 'Statius' and 'Ear of Dionysius' cases, the knowledge shown and the associations made were all clearly appropriate to the mind of Dr. Verrall, or, in the latter case, to Prof. Butcher's as well. It is not *impossible* that they might have been derived from the subliminal mind of Mrs. Verrall, but in that case we must credit her with supernormal knowledge of the classical works and books of reference from which alone that knowledge could have been drawn.

That many of the cases are in the nature of literary puzzles can hardly be doubted, and if this be so, some mind or minds must have designed them. It is too improbable to be seriously suggested that the coherence and design which is exhibited in the more complex cases was simply due to chance. It is constantly claimed that these puzzles have been set by that mind which inspired the scripts and the claim seems, on the whole, to be justifiable.

There was no person living who consciously and supraliminally designed the puzzles, so we are left with two alternatives, viz., that they were designed by the subliminal mind of someone living, or by the surviving mind of a deceased person. I think that we may reasonably narrow down these alternatives by restricting the possible authorship to members of the group of automatists and investigators on the one hand, and the surviving personalities of Myers and his associates on the other. It is, of course, possible that the source was quite extraneous to either of these groups, but there is no indication of any evidence that it was so.

Now any mind which possessed the requisite classical and literary knowledge could have designed the puzzles, and there were in both groups persons who fulfilled this condition. It is true that in the case of the living group there are some instances where the knowledge was not supraliminally possessed, as for example, the connection between 'In Memoriam' and 'Plotinus' and the others which I mentioned a few pages previously, but as we have no means of determining the extent of the subliminal knowledge of any person, this cannot be held to be decisive.

In speaking, as I have done, of a group of surviving personalities, it must be understood that I do so only as an hypothesis. Unless such hypothesis is *a priori* impossible or of so high an antecedent improbability as to be unworthy of serious consideration, it is permissible so to speak. There are those who, on other grounds, have already come to the conclusion that the death of the body entails the final extinction of anything which could be called a personality or mind, and for these no evidence, such as has been here presented, will avail to influence their decision. They are quite right in taking this attitude so long as they remain satisfied that the grounds of their original conclusion are adequate. For them survival is either impossible, or so improbable as to be practically impossible, so there is nothing more to be said about the matter.

However, there are many others, equally competent, who do not accept this conclusion, and for them the evidence of cross correspondences may possess validity. As it is only such persons, if any, who are likely to read this and similar books, it is to them alone that I address my remarks.

We have now arrived at the position that the two most probable hypotheses which we can make to account for the facts are telepathy between the automatists and/or the investigators, combined with subliminal in excess of supraliminal knowledge, and inspiration of some sort from the surviving personalities of Myers and his group. Both these hypotheses, we have agreed, are not so antecedently improbable as to be rejected *a priori*, and it only remains to weigh one against the other and to make a provisional decision based on an estimate of their relative probabilities.

We have, as I see it, four relevant questions to answer.

First. What is the probability that any member of the living group subliminally invented the plan of cross correspondences, devised the literary puzzles and foisted them on the other members of the group? In considering this question it must be remembered that if responsibility for the invention and execution of the plan be ascribed to the subliminal mind of one of the living group, we must also ascribe to that mind the intention to deceive.

Second. What was the probability that a member of the living group possessed the requisite subliminal addition to his or her normal knowledge? In all cases I think that it may be said that some member of the other group had the necessary knowledge when alive.

Third. Were the associations displayed more appropriate to one group than to the other, and what was the probability in the matter?

Fourth. Was the dramatic personation exhibited by the scripts such as to warrant us in ascribing authorship, and, if so, with what degree of probability?

Regarding the first question, we have independent evidence which tends to show that the subliminal mind may indulge in deception of this kind, although I do not know of any instances where it was carried to anything approaching the pitch and elaboration here shown, nor carried on continuously over so long a period of years.

As a rule these other cases of deception are simple impersonations, as when messages purporting to come from the surviving personalities of deceased human beings are given through a medium or automatist.

Moreover, there is the question of selection of the material for the puzzles and the combination of the various parts into a coherent whole. This represents a formidable task for some of the more complex cases. However, the fact that this task was actually performed by *some* mind, shows that it is not beyond the powers of the subliminal, for we cannot admit that the supra-liminal is necessarily superior in intelligence, if anything the reverse may be true.

But I suggest that it may seem unreasonable to attribute to the same level of consciousness intellectual powers of a very high order and a rather stupid spirit of trickery and deception. One would not expect a scientist of the first rank to publish a set of false statements and fallacious inferences, cunningly designed to deceive, for the sole purpose of bolstering up an erroneous hypothesis.

There is some internal evidence in the scripts which bears on the matter. If we study the 'Statius' and 'Ear of Dionysius' scripts, I think that we get a strong impression that the author of these was well acquainted with the plan but had had no actual experience of carrying it out. This seems to be the obvious meaning of the words used in the first script in the 'Ear of

Dionysius' case: 'This sort of thing is more difficult to do than it looked.'[1] If the communications were in some way inspired by Dr. Verrall, this remark is singularly appropriate.

The communicator's style and technique in these two cases seem somewhat different from those shown in the cases attributed to Myers. This is what we might expect if they were inspired by Dr. Verrall.

The second and third of these questions have been discussed pretty fully in passing, and it is unnecessary to add much here.

The 'Ear of Dionysius' case is, perhaps, the best evidence on the matter, not only on account of the richness of detail but also of the inaccessibility of the source of the knowledge. That source was a highly technical work by an American scholar, such that it would be read by few even among classical students; the clue was given by the name of Philoxenus of Cythera, a classical poet of whom very little is known.

The answer to the third question depends, of course, upon the attitude taken up as regards the second. If one of the automatists possessed the requisite subliminal knowledge, she might have made the associations. On the other hand, in the absence of such knowledge it is highly unlikely that they would have occurred by mere chance.

It must be remembered that where there are two or more independent conditions of which the probability has been assessed, the combined probability is the product and not the sum of the individual probabilities Thus, suppose that we assessed the probability in

[1] *Proc.*, S.P.R., Vol. XXIX, p. 199.

Question 1 as 3 to 1 against a member of the living group having devised the puzzles, i.e. probability $= \frac{1}{4}$, and in Question 2 as 4 to 1 against such member having the requisite subliminal knowledge, i.e. probability $= \frac{1}{5}$, the combined probability against assigning authorship to that group is $\frac{1}{20}$ or 19 to 1 against.

I do not suppose that any reader will feel disposed to attempt to assign a numerical value to any of these probabilities, such a thing is clearly impossible, but it is well to bear in mind that two independent probabilities reinforce each other to a greater extent than by mere addition.

The conditions contained in Questions 3 and 4 are not wholly independent, so the mode of combination of their probabilities would not be the same as for 1 and 2. However, if they be in the same sense they lend added weight, if they be in the opposite sense they may detract, but not necessarily to the same extent as they would add. For example, if we felt pretty sure that no member of the living group devised the puzzles or had the requisite subliminal knowledge, the fact that the dramatic personation was poor need not seriously upset our confidence. It might be that dramatic personation was not being aimed at.

Common sense is the only guide in this matter, mathematical treatment is not applicable.

Concerning the fourth question, some further discussion is necessary. It must be remembered that some of the automatists, in particular Mrs. and Miss Verrall and all the investigators, were personally acquainted with Myers and other members of the group in their lifetimes; of the other automatists, Mrs. Piper must have known Myers fairly well, for she stayed at his house for some weeks, she was also well acquainted with Hodgson as she had had a long series of sittings with him in America.

It must be admitted that in the case of Myers the characteristics or, as I have called it, the dramatic personation shown in the scripts is very unequal.

But in this connection I would refer to the remarks made by Sir Oliver Lodge, quoted on page 91, wherein he points out that the Myers personalities which come through the different automatists are not all exactly the same; the Myers element is in no case pure and undiluted.

The most striking instance of dramatic personation is in the 'Statius' case, concerning which Rev. M. A. Bayfield, a most intimate friend of Dr. Verrall's, writes:[1] 'These additional reasons for assigning to Dr. Verrall the scripts which we are examining can, I fear, be fully appreciated only by those who knew him somewhat intimately, for they consist in the exhibition in the scripts of two traits of his personality which, highly characteristic though they are, would not be likely to come under the notice of an ordinary acquaintance, or be known by hearsay to a stranger.' Concerning certain passages in the script, he writes:[2] 'All this is Verrall's manner to the life in animated conversation.' 'When I first read the words quoted above I received a series of little shocks, for the turns of speech are Verrall's, the high-pitched emphasis is his, and I could hear the very tones in which he would have spoken each sentence.'

[1] *Proc.*, S.P.R., Vol. XXVII, p. 244.   [2] ibid., p. 246.

He sums up in these words:[1] 'It remains to mention one more point which also impresses me strongly. We have here an extraordinarily faithful representation of Verrall in respect of a peculiar kind of impatience and a habit of emphasis which he had in conversation, and of his playfulness and sense of humour. In what way are these lifelike touches of character introduced? How are they worked into the essential matter of the scripts? Have they the air of being inserted by an ingenious forger (the unprincipled subliminal of some living person) *with a purpose*, in order to lend convincing *vraisemblance* to a fictitious impersonation; or do they give us the impression of being spontaneous and genuine? Unless I am inexcusably mistaken, no one accustomed to estimate the internal evidence afforded by a document of doubtful origin could hesitate as to the answer.' 'To me, at least, it is incredible that even the cleverest could achieve such an unexampled triumph in deceptive impersonation as this would be if the actor is not Verrall himself.'

It is, of course, difficult for those who have no acquaintance with the *dramatis personae* to form a judgment in this matter, but I think that the opinion of one who, like Mr. Bayfield, counted Dr. Verrall as his 'oldest and dearest friend' must carry considerable weight.

Mrs. Willett's acquaintance with Dr. Verrall was very slight, far too slight for her to have had so intimate a knowledge of his personality as to reproduce his characteristic mannerisms to the extent shown in the scripts, so that unless we can ascribe the whole thing to telepathy from some living mind, there seems a

[1] *Proc.*, S.P.R., Vol. XXVII, p. 249.

SUMMARY AND DISCUSSION 143

high probability that it was somehow inspired by the surviving consciousness of Dr. Verrall.

Finally, before submitting the case to the jury for their verdict, there is one general consideration which must be mentioned. We can understand, or at least we think that we can understand, pretty well what is meant by communication from a living person, whether from the supraliminal or subliminal part of the mind. It is true, perhaps, that if we tried to state definitely what is implied by this partition of the mind, we might get into serious difficulties. I, personally, think that we should most certainly do so.

But without going into the metaphysics of the thing, we have a rough idea sufficient for the purposes of the hypothesis.

We have experience of countless instances of supra-liminal mental events and we also have experiential knowledge of other events which look as though they were mental yet are clearly not supraliminal. It is these which we call subliminal. We may not under-stand fully their nature or *modus operandi*, but they are sufficiently familiar for us to feel at home with them.

The same may be said, though in a somewhat less degree, of telepathy; we do not understand it, but we have come across it sufficiently frequently for us to employ the conception of it in our hypotheses without feeling much discomfort.

Thus it is that we can put forward the explanation of telepathy from the living, combined with sublminal knowledge in excess of the normal, and feel more or less satisfied that we know what we are talking about.

But communication from, or inspiration by, the

surviving consciousness of deceased human beings is a very 'different pair of shoes.' I know that many, perhaps most, people would, at first sight, see no particular difficulty in the conception of survival, whether they accept it as fact or not. They might say: 'I know what I mean when I talk about the mind or consciousness of a living human being, I also know what I mean when I talk about his body; the two things are clearly distinguishable. By survival, therefore, I mean that the first goes on existing when the second has been destroyed.'

This attitude, however, involves a good many assumptions, both explicit and implicit, for which we have no sufficient warrant.

The only minds of which we have any experiential knowledge are embodied minds, we have no certain knowledge of a disembodied one. We do not know that the conditions of space and time to which we are accustomed prevail in the state of existence which the hypothetical disembodied mind must occupy; neither do we know that the familiar categories of cause and effect, sameness and difference and of number, apply in that state. They may do so but until we have some definite experience on which to found them, our opinions on the matter can never be more than assumptions, which, however plausible they may be, are not based on experiential knowledge.

Moreover, experience seems to be subject to certain fundamental laws or principles: these have been variously formulated; as an example I would cite the law known as the 'Law of Contradiction.' This states that two contradictory propositions cannot both be true at the same time; or the law of 'Excluded Middle.' A either is B or is not B.

These laws appear to us to be self-evidently true; we cannot conceive an exception. Yet we have no right to assume that they necessarily apply in a state of existence of which we have no knowledge whatsoever: the King's writ may run all over his dominions, but not necessarily across the frontier.

To discuss the matter further, would take us too far out on the perilous waters of metaphysical speculation, but I can give one example. Speaking for myself I think that I have an unescapable conviction of being one and only one person, my moods may vary but behind them all is one and only one 'me.' I cannot conceive myself as being split up into two, or as merging into someone else's self. I am I and no one else. Of course I may be unique in this, but I imagine that most people feel the same.

But Sir Oliver Lodge speaks of the Myers personalities as manifested through the various automatists not being all the same: there is some part of Myers present but the personality of the script is a compound or mixture.[1]

---

[1] It should be noted that this opinion, expressed by Sir Oliver Lodge, is only one possible interpretation of the facts. They may be explained equally well in the following manner. We derive our conception of the communicating personality solely from the internal evidence of the scripts. It is as though we were forming an estimate of the character of some one, of whom we had no other knowledge, by reading letters which he had written. Now, if these letters had been the joint production of two people, say, that they had been written by a secretary, not from dictation, but from notes supplied, they would exhibit a compound or mixture of characteristics. The scripts may be looked upon as being of this nature, the communicator inspires them in some way, but the automatist acts as secretary rather than as a mere amanuensis, and thus contributes a considerable share of the internal characteristics.

We may be unable, with our embodied minds, to conceive how two separate personalities can merge into one, yet if disembodied minds exist at all, the conditions of their existence may, for all that we know, be such that the hard and fast lines of demarcation between individualities no longer prevail. If, while I am in the body, I am I and no one else, it does not necessarily follow that when freed from the body this will remain true. It might be, as some have held, that the disembodied mind or soul is somehow reabsorbed into a cosmic soul and yet retains its personality.

Moreover, the *me* which I recognize as myself in this life is a composite entity, it is composed of both mental and physical factors. This is immediately obvious if one considers how great is the influence on the self of the state of bodily health, what sweeping change in character may be produced by drugs or injury to the brain. But, although it is generally agreed that there is a factor in the manifested personality due to the physical organism, there is wide divergence of opinion as to its extent and importance.

The tendency of physiologists and some psychologists is to assign to the physical the predominant share in the partnership, many authorities even go so far as to reduce mind to the level of a sort of by-product, an epiphenomenon as it is called, of the working of the cerebro-neural organism. If, however, these extreme views should be correct it is of little use to discuss the question of survival, for, while survival may remain conceivably possible, it seems so highly improbable as to be hardly worth consideration.

To discuss the matter in all its aspects is quite beyond

the scope of this book, but I have thought it right thus briefly to mention it, so that, in considering their verdict on the evidence put before them, my readers may avoid falling into the error of assuming that the naïve, uncritical hypothesis of survival, i.e. that that which survives is an exact replica of the personality which was manifested in this life, is the only possible alternative to complete extinction.

They are at liberty to hold that evidence establishes a probability that there is some sort of survival of personality, while leaving undefined the exact nature of that personality and the conditions in which it exists.

That so large a tincture of agnosticism should pervade our opinions is, in my opinion inevitable and not undesirable. Though it may be that the 'me' which I have recognized as myself in this life may cease to be after physical death, there may be a larger 'me' which survives.[1]

To some this may appear an unsatisfactory conclusion, and extinction of that which they have been accustomed to regard as being their total and only self, an unwelcome thought, but it must be remembered that if that self no longer exist it can no longer suffer any pain or disappointment, while, if there be a larger self which survives, that survival may be far more satisfying to it than would be any continuance of the partial manifestation which played its fleeting part in this life.

This then is the case for survival as presented by the evidence of cross correspondences and automatism, and I leave it to the jury of my readers to form their own opinions.

[1] See last sentence of the passage from *Human Personality*, quoted on p. 12.

APPENDIX I

To those of my readers who are sufficiently interested I would suggest three experiments.

First. Let them try to construct cross correspondences normally. Thus, let an author be chosen with whose works they are well acquainted, and then some topic or quotation be picked out. Then from another book by the same author or from a different part of the same book other quotations must be sought which bear allusively on this topic, yet avoid direct mention of it. Punning references may be employed. When this had been done let the two sets be submitted to some person, who will play the part of investigator, to see whether the puzzle can be solved. Should he fail to do so, a further clue can be sought which will bind it all together into a coherent and intelligible whole.

If this experiment be tried, it will, I think, be found that a good deal of research, knowledge and ingenuity is required and that, in the words of Mrs. Willett's 'Verrall' communicator, 'This sort of thing is more difficult to do than it looked.'

Second. Choose a book by an author with whose works you are well acquainted, and from it pick a passage by chance. You could open it at random and, with the eyes shut, put your finger on the page, then take the passage indicated. Do the same thing with another such book and then try to work out a cross correspondence between the two passages. This experiment will give an indication of how far pure chance is likely to have been responsible for the concordance found between the scripts of the automatists.

The third experiment is to try to obtain automatic writing.

Quite a large proportion of those who have tried have succeeded in obtaining automatic writing, but there is no reason to suppose that in any except a very few cases there was anything else involved beyond some level of the subliminal mind of the writer.

The process is quite easy; one simply sits holding a pencil with the hand resting on a sheet of paper in the attitude of writing and allows the mind to drift. Conscious attention must be withdrawn from the hand. Probably nothing will result from the first attempts, but with perseverance there is a fair chance of success.

Once the first scrawling motions are made experience will show what are the best conditions and the best methods. A planchette could also be tried, or some form of ouija board.

But I would add a most emphatic warning. Leave it all severely alone unless you are prepared to maintain a cool, detached and preferably rather sceptical attitude towards the phenomena. It should be treated seriously, of course, but not emotionally. If the experimenter is prone to see in every script messages from the dead or weighty pronouncements from august spiritual beings, then the experiment had better be dropped.

Scripts must be judged from the nature of their contents and in so judging it should be borne in mind that there is a level of the subliminal mind which is apt to be rather 'tricky' and is not above staging a false impersonation.

The very large bulk of the matter which comes through most automatists is only a kind of dream stuff, it is only on very rare occasions and with very few specially gifted automatists that anything supernormal, such as telepathy or clairvoyance, may occur. If the automatist is imbued with the idea that the spirits of the dead will communicate through the scripts, it is quite likely that the subliminal mind will endeavour to 'oblige' by supplying plausible sounding messages.

Where it is possible, those who desire to try the experiment should seek guidance and advice from some experienced person.

I repeat my warning: leave it alone altogether unless you are quite sure that you can adopt and *maintain* the cool, detached, scientific attitude, otherwise you will run the risk of self-deception and possible mental and moral disturbance.

LIST OF REFERENCES

FOR the convenience of those who wish to make a thorough examination of the question, I append a list of the Volumes of *Proceedings* in which may be found the full reports. It will be noticed that there are a great many cases of cross correspondence to which I have not referred.

Vol. XX, pages 1–432. Mrs. Verrall. 'On a Series of Automatic Writings.' Her methods are described and reports of the first cross correspondence cases, mostly simple, are given. It also gives examples of telepathic phenomena, etc.

Vol. XXI, pages 166–391. Miss A. Johnson. 'On the Automatic Writing of Mrs. Holland.' Description is given of the development of the phenomena and many cases of cross correspondence, including the 'Ave Roma Immortalis' case. Miss Johnson also gives the first clear exposition of the theory of cross correspondences.

Vol. XXII, pages 19–416. Mr. J. G. Piddington. 'A Series of Concordant Automatisms.' This contains reports of a large number of cases of cross correspondence, both simple and complex. It is a most important source of information.

Vol. XXII, pages 417–40. Mrs. Sidgwick. 'An Incident in Mrs. Piper's Trance.' This describes an incident, not a case of cross correspondence.

Vol. XXIII, pages 122–6. Mrs. Sidgwick and Mr. Piddington. 'Note on Mrs. Piper's Hodgson–Control in England in 1906–7. A discussion of features of the control.

Vol. XXIII, pages 286–303. Prof. A. C. Pigou. 'Psychical Research and Survival after Bodily Death.' A criticism of the cross-correspondence evidence for survival.

Vol. XXIV, pages 2–10. Miss A. Johnson. 'Supplementary Notes on the First Report on Mrs. Holland's Script.'

Vol. XXIV, pages 11–30. Mr. J. G. Piddington. Supplementary Notes on 'A Series of Concordant Automatisms.'

Vol. XXIV, pages 31–8. Mrs. Sidgwick, Mrs. Verrall and Mr. J. G. Piddington. Joint Introduction to a series of three articles on 'Further Experiments with Mrs. Piper in 1908.' This includes list of sittings and references.

Vol. XXIV, pages 39–85. Mrs. Verrall. 'Classical and Literary Allusions in Mrs. Piper's Trance.'

Vol. XXIV, pages 86–169. Mr. J. C. Piddington. 'Three Incidents from the Sittings: "Lethe," "The Sibyl," "The Horace Ode" Question.'

Vol. XXIV, pages 170–200. Mrs. Sidgwick. 'Cross correspondences between Mrs. Piper and Other Automatists.'

Vol. XXIV, pages 201–63. Miss A. Johnson. 'Second Report on Mrs. Holland's Script.' Contains reports on several cases of cross correspondence, including the complex case, 'Sevens.' Also a reply to Professor Pigou's criticisms.

Vol. XXIV, pages 264–318. Mrs. Verrall. 'A New Group of Experimenters.' A description of the phenomena of the 'Mac' group.

Vol. XXIV, pages 319–26. Miss A. Johnson. 'Sequel to the "Sesame and Lilies" Incident.'

Vol. XXIV, pages 327–8. Mr. J. G. Piddington. 'Postscript to the "Lethe" Incident.'

Vol. XXV, pages 113–75. Sir Oliver Lodge. 'Evidence of Classical Scholarship and of Cross-Correspondence in some New Automatic Writing.' This contains the report on the 'Lethe' case in Mrs. Willett's script and discussion thereon.

Vol. XXV, pages 176–217. Mrs. Verrall. 'Notes on Mrs. Willett's Scripts of February, 1910.' These bear on the 'Lethe' and other cases.

Vol. XXV, pages 218–303. Miss A. Johnson. 'Third Report on Mrs. Holland's Script.' Reports of cross correspondences. Mostly simple. Also note on the principle of Selection in the Production of Scripts.

Vol. XXV, pages 304–19. Mrs. Verrall. Note on the Cross Correspondence "Cup." '

Vol. XXV, pages 320–37. Mrs. Verrall. 'Miss Verrall's Script of March 16th, 1908: a Correction and an Addition.'

Vol. XXVI, pages 24–56. Mrs. Verrall. 'A Month's Record of Cross Correspondences.'

Vol. XXVI, pages 57–144. Dr. Joseph Maxwell, M.D. 'Correspondances Croisées.' Criticism of the evidence and theory of Cross Correspondences.

Vol. XXVI, pages 145–6. Editorial Note on above.

Vol. XXVI, pages 147–70. Mrs. Anna Hude. 'The Latin Message Experiment: A Criticism.'

Vol. XXVI, pages 171–3. Mr. J. G. Piddington. 'Note on Mrs. Hude's Paper.'

Vol. XXVI, pages 174–220. Mr. J. G. Piddington. 'A Hitherto Unsuspected Answer to the Horace Ode Question.'

Vol. XXVI, pages 221–30. The Right Hon. G. W. Balfour. 'Some Observations on Mr. Piddington's Paper.'

Vol. XXVI, pages 231–44. Mr. J. G. Piddington. 'A Reply to Mr. Balfour's Observations.'

Vol. XXVI, pages 245–50. Mr. J. G. Piddington. 'Two Tennysonian Quotations in Mrs. Verrall's Script.'

Vol. XXVI, pages 375–400. Mrs. Sidgwick. 'A Reply to Dr. Joseph Maxwell's Paper on "Cross Correspondences" and the Experimental Method.'

Vol. XXVI, pages 401–18. Appendices to above by Mrs. Verrall, Miss A. Johnson and Mr. J. G. Piddington.

Vol. XXVII, pages 1–156. Miss A. Johnson. 'A Reconstruction of some "Concordant Automatisms." This contains additional details of the 'Ave Roma immortalis.' Latin Message, 'Hope, Star and Browning,' 'Alexander's (Medici) Tomb,' 'Autos ouranos akumon' and 'Claviger (Light in the West)' cases, and discussion thereon.

Vol. XXVII, pages 221–43. The Right Hon. Gerald W. Balfour. 'Some Recent Scripts affording Evidence of Personal Survival.' The 'Statius' case.

Vol. XXVII, pages 244–9. Rev. M. A. Bayfield. 'Note on the same Script.'

Vol. XXVII, pages 250–78. Mrs. Verrall. 'A Further Study of the Mac Scripts.'

Vol. XXVII, pages 458–91. Mr. Hereward Carrington, Ivor Lloyd Tuckett, M.D., and Rev. M. A. Bayfield. 'A Discussion of the Willett Scripts.' Messrs. Carrington and Tuckett criticize the report on the 'Statius' case. Mr. Bayfield answers their criticisms.

Vol. XXIX, pages 1–45. Mr. J. G. Piddington. 'Cross-Correspondences of a Gallic Type.' This contains accounts of several fresh cases and criticizes the views expressed by Dr. Geley and Dr. Joseph Maxwell.

Vol. XXIX, pages 197–243. The Right Hon. Gerald W. Balfour. 'The Ear of Dionysius: Further Scripts Affording Evidence of Personal Survival.'

Vol. XXIX, pages 245–59. Mrs. Sidgwick. 'On the Development of Different Types of Evidence for Survival in the Work of the Society.' This includes a discussion of the Cross Correspondence evidence.

Vol. XXIX, pages 260–9. Miss F. Melian Stawell. 'The Ear of Dionysius: A Discussion of the Evidence.'

Vol. XXIX, pages 270–86. The Right Hon. Gerald W. Balfour. 'The Ear of Dionysius: A Reply.'

Vol. XXIX, pages 306–49. Mrs. W. H. Salter (née Miss Verrall). 'Some Experiments with a New Automatist.' Contains accounts of some fresh cases of cross correspondence.

Vol. XXX, pages 115–229. Mr. J. G. Piddington. 'Fresh Light on the "One-Horse Dawn" Experiment.'

Vol. XXX, pages 291–5. Sir Oliver Lodge. 'Note on Mr. Piddington's paper called "Fresh Light on the 'One-Horse Dawn' Experiment."'

Vol. XXX, pages 296–9. Mr. J. G. Piddington. 'A Reply to Sir Oliver Lodge's Note.'

Vol. XXXVI, pages 345–75. Mr. J. G. Piddington. 'One Crowded Hour of Glorious Life' cross-correspondence case.

Vol. XXXVI, 455–70. Mr. A. F. Hall. 'Criticism of Mr. Piddington's paper on "One Crowded Hour of Glorious Life" case.'

Vol. XXXVI, pages 471–6. Mr. J. G. Piddington. 'Reply to Mr. A. F. Hall.'

Vol. XXXVI, pages 477–505. Mr. J. G. Piddington. 'The Master Builder' cross-correspondence case.

Vol. XXXVI, pages 525–54. Mr. W. H. Salter. An Experiment in Pseudo-Scripts. An account of an attempt to determine how far chance could produce cross-correspondences.

Vol. XLIII, pages 41–318. Gerald William Earl of Balfour. 'A Study of the Psychological Aspects of Mrs. Willett's Mediumship, and of the Statements of the Communicators Concerning Process.' This paper, though it makes no direct reference to cross correspondences, contains most important discussion of the process and methods.

GLOSSARY

Of terms, and special uses of words, commonly
found in the literature of psychical research.

Agent. One who takes the part of transmitter in telepathic
communication.

Automatic writing. Writing executed without the conscious
use of thought or muscular control by the writer. The
term is also applied when the act of writing is consciously
directed but the origin of the words or ideas is unknown
to the writer.

Automatist. One who writes, speaks, or performs other
significant action, without conscious volition. The term
is somewhat widely applied, so as to include cases in
which only the mental action involved is involuntary.

Auto-suggestion. Suggestion applied to oneself. (See
Suggestion.)

Clairaudience. Perception as sound of an impression in some
way true to fact, and not perceptible to the ordinary
senses.

Clairvoyance. Perception of real objects or facts not within
range of the ordinary senses. (Strictly used of perception
in visual form; but the word often denotes paranormal
perception of other kinds.)

Communicator. A personality seeming to be that of a deceased
person or other discarnate being.

Control. (1) A personality regularly represented as using
and taking charge of a medium during trance; (2) The
direction of a medium's speech or action by another
personality.

Discarnate. Disembodied, opposed to incarnate.

157

Dissociation. Independent activity of a part of the mind, which behaves in some way like a separate individual.

Externalized. This word is used of an impression, arising within the mind, which is perceived as though coming from without.

Extra-Sensory Perception. (Abbreviated, E.S.P.). Perception without use of the known senses. A general term, used to include such conceptions as telepathy, clairvoyance and precognition.

Hallucination. A supposed sensory perception which has no objective cause within the range of the sense concerned. (A hallucination may or may not represent a fact underlying the impression received.)

Illusion. The misinterpretation by the mind of something actually perceived.

Influenced Writing. Writing in which the flow of ideas is affected as though by unspoken suggestion from another mind.

Medium. One able to respond to and give expression to paranormal influences, expecially those appearing to be personal influences.

Metagnome. An alternative and less question-begging term for 'Medium', introduced by Boirac. Driesch defines it as 'a person from whom supernormal phenomena originate or in express relation to whom these phenomena occur.'

Paragnosis. Equivalent to extra-sensory perception.

Paranormal. Outside accepted experience of cause and effect.

Percipient. One who takes the part of receiver in telepathic communication.

Phantasm. The appearance of a person (in less common usage, also of a thing or event) as conveyed to the mind in hallucination.

Precognition. Perception or awareness of future event, apart from information or inference.

Psychic. This word is applied in general science to all action that has a mental as distinct from a physical basis. In popular speech it has a wide usage denoting anything paranormal. In psychical research the word is largely avoided as ambiguous, but it can occur in either the scientific or in the popular sense.

Purporting. Professing or seeming. It is said that a phenomenon 'purports' to be due to some paranormal cause when the evidence for such a cause is intended to be taken without prejudice for or against.

Retrocognition. Perception or awareness of past event not known to or within the memory of the perceiver.

Script. A piece of automatic writing: the record of an automatist's utterance.

Subliminal. Lying beneath the 'threshold' of consciousness. Practically equivalent to subconscious, or to 'unconscious' as a psychological term.

Suggestion. The impressing of ideas or feelings upon the mind, one's own or another's, so that they become effective without conscious volition on the part of the mind impressed.

Supernormal. See paranormal. The word does not necessarily imply a superior level of action or being.

Telekinesis. The causing of material objects to move without touching them or subjecting them to any known physical force.

Telepathy. Transmission of an image, idea or impulse from one mind to another by paranormal action of the minds concerned.

Veridical. Conveying facts, or ideas that can be shown to have basis in fact.

Essential Books in Parapsychology

Some of the best books on consciousness are out of print and hard to find, yet they are still of great importance. Hampton Roads Publishing Company—in partnership with consciousness research pioneer Russell Targ—is proud to bring some of these texts back into print. All books in the series are quality paperbacks in an attractive series design, affordably priced.

Distant Mental Influence
Its Contributions to Science, Healing, and Human Interactions
William Braud, Ph.D.

Braud is highly-regarded in the field of transpersonal psychology. *Distant Mental Influence* represents twenty years of thinking and experiments in biochemistry and transpersonal psychology. These twelve articles reveal Braud's discovery of experiments capable of measuring human interconnection and person-to-person influence across space and time.
ISBN 1-57174-354-5 • 224 pages, $15.95

Dream Telepathy
Montague Ullman, M.D., and Stanley Krippner, Ph.D., with Alan Vaughan
Foreword by Gardner Murphy

In the 1960s and '70s, Ullman and Krippner headed the dream laboratory at the Maimonides Medical Center. Their report on their ten years of experimentation with the human power to communicate across the barriers of time, space, and sleep presages the use of dream telepathy in all areas of paranormal study.
ISBN 1-57174-321-9 • 304 pages, $16.95

An Experiment with Time
J. W. Dunne
Preface by Russell Targ

First published in 1927, *An Experiment with Time* presents a theory of time that has earned Dunne a place of honor among the twentieth century's brightest minds. Spurred by vivid dreams of the future, Dunne designed an experiment whose groundbreaking results resonate as clearly today as they did seventy-five years ago.
ISBN 1-57174-234-4 • 176 pages, $14.95

Experiments in Mental Suggestion
L. L. Vasiliev
Preface by Arthur Hastings, Ph.D.

A Soviet scientist convincingly demonstrates that the thoughts of one person can directly affect the physiology and behavior of a distant person.
ISBN 1-57174-274-3 • 224 pages, $14.95

Human Personality and Its Survival of Bodily Death
F. W. H. Myers
Preface by Jeffrey Mishlove, Ph.D.
Foreword by Aldous Huxley

Human Personality, the culmination of the research of the cofounder of the Society for Psychical Research, includes a complete synthesis of seminal nineteenth-century thought on the role of science in paranormal research.
ISBN 1-57174-238-7 • 384 pages, $16.95

Mental Radio
Upton Sinclair
Preface by Albert Einstein
Introduction by Professor William McDougall

In 1929, the world-famous author of *The Jungle* astounded his readers and the scientific world with a page-turning report of his wife Mary's telepathy, and argued that all humans have the ability to learn and use psychic skills. Includes the original preface by Albert Einstein.
ISBN 1-57174-235-2 • 224 pages, $14.95

Mind at Large
Edited by Charles T. Tart, Harold E. Puthoff, and Russell Targ

Mind at Large is a collection of essays from preeminent mental researchers, including Edgar Mitchell's call to train individuals to use the psychic arts, and Ingo Swann's "View from the Inside" as the subject in psi research projects.
ISBN 1-57174-320-0 • 256 pages, $16.95

Mind to Mind
René Warcollier
Preface by Ingo Swann
Interpretive Introduction by Russell Targ

Chemical engineer René Warcollier's series of experiments in telepathic communication are described here in precise detail, including many drawings and impressions. His research revealed surprising parallels between extrasensory communication and modern psychology.
ISBN 1-57174-311-1 • 144 pages, $14.95

Thoughts Through Space
A Remarkable Adventure in the Realm of Mind
Sir Hubert Wilkins and Harold M. Sherman
Foreword by Ingo Swann

In 1937, noted aviator and explorer Sir Hubert Wilkins, while flying dozens of trans-Arctic flights searching for a downed plane, mentally projected his thoughts toward Sherman who sat 2,500 miles away. When their notes were matched, a stunning pattern of accurate "hits" emerged, making *Thoughts Through Space* one of the most indisputable proofs of mental telepathy ever published.
ISBN 1-57174-314-6 • 480 pages, $14.95

Available from your bookseller or online.

Hampton Roads Publishing Company

... for the evolving human spirit

Hampton Roads Publishing Company
publishes books on a variety of subjects,
including metaphysics, health,
visionary fiction, and other related topics.

For a copy of our latest catalog, call toll-free
(800) 766-8009, or send your name and address to:

Hampton Roads Publishing Company, Inc.
1125 Stoney Ridge Road
Charlottesville, VA 22902

e-mail: hrpc@hrpub.com
www.hrpub.com